UNCTAD/ST/SEU/3/Rev.1

UNITED NATIONS CONFERENCE ON TRADE AND DEVELOPMENT
Geneva

The Palestinian financial sector under Israeli occupation

*Study prepared by the secretariat of UNCTAD
in collaboration with the secretariat of the
Economic and Social Commission for Western Asia*

UNITED NATIONS
New York, 1989

NOTE

Symbols of United Nations documents are composed of capital letters combined with figures. Mention of such a symbol indicates a reference to a United Nations document.

*

* *

The designations employed and the presentation of the material in this publication do not imply the expression of any opinion whatsoever on the part of the Secretariat of the United Nations concerning the legal status of any country, territory, city or area, or of its authorities, or concerning the delimitation of its frontiers or boundaries.

*

* *

Material in this publication may be freely quoted or reprinted, but acknowledgement is requested, together with a reference to the document number. A copy of the publication containing the quotation or reprint should be sent to the UNCTAD secretariat.

UNCTAD/ST/SEU/3/Rev.1

UNITED NATIONS PUBLICATION

Sales No. E.89.II.D.7

ISBN 92-1-112273-2

03900P

CONTENTS

		Paragraphs	Page
EXPLANATORY NOTES			iii
PREFACE		i - vii	iv

Chapter

I.	STRUCTURE AND CHARACTERISTICS OF THE ECONOMY - AN OVERVIEW	1 - 73	1
	A. Area and population	2 - 5	1
	B. Administration	6 - 11	5
	C. Aggregate economic performance	12 - 35	7
	1. Trends in output	12 - 20	7
	2. Savings and investment	21 - 27	11
	3. Prices and the impact of inflation	28 - 35	14
	D. Major developments	36 - 73	17
	1. Agriculture	37 - 42	17
	2. Industry	43 - 50	20
	3. Structure and direction of trade .	51 - 57	23
	4. Labour and employment in Israel ..	58 - 63	26
	5. Housing and Israeli settlements ..	64 - 73	30
II.	MONEY AND BANKING	74 - 228	33
	Introduction	74 - 76	33
	A. Pre-1967 situation: a brief historical account	77 - 82	33
	B. Post-1967 situation: policies and practices	83 - 205	34
	1. A brief review of Israeli military government orders	83 - 93	34
	2. Israeli banks	94 - 125	38
	3. Arab financial institutions and practices	126 - 194	49
	4. Attempts at re-opening banks	195 - 205	66
	C. A general assessment of the monetary sector and its prospects	206 - 228	68
III.	FISCAL DETERMINANTS	229 - 311	74
	Introduction	229	74
	A. Pre-1967 situation	230 - 234	74

CONTENTS (<u>continued</u>)

			Paragraphs	Page
Chapter				
	B.	Post-1967 situation	235 - 311	75
		1. Government expenditures	237 - 247	76
		2. Government revenues	248 - 250	82
		3. Revenues and expenditures of municipalities	251 - 258	84
		4. The tax system	259 - 311	87
IV.		EXTERNAL FINANCIAL RESOURCES AND THE DEVELOPMENT OF THE OCCUPIED PALESTINIAN TERRITORIES	312 - 365	100
		Introduction	312 - 313	100
	A.	Factor income from abroad	314 - 332	100
		1. Sources of factor income	315 - 319	100
		2. Components of factor income	320 - 327	102
		3. Role of factor income	328 - 332	107
	B.	Financial transfers	333 - 361	109
		1. Gross and net transfers to the occupied territories	333 - 336	109
		2. Components of transfers	337 - 361	112
	C.	External financial sources and the occupied territories' development	362 - 365	128
		1. The relative importance of different components of transfers	362	128
		2. Factor income and transfers within overall sources of Palestinian national income	363 - 365	129
V.		CONCLUSIONS AND RECOMMENDATIONS	366 - 426	132
	A.	General economic situation	367 - 375	132
	B.	Money and banking	376 - 390	134
	C.	Public finance	391 - 410	138
	D.	External resources	411 - 426	142

EXPLANATORY NOTES

- The term dollar ($) refers to United States dollars unless otherwise stated.

- An oblique stroke (/) between two years, e.g. 1980/1981, signifies a fiscal or crop year.

- Two dots (..) indicate that the data are not available, or are not separately reported.

- A dash (-) indicates that the amount is nil or negligible.

- JD represents Jordanian dinars.

PREFACE

i.   The structure and development of the economy of the occupied Palestinian territories (the West Bank and Gaza Strip) have been fundamentally influenced by Israeli policies and practices during the past 20 years of occupation. Various considerations, reflecting the interests of the occupation authorities, have prompted the Israeli military government to adopt measures which have had adverse effects on the very existence of the Palestinian economy. Nowhere in the economy has the effect of these measures been more detrimental than in the financial sector, which normally serves as the backbone of any economy.

ii.   As part of the 1986-1987 work programme of UNCTAD, this study investigates various aspects of the Palestinian financial sector by focusing on Israeli policies in this field, analysing the problems encountered by Palestinians in the financing of current economic activities and future development, and examining prospects for policy consideration. The study has been undertaken in collaboration with the Economic and Social Commission for Western Asia (ESCWA), which assisted in various stages of its preparation, including through the commissioning of a field report. The study is based on data from official sources, published and unpublished reports, studies and other references, and from field information compiled as part of the research required.

iii. The study comprises five chapters. Chapter I provides an overall view of the economy of the occupied territories by briefly analysing its aggregate performance during the past six years. Attention is focused on such major determinants as output, savings and investment, capital formation, prices and inflation and the performance of the major economic sectors. The objective of this chapter is to familiarize the reader with the structure, characteristics and operation of the territories' economy as it has evolved under occupation. Special emphasis is given to some of the major obstacles related to financing that have hindered progress in these sectors and the efforts needed to remedy the situation.

iv.   Chapter II analyses the different aspects of the monetary system under occupation. It examines the crucial role of the banking system in financing short-term and long-term economic activities. Emphasis is placed on its ability to provide financial intermediation by mobilizing and allocating savings in the economy. Special attention is given to the role of the Israeli banks and the need to promote local Palestinian banks and other specialized financial institutions aimed at meeting the growing development finance needs of the Palestinian economy. In the absence of an adequate banking system, the informal monetary sector has assumed increasing importance in facilitating the day-to-day banking needs of a large number of Palestinians, both within and outside the occupied territories. In this connection, the role played by Palestinian money changers and its prospects for the future of the economy have been examined at length.

v.   Chapter III deals with some of the fiscal determinants in the Palestinian economy. It concentrates on the significance of Israeli government and Palestinian municipal budgets by examining the scope and orientation of revenues and expenditures. The chapter examines the extent to which government expenditures have provided the basic social services for a rapidly growing population and created the necessary infrastructure for the development of the

Palestinian economy. Special attention is given to the examination of the two most important functions of the tax system, i.e. serving as the major source of government revenues and as an effective instrument of fiscal policy in influencing resource allocation in the economy. It examines the numerous changes that have been introduced by the occupation authorities in the tax system during the last 20 years without due consideration given to the specific needs of the economy of the territories.

vi. Chapter IV provides a detailed analysis of external financial flows to the occupied territories. It concentrates on an assessment of the magnitude of remittances of workers from the occupied territories employed in Israel and elsewhere. This is followed by an examination of transfers comprising aid from various Arab and non-Arab sources including international organizations and other governmental and non-governmental institutions.

vii. Chapter V presents a summary of the findings and conclusions of the study. An attempt is made to reflect on some recommendations with a view to improving the situation and rendering the financial sector capable of meeting the rapidly growing financial resource needs of the Palestinian economy.

Chapter I

STRUCTURE AND CHARACTERISTICS OF THE ECONOMY - AN OVERVIEW

1. Prior to embarking on the examination of the financial sector in the occupied Palestinian territories, it is considered necessary to provide an overview of the economy of the territories. This chapter attempts to meet this objective. It presents a concise analysis of the recent performance of the economy of the territories and of the developments and problems encountered in striving to maintain a sustained level of growth. It is intended to provide the substantive background for the analysis of the structures and operation of the financial sector and its potential for the future. The analysis is preceded by a brief historical account of some relevant issues pertaining to area, population and system of administration, with a view to supplying the reader with information providing a more comprehensive picture of the situation under which the economy of the occupied territories operates.

A.   Area and population

2.   The total land area of the occupied Palestinian territories is approximately 5,939,000 dunums,[1] of which 5,572,000 dunums are in the West Bank and 367,000 dunums are in the Gaza Strip.[2] Of this, an area of 2,267,000 dunums was under cultivation in 1966. By 1984, this area had declined to 1,768,500 dunums, or by almost 22 per cent of its 1966 level. Much of this is attributed to the occupation authorities gradually expropriating an increasing number of dunums and bringing them under their direct control.[3] By 1985, land under Israeli control had reached 3,070,000 dunums or about 52 per cent of the total area of the West Bank and Gaza Strip.[4]

3.   Much of the expropriated land was held by Palestinians in common for grazing and other purposes, both State land and land that was privately owned and farmed but not registered.[5] Land expropriated has included grazing land as well as orchards, land under field crops and land bordering established Israeli settlements to permit their expansion.[6] Land expropriated falls under various categories, namely; "Absentee property", "Registered State Domain", "Land requisitioned for military purposes", "Land closed for military purposes", "Jewish lands"; "Purchased land"; and, more recently, "dead land".[7]

4.   The population of the occupied territories has grown despite continuous emigration over the past 20 years of occupation. By 1985, the Palestinian population of the territories, excluding those in East Jerusalem, had reached close to 1,338,900 people (see table 1). Of this total, around 813,400 persons were living in the West Bank, 15 per cent of whom were refugees. Despite high rates of natural increase, the population of the West Bank has not yet regained its pre-1967 level. The population of the Gaza Strip had reached a total of 525,500 by 1985. Well over 60 per cent of the inhabitants are refugees living in eight over-crowded and impoverished refugee camps.[8] The Palestinian Arab population of East Jerusalem, which was annexed by Israel in 1967, stood at 130,000 in 1985.[9] Including these inhabitants, the population of the Palestinian territories occupied in 1967 was 1,468,900 in 1985.

5.   In general, emigration has given the territories a relatively low rate of
population growth, despite their registering high positive rates of natural
increase which have at times exceeded 3.5 per cent. One study estimates that
247,000 people became refugees during and immediately after the 1967 war,
(including East Jerusalem residents), while a further 312,000 persons (not
including East Jerusalem) left the territories permanently between
September 1967 and 1984 (see table 2).[10]/ When the population growth of the
first group from 1967 to 1984 (i.e. some 202,000) is added to the total number
of migrants since 1967 (i.e. 247,000 and 312,000), the total migrant
population originating in the territories can be estimated at 761,000 in
1984.[11]/ It can be further estimated that, by 1984, of the 761,000 migrants
from the territories, some 152,000 were in the labour force in the receiving
countries (i.e. in Jordan, the Gulf countries and elsewhere).[12]/

Table 1

Population estimates and sources of its growth

Years	Population at beginning of period (thousands)	Natural increase (thousands)	Balance of population movement (thousands)	Annual growth (percentages)	Population at end of period (thousands)
		WEST BANK			
1961[a]	805.5	...	...	...	...
1967[b]	595.9[c]	3.0	13.0	...	585.9
1968	585.9	13.0	15.8	0.5	583.1
1969	583.1	13.5	1.3	2.5	597.9
1970	597.9	14.9	5.0	1.7	607.8
1971	607.8	17.3	2.5	2.4	622.6
1972	622.6	18.1	7.3	1.8	633.5
1973	633.5	18.7	0.3	3.0	652.4
1974	652.4	20.1	2.8	2.7	669.7
1975	669.7	20.6	15.1	0.8	675.2
1976	675.2	22.5	14.4	1.2	683.3
1977	683.3	22.7	10.2	1.8	695.7
1978	695.7	21.6	9.4	1.8	708.0
1979	708.0	23.3	12.6	1.5	718.6
1980	718.6	22.9	17.3	0.8	724.3
1981	724.3	23.2	15.7	1.0	731.8
1982	732.7	24.5	7.9	2.4	749.3
1983	749.3	25.2	2.7	3.0	771.8
1984	771.8	27.4	5.8	2.8	793.4
1985	793.4	...	...	2.5	813.4

Table 1 (continued)

Years	Population at beginning of period (thousands)	Natural increase (thousands)	Balance of population movement (thousands)	Annual growth (percentages)	Population at end of period (thousands)
		GAZA STRIP			
1966	455.0[d]	...	...	...	...
1967[b]	389.7	3.3	12.2	...	380.8
1968	380.8	8.3	32.3	6.3	356.8
1969	356.8	10.0	2.9	2.0	363.9
1970	363.9	9.4	3.3	1.7	370.0
1971	370.0	11.2	2.4	2.4	378.8
1972	378.8	12.2	4.0	2.2	387.0
1973	387.0	12.8	1.7	3.7	401.5
1974	401.5	14.3	1.8	3.1	414.0
1975	414.0	15.0	3.5	2.8	425.5
1976	425.5	16.1	4.2	2.8	437.4
1977	437.4	16.3	2.9	3.1	450.8
1978	450.8	16.9	4.7	2.7	463.0
1979[e]	463.0	16.5	4.8	2.5	444.7
1980	444.7	16.9	5.1	2.7	456.5
1981	456.5	17.7	5.3	2.7	468.9
1982[f]	469.6	17.8	3.1	1.8	477.3
1983	477.3	18.2	1.0	3.6	494.5
1984	494.5	20.2	4.8	3.1	509.9
1985[g]	509.9	...	...	3.1	525.5

Source: Except for 1961 and 1966, figures were obtained from Israel, Central Bureau of Statistics, Statistical Abstract of Israel, 1985 (Jerusalem, CBS, 1986), table XXVII/1, p. 683.

a/ Includes 60,000 inhabitants of East Jerusalem. See Fawzi, A. Gharaibeh, The Economies of the West Bank and Gaza Strip (Boulder and London, Westview Press, 1985), p. 31.

b/ Figures for 1967 from census conducted in September 1967.

c/ Other sources put the population of the West Bank in June 1967 between 803,000 and 845,000. See George Kosseifi, "Forced migration of Palestinians from the West Bank and Gaza Strip", in Population Bulletin of ESCWA, No. 27, December 1985, p. 94.

d/ Egyptian estimates of 1966 put the total population of the Gaza Strip at 455,000 inhabitants. The discrepancy between the figures for 1966 and 1967 could be explained by the collective deportations and emigrations after the 1967 war. See Ziad Abu-Amr "The Gaza Economy Since 1948", a paper presented to the Welfare Association Symposium on Economic Development Under Prolonged Occupation, Oxford, 3-5 January 1986.

e/ The El-Arish population, about 30,000 inhabitants, was deducted after its return to Egypt.

f/ The population of the Rafah Area, about 7,000 inhabitants, was deducted after its return to Egypt.

g/ Provisional figures.

Table 2

Estimates of Palestinian migrant population and labour force,
selected years

Source	Year	Total migrant population from:		
		West Bank	Gaza Strip	Total
Kosseifi[a]				
(1)	VI-VIII 1967	148,000	99,000	247,000
(2)	Population growth 1968-84	112,000	90,000	202,000
(3)	IX-XII 1967	15,000	7,000	22,000
(4)	1968-1984	207,000	83,000	290,000
(5)=(3)+(4)	IX 1967-1984	222,000	90,000	312,000
(6)=(1)+(2)+(5)	VI 1967-1984	482,000	279,000	761,000
Israel CBS[b]	IX 1967-1984	156,000	97,000	253,000
		Total migrant working population from:		
		West Bank	Gaza Strip	Total
Israel CBS[c]	1980	12,500	3,700	16,200
	1984	8,400	7,600	16,000
Calculated[d]	1984	96,000	56,000	152,000
Zaghloul[e]	1980	110,000		

a/ These figures (calculated by G. Kosseifi, "The forced migration of Palestinians from the West Bank and Gaza Strip, 1967-83", in Population Bulletin of ESCWA, No. 27, December 1985, p. 95) use official Israeli data to calculate the difference between the actual population of the territories as officially reported and the level it would have been had there been no emigration since 1967 (on the assumption of a population growth rate of 3.2 per cent p.a.). Those who work temporarily abroad but maintain residence in the territories are not included in these figures.

b/ These figures are calculated according to the difference between officially registered residents at the end of each year (net migration balance) since September 1967 (from Israel, CBS, Statistical Abstract of Israel (Jerusalem, CBS, 1985), p. 703) and include the total migrant population which left the territories since September 1967 and resided abroad, including 22,000 East Jerusalem migrants.

c/ Israel Central Bureau of Statistics for 1980 from Israel, CBS, Statistical Abstract of Israel 1985 (Jerusalem, CBS 1985), p. 721 and for 1984 from Israel, CBS, Judea, Samaria and Gaza Area Statistics (Jerusalem, CBS, vol. XV, No. 2, December 1985). These sources provide an annual figure for territories' residents who are 'working abroad' and who are specified as 'not in the labour force'.

d/ These figures are calculated according to Kosseifi's above population estimates, assuming a crude labour force participation rate of 20 per cent.

e/ These figures (from I. Zaghloul, Transfers of Jordanians and Their Effect on the Israeli Economy (Amman, Central Bank of Jordan, 1984), p. 11., in Arabic) are calculated using several official estimates for the number of Jordanians (not including Gaza Strip residents) working outside Jordan and assuming that West Bank (origin) Palestinians constitute about one third of Jordanians working abroad.

B.   Administration

6.   From 1950, when the Hashemite Kingdom of Jordan assumed responsibility
for the West Bank in accordance with the terms of the "act of unity", and
until 1967, public administration in the West Bank was largely entrusted to
municipal authorities. The 1955 Jordanian Municipal Law and its amendments
gave municipal government the authority to act in 40 different areas including
town planning and zoning, regulation of the use of water, electricity,
business activities, transportation, public health, town protection and
others.[13]/ At the local level, municipal councils served as the highest
indigenous political institutions; they were composed of members who were
elected on the basis of proportional representation and held office for four
years. In the Gaza Strip, the 1934 municipal law, under the British Mandate,
provided for a Legislative Council and Executive Council, composed of both
elected and appointed members. These bodies had developed the capacity for
self-government and for formulating laws compatible with the interests of the
society.[14]/ From 1948 to 1967 when the Strip was under Egyptian
administration, no elections were held. An appointive system of local
government prevailed.

7.   Shortly after the 1967 war, the military command of the Israeli
occupation forces issued a proclamation whereby the Israeli Minister of
Defense assumed the authority over the territories which had previously been
exercised by Jordan and Egypt.[15]/ The proclamation further stipulated that
existing law in the areas would continue with such modifications as might
result from the establishment of the military government and from any
proclamation or order issued by the IDF Commander. Policy for the areas is
determined at the ministerial level, mainly by the Prime Minister and the
Minister of Defense. Policy implementation and day-to-day decisions are
entrusted to the Israeli military administration, assisted by personnel
recruited from the various government ministries and from non-government
agencies and local staff.[16]/ There is no institutional or formal mechanism
for local participation in the formulation of these policies. Legislative,
administrative and judicial authority is exercised through military orders and
proclamations, based mainly on the 1945 Emergency Regulations instituted under
the British Mandate, which were completely abolished under the Jordanian
constitution.[17]/

8.   Local government in the occupied territories now exists at two levels:
one comprising the Palestinian local bodies which operate under former
Jordanian law as amended by Israel, and the other involving Israeli
settlements incorporated into Israeli local and regional councils operating
under Israeli municipal law.[18]/ In the West Bank there are 460 municipal and
village councils and villages, in addition to 20 refugee camps, administered
by the United Nations Relief and Works Agency (UNRWA), and the Arab Jerusalem
municipality. Arab Jerusalem was annexed by Israel in June 1967. In the Gaza
Strip, there are four municipalities, seven village councils and eight local
committees.[19]/ Since 1976, no municipal elections have been held in the West
Bank, in defiance of Jordanian law. The last elections for village councils
and Chambers of Commerce were held in 1975 and 1972-1973, respectively. No
elections have been held in the Gaza Strip under the 20 years of Israeli
occupation. Most municipalities are now run by Israeli officials or local
inhabitants appointed by the authorities, as mayors have either been deposed
and/or have suspended operations in the wake of Israeli pressures and
intimidation or as a protest against their inability to carry out their
responsibilities.

9.   A major problem confronting these municipalities is the control exercised by the military authorities over local municipal government. "Municipal officials assert that military interference in their affairs has blurred the sources of law upon which municipal authority relies. The confusion resulting from existing municipal law and its legal relation to military order has often led to serious confrontations between indigenous local officials and occupation officials."[20] The hierarchical system of local, district and national planning committees, based on Jordanian law, was eliminated by the occupation authorities and its powers transferred to the 'Supreme Planning Council' newly created above the municipal government. The Council has the authority to amend, revoke or place conditions on municipal decisions. The Council's main goal is to implement the Israeli settlement policy in the occupied territories and to provide municipal services to Israeli settlements scattered over a wide area within the occupied territories.

10.   Israeli civilian administration in the territories was introduced in March 1981 with a view to preparing the ground for the implementation of the so-called "autonomy for residents" plan within the framework of the Camp David accords.[21] It separated the military branch from the civilian branch of the military government. The administration's jurisdiction includes all the civil powers of the military government but not the authority to enact primary legislation, which has remained in the hands of the Military Commander as the "source of authority in the occupied territories". The significance of the civil administration goes far beyond the exigencies which brought about its establishment. It represents the passage from an ad hoc military government to a more permanent system of rule over the local population.[22] In the area of justice, the activities and independent judgement of local courts are similarly constrained. The local courts are almost completely lacking in means of executing court decisions and judgements. This has increasingly weakened the legal framework within which contractual dealings are carried out.[23]

11.   The above developments have rendered an already weak local system of public administration in the territories incapable of meeting the growing needs of the population. Indeed, they have deprived the local population from effectively participating in the design, formulation and implementation of policies and programmes aimed at bolstering their economic and social development. The absence of a national central authority has further compounded the problem. As experience has shown throughout the developing world, a major limitation on the capacity of government to provide public services to a growing population and to mobilize human and material resources has been the inadequacy of public administration.[24] These shortcomings are magnified in the territories, where a weak and fragmented system of local government has been subjected to harsh treatment over the past 20 years. The inadequate and archaic fabric of government machinery in the territories is in need of urgent support to help create an administrative structure with capabilities at various levels aimed at providing usual government services and meeting the administrative needs of development efforts.

C.   Aggregate economic performance

1.   Trends in output

(a)   Israeli policies

12.   The most noticeable feature of the immediate post-1967 period was the
high rates of growth accompanied by changes in economic structures and
relations between the occupying power and the territories. However, subsequent
developments do not show the continuation of this trend.

13.   Israeli occupation of the territories since 1967 has brought about
radical changes in the structure of the territories' economy. Three decisions
taken by the authorities soon after occupation of the territories have altered
the economic situation, namely: to annex Jerusalem and so alter the structural
relationships in the economy of the territories; to adopt the so called "open
bridges" policy to Jordan to secure a market outlet for the territories'
agricultural produce, thus protecting similar Israeli output from competition;
and to provide for selective opening of the borders between Israel and the
territories to ensure a flow of goods and services beneficial to the Israeli
economy.25/

14.   With respect to agriculture, Israeli policy has since proceeded along a
number of axes involving the expropriation of land, increasing restrictions on
the types and quantities of crops to be grown and exported to the Israeli
market, and control of water resources. In the area of industry,
subcontracting arrangements have increasingly involved small-scale industries,
transforming them into ancillary industries catering to the needs of Israeli
industries through subcontracting arrangements. The closure of all the banks
and financial institutions that existed prior to occupation, as well as
Israeli banks' discriminatory policies on loans and deposits, virtually
deprived the territories' economy of its prime source of finance. Israeli
commercial policy has gradually resulted in the domination of Palestinian
imports by Israeli products, with a growing adverse effect on the balance of
trade of the territories.26/ Parallel to these developments, a rapidly
growing percentage of the Palestinian labour force has been obliged to seek
employment in Israel and/or to leave the territories in search of work
opportunities elsewhere.

15.   Consequently, the economy of the territories is at present characterized
by a high degree of fragmentation reflecting increasing distortion in the
structure of output and income, a widening gap between domestic and national
output, and a high degree of openness, all leading to a lack of internal
cohesion of the economy as a whole and its increasing subservience to the
economy of Israel. The problem is further compounded by the absence of
indigenous institutions capable of dealing with the adverse effects of
policies under occupation for the past 20 years.

(b)   Domestic product and national income

16.   After a period of relative growth, the domestic contribution to gross
national product (GNP) fell steadily during the period 1978-1984 (see tables 3
and 4). Developments during this period reflect a pattern of structural change
which brought about a rapid decline in the relative share of the traditional

sector - an approach witnessed in many developing economies during their initial period of economic transformation. The share of agriculture in gross domestic product (GDP) fell by more than 12 per cent in real terms over the period 1978-1984.

17.   Contrary to expectations, however, the structural changes have not brought about increased capacity within the modern commodity-producing sectors for the establishment of a more durable base for the sustained growth and development of the economy. The share of the industrial sector in domestic output stagnated over a period of 7 years. In fact, for much of the period this share too declined from its low level of 9 per cent to a mere 7 per cent of domestic output, only to rise again in 1984 to the initial level of 9 per cent registered in 1978. It has hardly shown any increase since 1972. Despite modest increases in the services sector, the overall share of domestic output in gross national product declined to a low level of less than 65 per cent in 1984.

18.   The GDP of the West Bank rose by only 1 per cent in 1984 and 1985. Obviously, the gradual deterioration of the economy during the period reflects the absence of sound planning or programming with appropriate policy measures based on a coherent economic policy for the development of the territories. On the contrary, indigenous efforts and proposals aimed at enhancing economic activities and contributing to development have been stifled on security, political and economic grounds as and when such efforts and proposals were considered to undermine Israel's security and create economically based Palestinian power centres and were potentially competitive with Israeli production.[27]

19.   Around 36 per cent of national disposable income in 1984 was generated outside the territories, mostly in the form of remittances of factor income consisting mainly of wages of Palestinian workers in Israel and the rest of the world, and partly as transfers from various private and official sources. The net effect of these has been a sizeable increase in private income and consumption, as well as in transfers (as taxes, social security payments and others) to Israel.[28] Similarly, private consumption expenditures have increased by an average annual rate of 3 per cent. Since 1978, private consumption has exceeded GDP, with margins varying from 3 to 18 per cent during the period, with an adverse effect on prices and the balance of trade.[29]

20.   It is the flow of external resources (i.e. factor income and transfers) that has made the high level of consumption possible and, at the same time, provided for a certain level of savings. However, lack of appropriate financial institutions and investment opportunities has prevented the mobilization of residual income and its allocation into productive areas. Hoarding, conspicuous consumption and placing of savings in safer and reliable currencies and accounts abroad have provided the main outlet for the use of such income in the territories. This is a feature that the economy of the territories cannot afford to sustain, given the 20 years of neglect and the unstable economic situation. Every effort is needed to encourage the mobilization of these resources and facilitate their allocation to productive areas with a view to creating the basis for sustained economic growth and development.

Table 3

Industrial origin of the gross domestic product of the West Bank and Gaza Strip at factor cost

(constant 1980 prices) 1978-1984

(Millions of Israeli shekels and percentages)

Year a/	Agriculture	%	Industry	%	Construction	%	Public Serv.	%	Transp./trade	%	GDP Total	% b/	GNP	GDP as % of GNP
1978	1,505	32	410	9	813	17	744	16	1,273	26	4,745	100	.. c/	..
1979	1,116	24	405	9	921	20	705	15	1,544	32	4,691	100	..	..
1980	1,763	32	407	8	846	16	697	13	1,717	31	5,425	100	..	..
1981	1,494	30	364	7	850	17	711	14	1,567	32	4,986	100	..	..
1982	1,665	31	398	7	891	17	722	13	1,714	32	5,390	100	..	..
1983	1,491	29	414	8	893	17	740	14	1,619	32	5,157	100	..	..
1984	1,488	28	471	9	859	16	773	14	1,760	33	5,351	100	..	..

Source : calculated from Israel, Central Bureau of Statistics, Judea, Samaria and Gaza Area Statistics (Jerusalem, CBS, 1985), vol. XV, Nos. 1 and 2, tables 6 and 13, pp. 168 and 175, and 72 and 79, respectively.

a/ Sources used for calculating aggregates in constant prices (i.e. Israel, Central Bureau of Statistics, Judea, Samaria and Gaza Area Statistics (Jerusalem, CBS, 1985), vol. XV, No. 2 have revised previously published estimates on which aggregates in current prices are based (i.e. Israel, Central Bureau of Statistics, Judea, Samaria and Gaza Area Statistics (Jerusalem, CBS, 1986), vol. XV, No. 1. Accordingly, the base year figures in this table and in table 4 for the two sets of aggregates do not correspond with each other.

b/ Decimal percentage points are rounded up to the nearest figure.

c/ Two dots (..) denote that figures are not available.

- 10 -

Table 4

Industrial origin of the gross domestic product of the West Bank and Gaza Strip at factor cost
(current prices) 1978-1984
(Millions of Israeli shekels and percentages)

Year	Agriculture	%	Industry	%	Construction	%	Public Serv.	%	Transp./trade	%	GDP Total	% a/	GNP	GDP as % of GNP
1978	409.1	34	105.0	9	195.4	16	165.6	13	339.0	28	1,241.1	100	1,668.9	72.7
1979	591.0	29	177.0	9	400.9	19	273.0	13	630.9	30	2,072.8	100	2,979.5	69.6
1980	1,762.7	33	406.9	7	845.6	16	689.8	13	1,644.7	31	5,349.7	100	7,409.2	72.2
1981	3,182.0	30	791.9	7	1,960.7	18	1,740.6	16	3,127.2	29	10,802.4	100	15,913.4	67.9
1982	6,407.1	26	1,709.9	7	4,511.3	19	3,832.5	16	7,716.3	32	24,317.1	100	36,571.5	66.5
1983	14,027.0	24	4,563.9	8	10,600.9	18	10,309.8	17	19,362.2	33	58,863.8	100	93,470.2	63.0
1984	54,038.0	18	26,927.0	9	50,063.0	17	60,577.0	21	104,110.0	35	295,715.0	100	455,805.0	65.0

Source : calculated from Israel, Central Bureau of Statistics, Judea, Samaria and Gaza Area Statistics (Jerusalem, CBS, 1985), vol. XV, Nos. 1 and 2, tables 6 and 13, pp. 168 and 175, and 72 and 79, respectively.

a/ Decimal percentage points are rounded up to the nearest figure.

2.   Savings and investment

21.   The growing domestic resource gap in the economy of the territories has increasingly been met from external flows. As indicated above, total disposable private income from all sources has increased at a rate much higher than the rise in gross national product. This rising trend does not seem to have been equally reflected in the level of personal savings (see table 5). Private savings have amounted to around one-fifth of gross disposable income for much of the period. This is partly due to higher propensities to consume, a deterioration in the balance of trade, lack of financial markets, anomalies in the structure of interest rates, and increasing inflationary pressure coupled with frequent depreciation of the Israeli currency. While domestic savings depict a negative trend, national savings amounted to an annual average of 28.3 per cent of GDP during the period 1980-1984. Although this is entirely attributed to net factor income and net current transfers from abroad, it is significant, bearing in mind that the territories have no institutional means of mobilizing and/or augmenting the meagre resources of individuals. This is a reasonable performance when seen against the figure of 23.3 per cent of GDP for total savings in all developing countries and 21.9 per cent for middle-income oil-importing countries. It is also higher than that of the industrial market economies.[30]/

22.   To a large extent, the level of total savings has been influenced by the strong impact of external forces and the structural changes in the economy of the territories. More importantly, it can be attributed to the initiative of the private sector and to its savings effort under very difficult circumstances. It should be noted, however, that the stagnating level of domestic sources of income would not have made such a level of consumption and savings possible were it not for the inflow of resources from abroad.

23.   In principle, the investment requirements of the economy should be met from the savings of three sectors, i.e. government, business, and household.[31]/ The first source is virtually non-existent in the territories. The economy has therefore been deprived of a source of finance which is usually called upon to render the basic public services to citizens and to undertake capital expenditures aimed at providing the economic and social infrastructures necessary for the successful launching of productive projects in agriculture, industry, construction and elsewhere. Similarly, the corporate source of savings is negligible due to the undeveloped state of this category of business institutions in the territories. It is largely the third source of domestic savings on which the economy of the territories has relied upon during the 20 years of occupation.

24.   As for investments, the household sector has also played an important role, despite various obstacles brought about by occupation, especially the non-existence of a financial structure with an adequate banking system to encourage and guide savings and investments in the economy. However, total private investments (table 6, column 3) have lagged behind private savings (table 5, column 2) throughout the period under review, reflecting poor financial intermediation, as well as a high degree of political and economic uncertainty and risks. Despite these unfavourable factors, the private sector's share in total gross domestic capital formation has reached over 80 per cent (see table 6).

Table 5

Savings and capital formation, 1977-1984

(Millions of current Israeli shekels and percentages)

Years	(1) Gross disposable private income from all sources	(2) Private savings	(3) Private consumption expenditures	(4) (2) as % of (1)	(5) Gross domestic capital formation a/	(6) (2) as % of		(7) (5) as % of	
						GDP	GNP	GDP	GNP
1977	974.7	126.3	838.4	13.0	183.3	17.4	13.1	25.3	19.0
1978	1,700.0	430.0	1,270.9	25.3	394.7	34.4	25.8	31.5	23.7
1979	3,025.0	682.0	2,336.7	22.5	701.2	32.1	22.9	33.0	23.5
1980	7,528.0	1,773.0	5,774.0	23.6	1,788.8	32.3	23.9	32.6	24.1
1981	16,110.0	3,373.0	12,776.7	20.9	3,264.9	15.8	21.2	29.2	20.5
1982	36,622.0	9,433.0	27,258.4	25.8	8,560.4	37.2	25.8	33.8	23.4
1983	90,025.0	20,155.0	71,300.4	22.4	18,578.3	32.2	21.6	29.7	19.9
1984	431,133.0	76,386.0	354,749.0	17.7	87,979.0	24.0	16.8	27.7	19.3

Source: Israel, Central Bureau of Statistics, Judea, Samaria and Gaza Area Statistics (Jerusalem, CBS, 1985), vol. XV, No. 2 tables 1, 2, 4, 7, 8, 9, 11 and 14, and Israel, Central Bureau of Statistics, Judea, Samaria and Gaza Area Statistics (Jerusalem, CBS, 1985), vol. XV, No. 1 tables 2, 4, 7, 9, 11, 14, pages 67-80 and 163-176, respectively.

a/ Includes changes in stock. Except for a few years (1978, 1980, 1982) there has been a net decrease in stock in the West Bank. For a breakdown of investment by sector and type of asset, reference may be made to table 6 in this document.

Table 6

Gross domestic capital formation by sector
and type of asset, 1978 - 1984
(Millions of Israeli shekels at current prices)

Years	Private sector			Public sector	Grand total
	Machinery, transport and other equip. (1)	Building and construction work (2)	Sub-total (3)	(govt.& local authorities) (4)	(5)
1978	65.3	247.3	312.6	45.8	394.7
1979	118.3	429.8	648.1	80.2	701.2
1980	220.5	1,148.1	1,368.6	150.8	1,788.8
1981	440.4	2,669.3	3,109.7	399.4	3,264.9
1982	1,056.5	5,967.6	7,024.1	1,102.9	8,559.4
1983	2,810.2	13,049.1	15,859.4	3,196.3	18,578.3
1984	11,966.0	59,662.0	71,628.0	18,727.0	87,979.0

Source: Israel, Central Bureau of Statistics, Judea, Samaria and Gaza Area Statistics, (Jerusalem, CBS, 1985), vol. XV, Nos. 1 and 2, tables 4 and 11, pages 70, 77, 166 and 173.

Note: Figures in column (5) do not reflect the total of columns (1) and (4). The latter columns have been adjusted for changes in stocks.

25. Total gross domestic capital formation amounted to an annual average of 31.3 per cent of GDP over the period 1980-1983. Although this is totally attributed to external flows, it compares favourably to the figure of 23.8 per cent for all developing countries and the figure of 21.1 per cent for industrial market economies.32/ The share of the private sector in total gross capital formation amounted to an annual average of 85 per cent during the period 1978-1984. The balance comprises the Israeli Government's small share, which is generally intended for infrastructural work mostly related to Israeli settlements in the territories.

26. As a result, physical and human infrastructure and government services for the inhabitants of the territories have remained very limited over the occupation period. Similarly, municipal services have been constrained due to the mounting budgetary difficulties. External assistance is increasingly being sought to provide some of the public services needed in such vital areas as health, water, education, electricity, road and others. There has been no government involvement in the productive sectors. In fact, official policy, or lack of it, has consistently acted against productive projects, even if these have involved local resources and entrepreneurs. Heavy investment is badly needed to provide an adequate infrastructure and to create a productive base for a self-sustaining economy in the territories.

27.   For the most part, private investment has been concerned with building
and construction works. Expenditure on residential buildings has absorbed more
than four-fifths of private investment. This building has been primarily
intended to meet the growing need for housing, to hedge against inflation,
which reached over 445 per cent in 1984, 33/ and to establish a presence on
land primarily aimed at thwarting Israeli land expropriation practices. In
addition, discouragement and obstacles acting against investment in productive
projects in agriculture and industry have led potential investors to move into
speculative dealings involving movable and immovable property and a range of
other commercial activities.

3.   Prices and the impact of inflation

28.   The increasingly close economic links with Israel have rendered the
territories highly susceptible to Israeli price movements and high rates of
inflation. Table 7 depicts the trend in general consumer price indices in the
West Bank and Gaza Strip and Israel since 1970.

29.   Much of the inflationary pressure in the territories is attributed to the
close economic links established with Israel. This pressure has been felt
primarily through the prices of increased imports of goods from Israel, which
have amounted to almost 90 per cent of all goods imported, the wages of
Palestinian workers in Israel and the declining value of the Israeli
currency, which also serves as the legal tender in the territories. It is
equally due to the declining capacity of the domestic economy and its
inability to meet the rising level of demand generated through increased
income from abroad in the form of factor income and transfers. Other domestic
factors such as the size of credit, government outlays and the extent of their
deficit financing are not likely to have played any significant role in
contributing to inflation.

30.   The impact of inflation on the life of ordinary citizens, civic
institutions and business enterprises in the occupied territories has been
overwhelming, particularly since 1974 and the devaluation of Israeli currency
in that year. Prior to 1974, inflation was associated with high rates of
growth in real income and output, thus benefiting those who participated in
their generation. The most important visible subsequent outcome of this
phenomenon was the sharp and often erratic depreciation of the Israeli
currency, especially when measured against the Jordanian dinar, which is the
second legal tender in the West Bank. Table 8 shows, for instance, that the
market exchange value of the Israeli shekel dropped from Jordanian fils
1000.0 per shekel in 1971 to 1.2 fils per shekel in 1984.

31.   The severe and noticeably erratic deterioration in the exchange value of
Israeli currency has made economic planning and business activity in the
territories extremely difficult and unusually risky. An overriding objective
for all businessmen has been the preservation of the real value of their sales
and goods in stock. One immediate measure they took for this purpose was to
curtail their credit facilities to customers almost to zero, or else convert
the unpaid value of goods to Jordanian dinars at the prevailing exchange
rate - a measure which often proved unfair to buyers. At any rate, the
deterioration in the level of prices during the period 1975-1984 was extremely
hard on consumers, as it subjected them to harsh inconsistencies in the
pricing system. On the other hand, it also increased the risk margin for
sellers and eventually drove some out of business.

Table 7

General consumer price index

	West Bank	Gaza Strip	Israel	Remarks
1970	..	..	106.1	Base 1969 = 100
1971	125.9	128.1	118.8	" "
1972	148.1	153.1	134.1	" "
1973	179.9	190.3	160.9	" "
1974	256.5	294.3	224.8	" "
1975	367.4	452.7	313.1	" "
1976	114.9	113.2	411.2	Base for occupied territories is Jan. 1976 = 100. Base for Israel 1976 = 100.
1977	156.3	151.5	134.6	
1978	235.1	216.4	202.7	
1979	395.3	373.0	361.4	
1980	946.2	954.7	834.9	Base for Israel 1980 = 100
1981	2,025.2	2,000.5	216.8	
1982	4,199.5	4,294.0.	477.7	
1983	10,069.0	10,784.6	1,173.5	
1984	46,384.2	51,006.8	5,560.4	

Sources : Figures derived from Israel, Central Bureau of Statistics, Statistical Abstract of Israel 1975 (Jerusalem, CBS, 1975), p. 694; Israel, Central Bureau of Statistics, Statistical Abstract of Israel 1978 (Jerusalem, CBS, 1978), p. 774 ; and Israel, Central Bureau of Statistics, Statistical Abstract of Israel 1985 (Jerusalem, CBS, 1985), pp. 714 and 265.

Table 8

Exchange rate for the Jordanian dinar and Israeli shekel

Year	IS per JD	Jordanian fils per IS
1971	1.00	1,000.0
1972	1.26	793.7
1973	1.34	746.2
1974	1.72	581.4
1975	2.05	487.8
1976	2.91	343.6
1977	3.20	312.5
1978	5.48	182.5
1979	8.37	119.5
1980	16.96	59.0
1981	34.23	29.2
1982	68.06	14.7
1983	154.97	6.4
1984	807.07	1.2

Source: a leading moneychanging office in Nablus, the West Bank, 1986.

Note: 1000 fils = 1 Jordanian dinar).

32. The collapse of sale credit facilities, during the inflationary period 1976-1985, was especially serious in certain farming sectors, where producers were used to procuring their farming inputs from major suppliers on the basis of loans which they usually settled after the sale of their produce. Coming at a time when the farmers had practically no alternative source of seasonal credit, the collapse of "in-kind" credit arrangements was particularly difficult to sustain.

33. The pronounced and continuously increasing differential in the consumer price indices of the territories and Israel has lead to a fall in the value of sales to Israeli buyers of output from local markets in the territories. In fact, it is now frequently reported that an increasing number of residents in the West Bank and Gaza Strip prefer to buy some of their consumer and durable goods from neighbouring Israeli towns, as prices there do not appear to be as high. This dual impact on demand in local markets has been an important factor in precipitating the current stagnation in economic activity in the territories.

34. The rising rate of inflation, especially since 1980, gradually resulted in a decline in the real disposable income of most income groups and was accompanied by a widening gap between the monetary income of families and the cost of maintaining their standards of living at the levels prevailing during mid-1970s. The grinding impact of this situation has been particularly hard on workers paid in Israeli currency, which includes all workers in Israel (close to 40 per cent of the employed labour force) and those working for the Israeli Civil Administration (around 10 per cent). The impact of inflation on the purchasing power of this category of income earners can be judged from the fact that the Jordanian dinar value of the Israeli shekel salary of a new college graduate (say, working as a teacher in a government school) dropped from JD 105 in 1976 to JD 65 in early 1985. Likewise, the value in Jordanian dinar terms of wages paid to unskilled Palestinian labourers employed in Israel has dropped from around JD 5 per day in the early 1970s to only JD 3 per day in the 1980s.

35. These high rates of inflation have no doubt affected the economic status of the middle and low-income groups especially and caused a sharp drop in the standard of living of the professionally privileged income group (e.g. a medical doctor working for the Government receives around $300-400 a month). The standard of living for most income groups would have dropped to very low levels had it not been for the effective role played by remittances earned abroad. However, the compensatory role of remittances is expected to be greatly undermined in the wake of the severe economic recession in the Gulf States and Jordan because of its grave ramifications for the employment potential and wage levels of emigrant Palestinian workers. Should all these adverse factors continue to bear on the occupied territories, it is certain that poverty and unemployment will undergo a dramatic surge over the next few years.

D. **Major developments**

36. The 20 years of occupation have resulted in significant structural
changes in the economy of the territories. As noted earlier, the traditional
sector has gradually given way to areas within the efficient modern sector,
which generally enjoys higher rates of productivity. The agricultural sector
has lost its predominant role in terms of its contribution to total output and
employment, largely in favour of services which have gradually emerged as
areas closely linked to the Israeli economy. The industrial sector has
virtually stagnated under occupation, despite its subcontracting arrangements
with Israeli enterprises. In fact, the composition and pattern of output of
the commodity-producing sectors themselves have slowly undergone changes
largely geared to meeting the requirements of the Israeli market. Developments
in these and other sectors indicate an increasing alignment of the economic
performance of the territories with the economic interests of Israel rather
than the creation of structures for an independent and self-sustaining economy.

1. **Agriculture**

37. Agriculture remains the backbone of the territories' economy, despite its
declining contribution to gross domestic product. In addition to being a
significant source of employment, it also provides the raw material basis for
immediate consumption and for industrial activities, as well as serving as an
important source of foreign exchange. For an initial period of over a decade,
agriculture was marked by high rates of growth. This was largely the result of
marked rise in the productivity of certain high-priced products rather than a
corresponding rise in aggregate output.[34]/ Since the early 1980s, however,
agricultural output has undergone a steady decline, especially in respect of
field crops and fruits grown under dry farming conditions where productivity
largely depends on the amount of rainfall.

38. Given the nature of agriculture, small improvements resulted in
considerable increases in output, especially of cash crops. Measures such as
improvements in the use of implements and the introduction of new equipment
and techniques, including drip irrigation, fertilizers, improved seeds and
other inputs requiring relatively small amounts of capital, were instrumental
in increasing output in relation to labour and land inputs. Most of these
measures were financed from the farmers' own resources through business
savings and by short-term borrowings from the informal financial market
involving merchants, money-lenders and commission agents. The capacity to
self-finance and borrowing limits were, however, over-stretched. The
contribution of government resources, which is crucial for increasing
efficiency in agriculture, has been virtually non-existant in the territories.
Israeli government loans, which continued only until 1970, involved no more
than token amounts. As in other areas, this sector was soon severely
handicapped by the lack of a credit system and began to feel the adverse
effect of the closure of local banks and other financial institutions. The
result has been severe hardship for small-scale family farms which have
constituted the bulk of production units and whose sources of finance have
been very limited.

39.   Growing limitations on the availability of private and public finance,
coupled with changing output and cropping patterns and markets, as well as
growing dependence on Israeli trade policies, have imposed severe constraints
on agricultural producers. Lack of official support for development projects,
inadequate infrastructure in terms of transportation, power, irrigation
schemes, research, experimental and other related physical and institutional
facilities have added to the difficult problem of inducing further increases
in private economic activity in agriculture. The impact of these features has
been further compounded by various administrative and legal constraints
imposed by the occupation authorities. These include severe restrictions on
the use of existing water resources and the tapping of new sources, the
uprooting of olive and citrus trees and their non-replacement by new ones,
land expropriations, and other practices detrimental to Palestinian
agriculture.

40.   In contrast, as part of a process of settling an increasing number of
Israelis in the territories, a plan for the agricultural establishment of
these settlers has envisaged a total of 55,000 dunums for cultivation and
145,000 dunums of marginal land for pasturage. In 1984, approximately
50,000 dunums of land were under Jewish cultivation in the West Bank,35/
much of it in the fertile lands of the Jordan Valley, where a total of 4,000
Israelis have been settled. A similar pattern of expropriation of land and its
allocation for Israeli settlements has been seen in the Gaza Strip, especially
since 1979. In 1985, out of a total of 100,000 dunums possessed by the
occupation authorities in the Strip, 22,250 dunums were occupied by
settlements, giving 10.4 dunums of land per Israeli settler.36/

41.   Consequently, the total cultivated area in the territories has decreased,
with no new measures to replace losses through land reclamation and irrigation
programmes (see table 9). Cultivated land declined from around 37 per cent of
the total land area in the West Bank in 1966 to about 28 per cent in 1984, and
in the Gaza Strip from 51 per cent of total area in 1966 to 50 per cent in
1984. In addition to land seizure, lack of private and public finance has also
forced farmers to either leave land fallow or abandon it altogether in pursuit
of more rewarding employment.

42.   The adverse effect of all these factors on agricultural output,
employment and income should not be underestimated. Agricultural output and
income in the West Bank showed a steady decline during the period 1981-1985
(see table 10). The decline in the level of employment in agriculture was less
drastic over the same period. However, employment in agriculture declined from
a total of 60,000 in 1970 to 37,100 in 1985, or by some 38 per cent. In terms
of total employment in the territories, the share of agricultural employment
also declined sharply from 38.7 per cent in 1970 to 24.4 per cent in 1985 (see
table 14 below). This drop has been partly offset by increases in employment
in the services sector and partly by employment in Israel and other countries.
Industry, as the potentially crucial sector of the economy, has provided no
employment opportunities to absorb the labour released from agriculture.

Table 9

Cultivated land in the West Bank and Gaza Strip
before and after Israeli occupation in 1967
(Thousands of dunums)

	West Bank			Gaza Strip		
	1966	1982[a/]	1984	1966	1982[a/]	1984
1. Total cultivated land	2,080.0	1,600.6	1,584.8	187.0	164.6	183.7
Cultivated as per cent of total area	37.3	28.7	28.4	51.0	44.8	50.0
2. Irrigated land	100.0	78.6	101.3	75.0	93.7	..
Irrigated as per cent of cultivated area	4.8	4.9	6.4	40.1	56.9	..

Sources: Meron Benvenisti (West Bank Data Base Project), A survey of
Israel's Policies (Washington and London, American Enterprise Institute for
Public Policy Research, 1984), p. 13; Sara Roy, (West Bank Data Base
Project), The Gaza Strip Survey (Cambridge, Harvard University Press, 1986),
p. 38; UNCTAD, "Selected statistical tables on the economy of the occupied
Palestinian territories" (UNCTAD/ST/SEU/1), table 19, p. 21; ESCWA, Food
Security in the West Bank and Gaza Strip (Baghdad, ESCWA, 1985), p. 34.

a/ Refers to agricultural year 1981/82.

Table 10

Output, employment and income originating in agriculture, 1980-1985 a/

	1980-1981	1981-1982	1982-1983	1983-1984	1984-1985
	(Millions of current dollars)				
Total value of output	387	436	445	314	389
- West Bank	296	346	341	309	297
- Gaza Strip	91	90	104	105	92
Income generated in agriculture	303	324	304	271	265
- West Bank	237	266	235	201	204
- Gaza Strip	66	58	69	70	61
	(Thousands)				
Total agricultural employment	36.9	39.6	38.0	37.4	37.1
- West Bank	28.5	31.35	29.25	29.64	28.3
- Gaza Strip	8.4	8.25	8.75	7.76	8.8

Source: (i) Value of output and income originating in agriculture for the years 1980-1981 and 1984-1985 are calculated from Israel, Central Bureau of Statistics, Statistical Abstracts of Israel, 1984 and 1986 (Jerusalem, CBS, 1984 and 1986), pp. 769 and 713, respectively. Figures for 1981-1984 are calculated from Israel, Central Bureau of Statistics, Judea, Samaria and Gaza Area Statistics (Jerusalem, CBS, December 1985), vol. XV, No. 2, pp. 97-103. Israeli shekels are converted to United States dollars according to the annual average exchange rate, International Monetary Fund, International Financial Statistics (Washington D.C., IMF, April 1986), p. 273;

(ii) Employment figures are for calendar years and are calculated from Israel, Central Bureau of Statistics, Statistical Abstract of Israel, 1986 (Jerusalem, CBS, 1986), table 21, p. 705.

a/ Prices are adjusted to April of each year.

2. Industry

43. The industrial sector has stagnated during much of the occupation period. In the early years of occupation, the authorities focused attention on developing industry, even though support was limited. In later years, the emphasis was shifted to the enforcement of routine industrial regulation.[37] In the late 1970s, Israeli government support for industrial development in the territories not only came to an end but was subsequently followed by a policy statement in 1984 which discouraged the development of both industry and agriculture in the territories.[38] The industrial sector has therefore been operating under increasingly difficult circumstances and has been deprived of a strategy guideline to assist in determining the degree of emphasis to be placed on issues crucial to industrial development.[39]

44. Consequently, the share of industry in gross domestic product stagnated at around 9 per cent between 1978 and 1984 (see table 11). The decline during the period 1980-1983 led to an annual average share of as little as 8 per cent. Including construction, this share amounted to 25 per cent in 1983, which is low given the relatively high level of per capita income of the territories. In 1983, the corresponding share of industry, including construction, was 31 per cent of GDP in Jordan, 25 per cent in the Syrian Arab Republic, 33 per cent in Egypt, and 27 per cent in Israel.[40/] The relatively high level of per capita income should provide a significant market to induce industrial expansion. Economies under colonial or protectorate administration and having a per capita income of up to $200 have had a share of manufacturing ranging from 7 to 11 per cent of GDP,[41/] as compared to only 9 per cent for the territories which had a per capita GDP of $848 in 1984.

Table 11

The share of industry in total employed persons, gross capital formation and gross domestic product, 1978-1985

Year	Employed persons (1)	As percent of total	Gross capital formation (2)	As percent of total	Gross domestic product (3)	As percent of total
1978	-	...	65.3	16.5	105.0	9
1979	23,184	16.8	118.3	16.9	177.0	9
1980	22,917	16.3	220.5	12.3	406.9	7
1981	22,416	16.0	440.4	13.5	791.9	7
1982	22,258	15.5	1,056.5	12.3	1,709.9	7
1983	22,862	15.8	2,810.2	15.1	4,563.9	8
1984	24,613	16.3	11,966.0	13.6	26,927.0	9
1985	24,584	16.1	..	..	..	.

Source: Column (1) is computed from Israel, Central Bureau of Statistics, Statistical Abstract of Israel, 1986 (Jerusalem, CBS., 1986), table XXVII/21, p. 705. Columns (2) and (3) are derived from tables 6 and 4, respectively.

45. The most recent survey of the industrial sector clearly depicts the consequences of the constraints confronting this sector in the territories.[42/] By 1984, there were 4,006 industrial firms operating in the territories (2,991 in the West Bank[43/] and 1,015 in the Gaza Strip). Of these, 13 per cent were engaged in garage and minor repairs, iron smithing and simple manufacturing, including that of furniture; 11 per cent in quarrying and manufacture of cement block and floor tiles; 13 per cent in carpentry; 20.5 per cent in garment manufacturing; 2 per cent in shoe making, leather and plastic goods; and the remaining 40.5 per cent in miscellaneous products. There were as many as 24,600 persons employed in these activities, constituting 16.3 per cent of total employed persons, compared to 21,000 employed in the territories in 1970, or an average annual increase of only 240 persons over 15 years. By 1985, this number had almost stagnated. Around 98 per cent of establishments in 1984 employed 10 or less persons, and they

were mostly financed by owner-capital. The majority of the firms surveyed were only working at around 50 per cent capacity due to financial constraints, as well as administrative, legal and other obstacles.

46.   On the whole, the sector has been forced to operate within limits imposed by three rival forces acting simultaneously on the scene, namely the domestic, Israeli and Jordanian markets. Domestically, industry has managed to sell more than twice as many products as it has sold to Israel. However, the sector is increasingly faced with competition from Israeli industries, which enjoy generous government support in the form of subsidies, credit on reasonable terms, tax incentives, concessions on foreign exchange earnings, protective customs duties and various infrastructural facilities, including research and training programmes. The lack of an appropriate body to regulate trade and adopt a rational import policy has had adverse effect on the balance of payments and the possibilities for an import substitution and export promotion drive. The imposition of value added tax (VAT) has further reduced the advantage enjoyed by Palestinian industry up to 1976 over comparable Israeli products.

47.   Local industry is also being confronted with competition from Israeli plants built in close proximity to the Israeli settlements in the territories.44/ Israeli settlement policy is complemented by an industrial plan for the Jewish areas in the West Bank which is designed to attract Israeli industry and labour to this "hinterland". The plan proposes that the largest Israeli industrial concentrations be located within the most densely populated regions of the West Bank and near the major Israeli population areas.45/ Six Israeli industrial parks, occupying an area of 1,260 dunums, had become operational by 1983 in the West Bank, employing 2,500 workers, 70 per cent of whom were Israelis. Between January and November 1985, the Israeli Government approved investment by Israeli industrial enterprises worth $27 million in the West Bank. Government grants amounted to $11 million. The region is classified as Development Area A+ and A and is thereby entitled to massive government assistance. 46/

48.   The occupation authorities are deploying a significant amount of resources for the construction of export-oriented factories in the occupied territories with the sole purpose of providing jobs for the settlers and to compete with the output of Palestinian industries in the territories and abroad where Israel can also benefit from free trade arrangements with both the United States and the European Community. For the first seven months of 1986, the government had planned to provide $19.5 million as grants to entrepreneurs - nearly one third more than was actually spent in all of 1985.47/ Current policy is to build only capital-intensive, sophisticated factories to achieve two objectives: to minimize the need for settlers to commute to work in Israeli cities; and to limit reliance on Palestinian Arab employment. As part of a long-term plan, an additional seven industrial parks are envisaged by the year 2010 which will create jobs for a total of 83,500 Israeli workers and only 23,000 Palestinian workers. By contrast, future policy towards Palestinian industry is aimed at dispersing it outside urban centres and developing workshop areas in villages. While Palestinian industries will be allowed to operate within Israeli industrial parks in the occupied territories, they will not be eligible for Israeli incentives.48/ At any rate, proposals have seldom received the attention or been provided with the support and resources they need. Even when resources have been raised, lack of infrastructural facilities (such as electricity,

water, drainage, transportation and so on) has prevented their implementation. In general, industry has not been able to respond to the changes that have taken place in agriculture and other sectors by providing job opportunities and satisfying increased demand for industrial output.

49. Regarding the Israeli market, there is minimal penetration of industrial goods from the territories, except for shoes, textiles, woodwork, building materials and certain processed food products. Much of this business has been organized through subcontracting arrangements between Israelis and Palestinian local producers which, on the whole, have contributed to only small increases in value added and employment in industry. Subcontracting has appealed to Israeli producers because of the availability of cheap labour and lower overheads in the territories. These branches of Palestinian industry have therefore been playing a complementary role to Israeli industry. Although subcontracting may also lead to some degree of specialization in the concerned industry branch of the territories, it does not reflect the actual needs of the Palestinian economy. The pattern is not similar to that emerging among economies where relations are governed by national considerations. 49/

50. As for the Jordanian market, large scale expansion of industrial exports is limited for two reasons, i.e. the policy of protecting similar domestic industries and maintaining the Arab boycott of products for which the equipment and raw materials are not imported from and/or through Jordan. It was recently reported that the Jordanian authorities have begun to relax some of the restrictions on the entry of industrial goods from the territories. However, economic recession in the once prosperous countries of the Gulf may not allow a more rapid absorption of industrial goods from the territories. While efforts need to be intensified in order to increase the ability of industrial output from the territories to enter international markets, it is primarily the share of the domestic market in the territories that is crucial for the expansion and development of Palestinian industry.

3.   Structure and direction of trade

51. An important aspect of the territories' economy is its longstanding international trade links. Historically, the West Bank has supplied neighbouring Arab countries with certain commodities and manufactured goods, especially olives, olive oil, building stone and soap, which had a stable market abroad. Similarly, the Gaza Strip developed well-established markets for its citrus fruits in a number of East European countries (inheriting some of those established by the pre-1948 Palestinian Arab citrus industry) and more recently in the Arab world. As with other developing economies, chances for the growth of the economy have always depended upon opportunities for expanding international trade relations. This is especially so in view of the relatively small local market and the difficulties in producing competitively many of the capital goods required for development or the consumer goods demanded by a population increasingly influenced by regional consumption patterns.

52. There are three ways in which the Israeli occupation of the West Bank and Gaza Strip influences the territories' trade. First, and most significantly, is the effect of occupation itself in creating factors which alter the established patterns and practices of trade and over which the Palestinian economy has little or no power. These include most prominently the physical

barriers imposed by occupation between the territories and their hinterland, the sectoral developments which have occurred as a direct result of the domination of the territories' economy by the much more advanced Israeli economy, and the boycott policies adopted by Arab countries to prevent the import of Palestinian exports containing any measure of Israeli produced or imported raw materials. Secondly, Israel has developed a policy with regard to trade with the territories which has resulted in a number of measures having a negative impact on their trading position. Finally, there are various trading procedures and practices which also adversely affect the ability to trade competitively.

53. The major consideration influencing Israeli policy towards trade with the territories is that Israeli exports should be able to flow freely there while exports to Israel should be closely controlled to safeguard the interests of Israeli producers. This is a deliberate and calculated policy decision, established early in the occupation period and scrupulously applied since. The existing patterns of trade between Israel and the territories reflect this consideration, and official statements confirm this orientation. In announcing new policy guidelines for export procedures to Israel, a government official affirmed that Palestinian products "threaten Israeli firms with unfair competition".50/ Meanwhile, Israeli policy allows the free flow of Israeli agricultural and industrial goods to the territories, disregarding the effects on Palestinian producers.

54. A number of specific measures have been enacted since 1967. To begin with, some of the territories' most lucrative cash crops (cucumbers, tomatoes, eggplant, melons, etc.) which could compete with Israeli produce are generally banned from Israeli markets, or, if allowed to enter, they are only imported in small and controlled quantitites, thus protecting Israeli producers of these commodities. Additionally, exports of Palestinian agricultural output, notably the Gaza Strip's citrus fruit, to Western Europe and other markets secured for Israeli produce is forbidden and strict punishments are imposed for contravention of this regulation.51/ In order to prevent 'the threat of competition' from Palestinian manufactures, a new military order enforces complex labelling guidelines for all Palestinian products (specifying manufacturer, contents, weight, etc.),52/ adding further costs to an already burdened manufacturing process.

55. Furthermore, most Israeli links with the territories' industrial exports are geared to taking advantage of the labour-intensive stages of the production process, for example in textiles and clothing and certain wood and metal products associated with the construction sector. These are most profitably subcontracted to the labour-surplus Palestinian economy for export to Israel in partially or fully finished form. Little or no control is exerted over the quality and quantity of goods entering the territories to safeguard the interests of local production capacity.53/

56. In 1985, the occupied territories exported $283 million of industrial and agricultural goods to Israel, Jordan and the rest of the world (see table 12). The trend in exports has declined in recent years, after having peaked at $403 million in 1981. The trend in imports has been similar. After having reached the highest level of $785 million in 1983, imports fell to $668 million. External trade has exhibited a deficit which grew at an average

Table 12

Selected external trade indicators, occupied Palestinian territories (OPT) and Israel, 1978-1985
(Millions of current United States dollars and percentages)

	1978	1979	1980	1981	1982	1983	1984	1985a/
Total OPT exports	263	272	343	403	391	382	300	283
Exports to Israel	158	169	224	289	258	285	196	192
As a percentage of the total	60%	62%	65%	72%	66%	74%	62%	68%
Exports to Jordan	95	92	107	105	125	93	115	85
As a percentage of the total	36%	34%	31%	26%	32%	24%	36%	30%
Industrial exports	165	174	233	300	286	293	242	191
As a percentage of the total	62%	64%	68%	74%	73%	76%	77%	71%
Agricultural exports	103	99	110	103	104	93	73	78
As a percentage of the total	38%	36%	32%	26%	27%	24%	23%	29%
Industrial exports to Israel	125	137	179	245	225	245	172	153
As a percentage of industrial exports	75%	79%	77%	82%	79%	84%	71%	76%
As a percentage of total exports	47%	50%	52%	60%	58%	63%	54%	54%
Agricultural exports to Jordan	60	56	(49)	(51)	65	46	45	49
As a percentage of agricultural exports	63%	61%	44%	49%	62%	50%	62%	62%
As a percentage of total exports	23%	20%	14%	13%	17%	12%	14%	17%
Israeli non-milit. imports	4520	6499	6835	7351	7430	7746	7364	7034
OPT exports to Israel as a percentage of Israeli imports	3.5%	2.6%	3.3%	3.9%	3.5%	3.7%	2.7%	2.7%
Total OPT imports	456	568	665	737	729	785	686	668
Total OPT imports from Israel	404	493	583	664	648	713	620	598
OPT imports from Israel as a percentage of OPT imports	89%	87%	88%	90%	89%	91%	90%	89%
Israeli non-milit. exports	2444	3128	3922	4273	4098	3900	4595	4824
OPT imports from Israel as a percentage of Israeli non-milit. exports:	16%	16%	15%	16%	16%	18%	13%	12%
Trade balance (deficit)	193	392	321	334	338	403	387	385

Sources: (1) Figures for 1985 calculated from Israel, Central Bureau of Statistics, Statistical Abstract of Israel 1986, (Jerusalem, CBS) p. 693; figures for 1982-1984 are calculated from Israel, Central Bureau of Statistics, Judea, Samaria and Gaza Area Statistics (Jerusalem, CBS, vol. XV, No. 2, December 1985) pp. 6-7; figures for 1978-1981 calculated from Israel, Central Bureau of Statistics, Administered Territories Statistics Quarterly (Jerusalem, CBS, vol. XI, July-September, 1981) pp. 6-7, and Israel, Central Bureau of Statistics, Statistical Abstract of Israel 1984 (Jerusalem, CBS, 1984) (1978-81 figures transformed from Israeli shekels into United States dollars according to annual average exchange rates in International Monetary Fund, International Financial Statistics (Wash. D.C., IMF, 1985) pp. 364-7.

(2) Israeli trade figures: from International Monetary Fund, International Financial Statistics (Wash. D.C., IMF, 1986) p. 409.

a/   Figures for 1985 are provisional.

annual rate of 14 per cent between 1978 and 1985; in 1985, it stood at some $100 million more than the total value of exports in that year. The deficit with Israel in 1985 was even larger and has been growing constantly since 1967. It is only the trade surplus with Jordan that helps to lessen the burden in trade relations with Israel. However, that surplus has recently shown incipient signs of a downward trend, falling to $75 million in 1985.

57. The direction and composition of trade are highly concentrated. Some two thirds of exports are destined for Israel,[54]/ while most of the rest go to or through Jordan and only a small proportion to other countries. Industrial exports account for an increasing share of total Palestinian exports, reaching a record 77 per cent in 1984.[55]/ Since 1978, between 79 and 88 per cent of exports to Israel have consisted of industrial goods. This growing percentage indicates domination by the Israeli market of the territories' export capacities. This is partially offset by industrial exports to Jordan and agricultural exports to/through Jordan. These, however, have recently accounted for a declining proportion of the territories' exports. On the whole, while the territories do not supply a significant part of Israel's imports (around 3 per cent of Israeli non-military imports), their own trade relations are increasingly influenced by Israel. An average of 16 per cent of Israeli exports are destined for the territories, making the Palestinian economy the second largest Israeli (non-military) export market after the United States.[56]/ Despite the recent slump in Palestinian trade and economic activity, there remains a substantial movement of goods and services between the territories and neighbouring economies which continues to require a flexible and effective system for financing and regulating the transactions involved.

4. Labour and employment in Israel

58. Crucial to the economy of the territories is the relationship between weak local productive capacity and the high proportion of national income generated from sources outside the territories. The phenonomon of migrant labour providing a substantial part of national income through remittances is not uncommon, internationally or regionally,[57]/ nor is it necessarily a negative one: if carefully channelled, it can be a growth-inducing source of income in a labour-surplus economy struggling to develop its indigenous potential. Since the beginning of the Israeli occupation of the West Bank and Gaza Strip, labour force development there has undergone a number of significant transformations, in terms of size, location of work and sectoral composition.

59. Perhaps the most noticeable effect of occupation has been the inability of the local economy to absorb its own labour force, leading to the phenonemon of migration abroad or to work in Israel. Consequently, the size of the locally employed labour force remained stagnant over 15 years (see table 14). An important feature of the territories' labour force in the past few years has been its increasing rate of growth, outstripping that of population (see table 13). Between 1983 and 1985, while population grew by an average annual rate of 2.9 per cent, the labour force grew by 3.3 per cent, so that an average of 7,000 new jobs are now required each year (assuming full employment). The difference between growth in population and labour force has been manifested by an increase in the crude participation rate. A main factor contributing to this development is a decrease in labour migration to Arab countries.[58]/

Table 13

Population, aged 14 and above, by labour force characteristics, 1979-1984

Year	Pop. grand total (000)	Total labour force (000)	Employed		Unem- ployed	Percentage of labour force unemployed	Labour Force	
			Total (000)	Thereof in Israel			Percentage of total population	Percentage employed in Israel
1979	641.6	213.9	212.4	74.1	1.5	0.7	33.3	34.6
1980	643.7	218.5	215.7	75.1	2.8	1.3	33.9	34.4
1981	650.0	218.1	215.9	75.8	2.2	1.0	33.6	35.1
1982	652.3	225.2	222.9	79.1	2.3	1.0	34.5	35.5
1983	682.3	235.9	232.5	87.8	3.4	1.4	34.6	37.8
1984	701.2	248.0	241.3	90.3	6.7	2.7	35.4	37.4
1985	722.4	251.3	242.1	89.2	9.2	3.6	34.8	35.4
1985 I-III	712.5	249.5	240.1	90.4	9.4	3.7	35.0	37.6
IV-VI	723.2	253.5	244.5	90.1	9.0	3.5	35.1	36.8
VII-IX	728.9	244.2	234.0	90.5	10.2	4.2	33.5	36.8
X-XII	726.1	257.9	249.8	86.4	8.1	3.1	35.5	33.5

Source: All figures, except for 1985, calculated from Israel, Central Bureau of Statistics, Judea, Samaria and Gaza Area Statistics (Jerusalem, CBS) vol. XV, No. 2, December 1985, p. 27. Figures for 1985 calculated from Israel, Central Bureau of Statistics, Judea, Samaria and Gaza Area Statistics (Jerusalem, CBS) vol. XVI, No. 1, 1986, pp. 29 and 36.

Note: Quarterly data for 1984 and 1985 are 'original data' (i.e. not 'seasonally adjusted data').

Table 14

Employed persons, by selected economic branch and place of work

Years	In Israel				Total		In occupied Palestinian territories				Total	
	Other branches	Const-ruction	Indus-try	Agricul-ture	%	000	Other branches	Const-ruction	Indus-try	Agricul-ture	%	000
1970	9.7	54.3	11.6	24.4	100	20.6	39.1	8.4	13.8	38.7	100	152.7
1975	12.9	54.4	18.4	14.3	100	66.3	46.4	7.3	14.5	31.8	100	138.6
1976	14.6	50.3	19.7	15.4	100	64.9	46.0	8.2	14.4	31.4	100	140.9
1977	17.2	45.3	21.3	16.2	100	63.0	46.2	9.1	14.2	30.5	100	141.4
1979	16.2	46.2	22.8	14.8	100	74.1	45.1	10.1	16.8	28.0	100	138.0
1980	18.0	47.4	20.9	13.7	100	75.1	45.7	9.6	16.3	28.4	100	140.6
1981	18.1	51.0	18.2	12.7	100	75.8	47.0	10.7	16.0	26.3	100	140.1
1982	16.7	52.8	17.7	12.8	100	79.1	47.0	9.9	15.5	27.6	100	143.6
1983	18.8	50.4	18.6	12.2	100	87.8	47.8	10.1	15.8	26.3	100	144.7
1984	19.5	48.3	18.0	14.2	100	90.3	48.5	10.4	16.3	24.8	100	151.0
1985	18.8	47.6	17.8	15.8	100	89.2	48.5	11.1	16.1	24.4	100	152.7

Source: From Israel, Central Bureau of Statistics, Statistical Abstract of Israel 1986 (Jerusalem, CBS, 1986), p. 705.

60. Associated with an overall recessionary climate, it is not surprising
that this growing labour force found it increasingly difficult to obtain
employment. The rate of unemployment in the territories had by 1985 risen to
3.7 per cent, with an average unemployed figure of 9,200 for the year. In the
fourth quarter of 1985, the first signs of an improvement were witnessed, with
the most significant fall in the number of unemployed Palestinians since the
preceding decade.59/ At the heart of this unemployment situation lies the
fall in work opportunities for Palestinian workers in Israel and in the Arab
countries, as these workers tend to face dismissal in periods of economic
crisis in both markets.60/ The nature of the local economy, which is
dependent upon external demand for its output and labour, is such that there
are few local alternatives.61/

61. Apart from employment opportunities elsewhere, there exist two markets
for Palestinian labour, i.e. in the territories themselves and inside Israel.
The main sectoral trend in the territories' resident labour force, which has
greatly influenced labour developments in other sectors, has been the sharp
decline in the proportion (and numbers) employed in agriculture (see
table 14).62/ While employment in other local sectors grew steadily into the
1980s, its growth in industry was directly linked to subcontracting for
Israeli industry. By 1985, 25 per cent of resident Palestinian labour was in
agriculture, 16 per cent in industry, 11 per cent in construction, and over
48 per cent in other sectors (mostly in public services and commerce).

62. Since 1967, an increasing proportion of the Palestinian labour force has
been drawn into work in Israel. In 1970, the 21,000 Palestinians working in
Israel constituted only 12 per cent of the labour force. The number and
proportion peaked in 1984, with 90,300 Palestinians working in Israel,
constituting some 37 per cent of the total Palestinian work force. By 1985,
the figure had dropped to 89,200, though this still represented just under
37 per cent of the total. Israeli demand for Palestinian labour exhibits
trends somewhat similar to those in the local labour market. The share of
Palestinian labour employed in Israeli agriculture fell from 24 per cent of
the territories' labour force employed in Israel in 1970 to 16 per cent in
1985. Employment of Palestinians from the territories in Israeli industry rose
in the 1970s only to fall to 18 per cent by 1985. Construction activity in
Israel has always been the main employer of labour from the territories. The
share of the migrant labour force in this sector fell from its high of
54 per cent early in the 1970s to 48 per cent in 1985, another reflection of
the Israeli recession.63/

63. While the migration process is a necessary response to deteriorating
economic conditions in the occupied territories, it has had an important role
in maintaining subsistence. This is achieved by channelling part of factor
income into the local economy and providing resources for the continued
operation of some farms which might otherwise not be able to survive under
prevailing circumstances. The process of 'labour export', while originally a
side-effect of the operation of constraints upon the Palestinian economy, has
increasingly become a crucial element in sustaining and influencing it. The
role that this process has played in the generation of financial resources for
the weakened Palestinian economy is of a significance that cannot be
underestimated.

5.   Housing and Israeli settlements

64.   Despite the growing need for more and better housing, the housing sector remains one of the most neglected areas of the territories' economy. By the end of 1983, the population of the territories, excluding East Jerusalem, was estimated at 1,266,000. Statistics for 1983 put over 7 persons per household for 49 per cent of population in the West Bank and 45 per cent of the population in the Gaza Strip.[64]/ The total population was served by 181,611 housing units, giving it an average of almost seven persons per unit. In practice, however, a more skewed distribution in dwelling is reported, whereby 32 per cent of the population lives in one-room units and 46 per cent in two-room units.[65]/ On average, this gives a density of three persons per room. About 40 per cent of families live in houses with three or more persons per room. At the same time, the proportion of Israeli families living under similar conditions did not exceed 1.3 per cent in 1982.[66]/

65.   The supply of housing over the years has not kept pace with the population increase. During the period 1967-1982, the housing industry satisfied housing needs of 38,589 units resulting from population growth, but only contributed a total of 6,721 units towards replacing an estimated 140,000 dilapidated and substandard units.[67]/. Much of this accomodation has been constructed by the private sector in the West Bank, mainly as a result of the rising demand of an expanding population for dwellings, increases in income, lack of alternative investment opportunities, unwillingness to invest in other branches of the economy because of the prevailing uncertainties, and people's determination to assert their rights to the land in the face of continuous threats of confiscation.[68]/ There has been no systematic planning and zoning to accommodate the normal expansion of the Palestinian communities. The choice of building sites is, therefore, in a number of instances determined by the intent to prevent the execution of Israeli road and settlement construction programmes, despite the hardships resulting from lack of public services such as transport, water, electricity and sewage.[69]/

66.   There has been no construction of residential buildings for Palestinians by the public sector in the West Bank since 1968 and in the Gaza Strip since 1978, except for some housing projects for the resettlement of refugees in the Gaza Strip.[70]/ The burden of residential construction has otherwise fallen entirely on private individuals with their meagre sources of finance. The Jordanian-Palestinian Joint Committee was able to make a modest allocation of around JD 27 million between 1979 and 1985, benefiting a total of 3,990 families.[71]/ However, the restrictive practices of the occupying authorities, in terms of administrative obstacles to issuing building permits and the transfer of funds from abroad until 1985, have stifled local efforts and effectively barred a potentially large number of families from procuring decent housing.[72]/ Alleviating current shortages in housing, upgrading substandard existing units and accommodating for national growth in population and return migration of Palestinians from abroad, especially from the oil-producing countries of the Gulf, would necessitate the construction of dwelling units at a rate of around 50,000 units per year for the next few years.[73]/

67. By contrast, the establishment of Israeli settlements in the occupied
territories has gone on unabated since 1967 in violation of international
law.74/ It has moved in parallel with Israeli land acquisition policies,
including measures under such schemes as expropriation of property, seizure of
possessions and restrictions on use, all of which have assured a virtually
unlimited reserve of land for Israeli settlements.75/ Currently there are
over 150 non-military highly subsidized Jewish settlements in the West Bank
(excluding East Jerusalem) and the Gaza Strip. These have a total population
of more than 52,000 settlers, almost equal to the figure of 52,500 Israelis
projected to be settled in the occupied territories by 1985.76/ Including
para-military settlements, a total of 267 Israeli settlements have been
constructed in the territories, presently accommodating around 55,000 Israeli
settlers.77/ Against this, net total Palestinian migration out of the
territories is estimated at more than 760,000 during the period 1967-1984.

68. The settlement policy is aimed at establishing an Israeli civilian
presence in the territories that would make it difficult for the Palestinian
communities to form an integrated entity and would isolate them from each
other, thus decreasing the possibility of unified action by them. The pattern
of settlements that has emerged reflects these considerations.78/ Although a
limited area of land is allocated for housing, in presently utilized
settlement areas, it could accommodate 800,000 to a million settlers (based on
a gross density of two families per dunum). In 1979, the Government also
allowed private Israeli citizens to buy Palestinian land, and three years
later land developers obtained approval to build private settlements. By the
end of 1985, the Higher Planning Committee had processed 191 plans for Jewish
built-up areas. The total area involved covers tens of thousands of dunums and
is intended to accommodate over 500,000 settlers.79/

69. The concentration of Israeli settlements in the metropolitan areas near
the so-called "green line" (i.e. the pre-1967 borders of Israel), a trend
which first appeared in 1981, has become more pronounced. Israeli settlers
wanting to move to such areas were offered an aid package consisting of a
mortgage of 11.5 per cent, an interest free loan for 65.5 per cent of the
cost, and an extra loan carrying 6 per cent interest. They receive the
confiscated land for only 5 per cent of its actual value. Businesses and
enterprises wishing to relocate just across the "green line" will get a grant
of 30 per cent of their cost and carry loans for the rest at 0.5 per cent
interest.80/ As a result, in 1985 three quarters of Israeli settlers were in
these Arab urban centres, where some 340,000 Palestinians are living.81/
Most of the Palestinian villages and towns have been prevented from
cultivating the land near these settlements or building on it. In fact, many
roads and other infrastructural facilities connecting these settlements are
extended through such land.82/

70. Major roads have by-passed Palestinian villages and connected Israeli
settlements with Israeli cities beyond the "green line". Once completed, the
network of roads and other settlement facilities will force Palestinian
sources of production to increase their links with Israeli regions, thus
increasing their dependence. Efforts are underway to extend Israeli
settlements into remote areas, while work on the expansion of the existing
ones continues. The strategy is to achieve "maximal distribution of a large
Israeli population in areas of high settlement importance...". 83/ The

infrastructure of the existing settlements is sufficient to double or even triple the present number of settlers. In addition to having built over 2,800 homes in existing settlements in recent years, attempts are underway to end the freeze on the establishment of new settlements and proceed with the construction of another 13 settlements in both Gaza and the West Bank.[84]/

71. As part of the overall financial and other incentives aimed at inducing Israelis to settle in the occupied territories, the Government of Israel invested a sum of almost $2 billion in settlements in the West Bank between 1968 and the end of 1985. This does not include investment in military installations. In recent years, the level of annual capital outlay has been $200-250 million. According to the State Comptroller's report in 1984, Israeli Government expenditures, including those of the World Zionist Organization (WZO), on settlements in the West Bank alone had amounted to around $220 million in 1983.[85]/ Investment allocations for 1985 amounted to $150 million; $95 million was for new projects, out of which 41 per cent was for housing and roads, 42 per cent for WZO settlements, and 11.6 per cent for industrial development related to these settlements. Allocations for the development of industrial parks increased by 168 per cent over 1984.[86]/ Outlays on settlements by the WZO alone (not including government contributions) for the period 1977-1985 amounted to approximately $292 million. In 1985, WZO's expenditure per Israeli unit (family) came to $165,000 in the Jordan Valley and about $80,000 in the highlands.[87]/

72. By comparison, total public capital formation (including that of Palestinian municipalities) for the benefit of Palestinians in the West Bank amounted to a sum of $300 million during a period of 17 years, i.e. 1968-1984, or an average of only $17.6 million per annum. On a per capita basis, public investment outlays on Israeli settlements in the West Bank, in 1983, amounted to $8,000 per Israeli settler as against $52 per Palestinian inhabitant of the West Bank.[88]/

73. An effective remedy for the shortcomings in the various sectors of the Palestinian economy, as enumerated above, requires serious efforts aimed at mobilizing human and material resources at all levels. In a dynamic setting, the 20 years of indifference towards the development of the territories makes it essential to avoid any further delay. Sizeable amounts of resources are needed to compensate for the inaction of the past. Given the present unfavourable circumstances under which the territories' economy operates, not much of the material resources required for development can be raised from domestic sources. The lack of an adequate and responsive financial system has been one of the major determinants of the difficulties encountered. A relaxation of the constraints that have so far impeded local efforts would certainly create an environment conducive to entrepreneurial initiative and promote the role of local institutions in the process of development. External support would be crucial for enhancing the pace at which progress can be achieved. The extent to which external contributions can provide such necessary support will be a profound test of the willingness of the international community to assist the Palestinian people in their endeavour to create a sound basis for the sustained growth and development of their economy.

Chapter II

MONEY AND BANKING

Introduction

74. All indigenous financial institutions of the West Bank and Gaza Strip ceased to function following the territories' occupation by Israel in 1967. Branches of Arab and non-Arab banks and other financial institutions were closed down by the Israeli military authorities and replaced by those of some Israeli banks and institutions. However, the inability of these branches of Israeli banks to engage actively in financial intermediation and the multiple currency standard imposed on the territories led to the emergence of the informal monetary sector, with the money changers playing a vitally important role. Nevertheless, the resource base of this sector has remained precarious and its institutional fabric vulnerable to various unpredictable developments and measures. As a result, the day-to-day financial needs of the economy and its future development requirements have for long been undermined.

75. Economic management during the 20 years of occupation has not been guided by or associated with a central indigenous body directing an overall and well-defined monetary policy. Indigenous institutional arrangements for this purpose are non-existent. While the Central Bank of the occupation authorities may preoccupy itself with certain aspects of the territories' monetary system and its operation, this effort has had no links with and/or participation of the inhabitants of the territories. As a consequence, the financial system remains both economically and politically fragmented, inadequate in terms of resources, and technically incapable of meeting the growing financial needs of the territories.

76. This chapter examines certain aspects of the monetary system in the territories and explores the possibilities for action with a view to improving the situation.

A. Pre-1967 situation: a brief historical account

77. With the advent of the British military administration in Palestine (1917-1918), the Egyptian pound was introduced throughout the whole country and declared legal tender.[89/] The introduction of the Egyptian currency as legal tender rested on two factors, i.e. its stability due to its link with the pound sterling and the need to meet Palestinian trading requirements, especially as approximately half of Palestine's trade was carried on with Egypt and the United Kingdom.[90/] This arrangement brought about an interlocking of the economies involved and increased their interdependence.

78. Under the League of Nations mandate, the British civil administration in Palestine established the Palestine Currency Board in 1926 with a view to providing for and controlling the supply of currency to Palestine. In 1927, the Board issued the Palestinian pound, which was linked to the pound sterling and remained in circulation until the end of the mandate in 1948. The Government of Transjordan also adopted the new currency for its own territory until the end of the British mandate.[91/]

79. The introduction of the new currency was accompanied by the development
of a modern banking system where foreign and local banks and credit
co-operative societies began catering for a steadily growing clientele.
However, as the Currency Board was not comparable to a Central Bank, which
also fulfils certain other banking functions besides acting as the currency
authority, foreign banks pursued a conservative policy in their operations.
As a result, almost all major foreign banks refrained from financing any local
investment, remitting abroad whatever funds they disposed of beyond their cash
holdings and amounts advanced to Palestinians.92/ Nevertheless, lenient
banking legislation induced the establishment of local financial institutions,
i.e. banks and credit co-operatives, aimed at meeting financial intermediation
needs within the economy.

80. With the division of Palestine and the creation of the State of Israel in
1948, the stocks of the Palestine Currency Board were largely transferred to
Haifa, under Israeli jurisdiction, and partly to Amman, Transjordan. As per
an agreement between the Anglo-Palestine Bank, Ltd., and the Government of
Israel, an Issue Department was set up by the Bank and a new currency, the
"Israel pound", was issued. The arrangement continued until the creation of
the Bank of Israel in 1954.

81. A similar currency conversion arrangement was resorted to by what had
then become the Hashemite Kingdom of Jordan93/ to issue a currency of its
own. By 1950, the Jordan Currency Board was established and the Jordanian
dinar was declared as the legal tender throughout the Kingdom, including the
West Bank.94/ The role of the Jordan Currency Board was confined to
maintaining sterling deposits against the issue of Jordanian dinars. It had
thus no control over the supply of money.95/ It was not until 1964 that the
Board was replaced by the Central Bank of Jordan, which was entrusted with all
the functions of a central monetary authority.96/

82. The 1950 developments in Jordan were followed, in 1951, by arrangements
between Barclays Bank and the National Bank of Egypt to replace the Palestine
pound in the Gaza Strip, which had come under Egyptian rule. Accordingly, the
Palestine currency was replaced by the Egyptian pound. The Palestine pound
was thus redeemed and ceased to be legal tender. The Palestine Currency Board
was liquidated and its remaining assets were transferred to Barclays Bank,
which began to serve as Crown Agent for the Colonies and for any redemption of
Palestine currency which would take place.

B.   Post-1967 situation: policies and practices

1.   A brief review of Israeli military government orders

83. A total of 122 military orders, issued from June 1967 up to the beginning
of 1983, govern banking and monetary activities in the West Bank and
Gaza Strip. A number of these reflect attempts over the past two decades to
modify earlier orders, thus creating a complex set of financial rules for the
territories. The military authorities have been entrusted, via an "Examiner
of Banks",97/ with power over banking and monetary operations, including the
licensing of banks and foreign exchange dealings, administering bank assets
and liabilities, closing and/or liquidating banks, establishing the level of
credit, interest rates, and liquidity, and determining a wide range of other
banking and monetary regulations.98/ These and other provisions of the
military orders have either cancelled or amended Jordanian and Egyptian

financial laws and regulations in force in the territories up to June 1967.
They have gradually subjected financial activities in the West Bank and
Gaza Strip to the provisions stipulated under Israeli rules and regulations.
The annexation of East Jerusalem by Israel has placed the sector under the
direct control of Israeli financial legislation in force within the post-1948
boundaries of Israel. The authorities have, however, allowed money-changing
operations, which existed prior to 1967, to continue since the
annexation.99/ On the whole, the major areas subjected to military orders
can be classified under two main headings, namely operation of banks and
currency dealings.

(a) Operation of banks

84. There were eight commercial banks operating in the West Bank and three in
Gaza Strip on the eve of Israeli occupation in June 1967. The total number of
branches had by then reached 26 in the West Bank and 4 in the Gaza Strip
(see table 15).

Table 15

Commercial banks and branch locations (May 1967)

Name of bank	Location of branches
I - West Bank	
1. Arab Bank	Nablus, Jerusalem, Hebron, Ramallah, Jenin, Tulkarm
2. Cairo-Amman Bank	Nablus, Jerusalem, Hebron, Ramallah, Jenin
3. Ottoman Bank	Nablus, Jerusalem, Ramallah, Bethlehem
4. Jordan National Bank	Nablus, Jerusalem, Hebron
5. Jordan Bank	Nablus, Jenin, Jericho
6. Arab Real Estate Bank	Nablus, Jerusalem
7. The British Bank of the Middle East	Jerusalem
8. Bank Intra	Nablus, Jerusalem
II - Gaza Strip	
1. Bank of Alexandria	Gaza
2. Arab Bank	Gaza
3. Bank of Palestine	Gaza, Khan Younes

Source: Interviews with officials in respective banks.

85. The above-mentioned banks, especially those in the West Bank, rendered
services of a relatively high standard and played an important role in
developing such sectors as trade, tourism, small-scale industries and certain
forms of agricultural ventures. In June 1967, the total assets of these
branches in the West Bank alone are estimated to have been more than
15 million Jordanian dinars (JD), accounting for over one fifth of total
assets of Jordan's commercial banking system, with deposits of about
JD 14 million and credit of around JD 10 million.100/

86.   Following the occupation of the territories, all commercial banks and
their branches, along with other financial institutions (e.g. the Agricultural
Credit Corporation and the Industrial Development Bank), were closed down by
Israel, both in the West Bank and Gaza Strip.[101]/ Their accounts were
frozen, documents removed and cash transferred to the Central Bank of Israel
as deposit accounts in the banks' names. The conversion to Israeli currency
of the Jordanian dinar and Egyptian pound was prohibited, only to be allowed
at a later date. Jordanian State funds were added to the account of the
military Government with the Central Bank of Israel.[102]/ In fact, the role
played by the Central Banks of Jordan and Egypt up to 1967 was taken over by
the Bank of Israel. "Examiners of Banks" were appointed and entrusted with
the power to issue bank licences, inspect and freeze accounts, determine
maximum permissible levels of interest rates and methods of accumulation of
funds, establish the minimum liquidity ratio and perform a number of other
functions.[103]/

87.   For its part, the Jordanian Government formally declared the closure of
the branches and froze their deposits and credit facilities, while retaining
their legal/official existence in the West Bank.[104]/ Subsequently, it
allowed deposits to be withdrawn at a pace that did not undermine the
liquidity of the Jordanian banking system itself. To make this possible, an
estimated 3.4 million Jordanian dinars of the Central Bank were made available
to support the banking system's ability to meet claims on deposits. By
mid-1975 about 80 per cent of the pre-1967 deposits had been paid out, leaving
about JD 2 million outstanding. On the asset side of the account, about
30 per cent of outstanding debts were collected, repayment being specially
concentrated on those instances where the headquarters of the commercial banks
held bills in Amman. No effort was made by the Jordanian authorities to
enforce repayments of debts to the Industrial and Agricultural Development
Banks, which are public development finance institutions.[105]/ The closure
of banks in 1967 signalled the beginning of hardship for the economy of the
territories until such time as the inhabitants could devise arrangements to
accommodate the situation by satisfying their immediate minimum monetary
needs. As a result, the overall mobilization of savings and their optimal
allocation within the economy began to encounter severe constraints.

(b)   Currency dealings

88.   Upon the closure of the Arab banks in the West Bank and Gaza Strip,
Israeli currency was declared legal tender in the territories. The Jordanian
dinar was also allowed to continue to serve as legal tender and circulate in
the West Bank. Its conversion into Israeli pounds was allowed at rates
officially established with the involvement of IMF and subsequently adjusted
whenever changes in the international value of the two currencies warranted.
This began to facilitate both the recovery of business activity within the
West Bank and the restoration of trade across the Jordan River.[106]/ The
Egyptian pound, however, was declared illegal and gradually withdrawn from
circulation, thus leaving the Israeli pound as the only legal tender in the
Gaza Strip. Although residents were allowed to continue holding Egyptian
pounds, the authorities encouraged the conversion of these holdings into
Israeli pounds at exchange rates established for different denominations of
the Egyptian currency. Any commitments made in Egyptian pounds were
considered to have been made in Israeli currency at conversion rates
determined by the international values of the currencies involved.[107]/
Subsequently, in 1981, the Bank of Palestine was allowed to resume operations

and was accorded special status with respect to old deposits which were maintained in Egyptian pounds.108/ However, it was not allowed to deal with any other currency except the Israeli shekel. As such, the Israeli currency continues to serve as the only official means of exchange, making the Gaza Strip less independent than the West Bank. Nevertheless, both the Jordanian dinar and the Egyptian pound do unofficially circulate in Gaza.109/

89. In line with the general monetary policy of the Government of Israel, dealings in foreign exchange in the territories appear to have prompted the issuance of a large number of military orders. All transactions in foreign exchange, gold, and bonds can only be carried out with licensed dealers designated to operate as individuals and/or institutions (i.e. banks).110/ These regulations effectively replaced the Jordanian and Egyptian foreign exchange regulations in force in the territories up to 1967. Accordingly, money changers are not allowed to: transfer foreign exchange, including Jordanian dinars, outside the territories unless the foreign exchange was originally brought in and declared and/or purchased in Israel; export or import Israeli pounds; undertake business transactions which would result in transfers of sums outside the territories and which establish a right to earnings outside; make payments to or take receipts from outside the territories or transfers of right, and to intermediate in foreign transactions outside the territories.111/ However, residents of the territories since 1985 have been allowed to bring Jordanian dinars over the bridges from Jordan, with no limits on the amount, provided it is declared upon arrival.112/ Foreign exchange, including Jordanian dinars and Israeli pounds, illegally transported into the territories is liable to confiscation and transfer to the so-called "development fund" for the territories established by the military authorities. The amount of such foreign exchange thus transferred to the "fund" is not known, despite the fact that such confiscations have taken place from time to time when the monetary authorities have tightened their control over the money changers.113/ It is further stipulated that those who hold foreign exchange should eventually sell it. Delays in its sale will force the holder to a sale at the conversion rate set by the authorities.114/

90. In the Gaza Strip, residents are allowed to receive foreign exchange from outside, maintain foreign exchange accounts with banks (i.e. Israeli banks) or keep in their possession an amount of $3,000 per person. This can be obtained partly in cash ($500) and partly in cheques and drafts and disposed of for travel, purchase of goods and services, and transfer for various purposes.115/ Israeli citizens are equally subject to these provisions.116/

91. As a result of the post-1967 developments, a monetary system based on a combination of Israeli and Jordanian currencies is effectively in operation in the occupied territories. The United States dollar is also in use along with the two currencies. There is no specific currency system belonging to the territories themselves, as was the case during and after the Mandate until 1967. The emergence of the two currencies has been further strengthened by the territories' trading realities and the consumption/saving/investment habits of their inhabitants. It now reflects the political and economic status of the territories thus closely binding them to the economies of both Israel and Jordan. It may be inferred that the circulation of the two currencies as legal tender in the territories carries with it the premium accruing to the monetary authorities of the two countries, perhaps in return for the use of their currencies.

92.   However, the continuous depreciation of the Israeli currency has led the
inhabitants of the territories to resort increasingly to the use of the
Jordanian dinar, which has remained a stable currency. Moreover, strong
financial links have been maintained with Amman for various reasons which will
be dealt with in the subsequent sections. The shift to dinars has further
reduced dealings with branches of the Israeli banks established in the
territories where bank deposits in dinars incur a commission instead of
earning interest.[117]/ Parallel to the dinar, the United States dollar is
also used as a unit of account and store of value in view of its relatively
stable nature.[118]/ Coupled with the minimal use of the branches of Israeli
banks, this practice has led to an accumulation of these currencies and
increased hoarding by the population of the territories.

93.   The Israeli currency is thus confined to meeting part of the "transaction
demand" for money and serves almost exclusively as a medium of exchange.
However, the volume and velocity of the currency in circulation have been
determined by the extent to which it has been used in transactions with or
through Israeli individuals and institutions. It is used as a medium of
exchange for small daily transactions and is received in wage payments by
residents from the occupied territories working in Israel. The lack of
confidence in the Israeli shekel resulting from the fact that it is the
currency of the occupying power has been particularly compounded by a series
of devaluations starting in 1974, the benefits of which could not be sustained
in view of the successive declines in the shekel's international value
following very high (three-digit) rates of inflation. Accordingly despite the
closely structured links that have emerged, since 1967, between the economy of
the territories and that of Israel, the use of the latter's currency has not
made much headway in serving the basic functions of money in the territories.

2.   Israeli banks

94.   Shortly after the start of occupation, Israeli authorities permitted the
opening of branches of Israeli banks in the occupied territories. According
to the Bank of Israel, there were, at the end of 1984, 30 branches of Israeli
banks in the West Bank (excluding East Jerusalem) and Gaza Strip distributed
as shown in table 16. If branches in East Jerusalem are also included, the
number rises to 36.

95.   However, a field survey of Israeli banks in the occupied territories
(including East Jerusalem) revealed that only 22 bank branches were serving
Palestinian towns in May 1986 (see table 17). This leads to the conclusion
that 14 branches are located in major Israeli settlements where they
exclusively serve Israeli settlers. It also explains why the branches serving
Arab towns are only rarely used by Israeli settlers. The distribution of
branches indicates that each branch generally has a monopoly of banking
business in its own town,[119]/ except in Jerusalem and Ramallah. A review of
the list further reveals that all banks in the territories are Israeli-owned,
except Barclays.

Table 16

Branches of Israeli and non-Arab Banks
(end of 1984)

Name of bank	Number of branches
Barclays Discount	1
Israeli Discount	5
United Mizrahi	4
Bank Hapoalim	4
Bank Leumi Le-Israel	15
Bank Ein Hai	1
TOTAL	30

Source: Examiner of Banks, Annual Statistics of Israel's Banking System, 1980-1984, (Jerusalem, Bank of Israel, 1985), p. 35.

Table 17

Israeli banks in Arab towns
(May 1986)

Location	Leumi	Discount	Barclays[a/]	Hapoalim
1. West Bank				
Hebron	1			
Bethlehem	1			
Beit Jala	1			
Jerusalem	2	2	1	1
Ramallah	1	1		
Jericho		1		
Nablus	2			
Tulkarm		1		
Qalqilia	1			
Jenin	1			
Sub-total	10	5	1	1
2. Gaza Strip	3	1		1
TOTAL	13	6	1	2

Source: Field survey.

a/ A corporation jointly owned by Barclays Bank of the United Kingdom and Discount Bank of Israel.

(a)   Resource base

96.   Branches of Israeli banks in the occupied territories derive their
resources from funds deposited by the Government of Israel and by the general
public in the territories. They are not widely used by the Palestinian
population. A review of the assets and liabilities of these branches, as
portrayed in table 18, does not reveal the exact monetary relations existing
between the branches operating in the territories and their headquarters in
Israel. It equally does not distinguish between branches in Palestinian
towns and those in Israeli settlements.

97.   From an operational point of view, however, the table indicates that
the branches do not really act as financial intermediaries within the
territories by accepting deposits and lending them to individuals and
business institutions in the West Bank and Gaza Strip. Despite an increase
in deposits, total credit extended by the Israeli banks to the public
declined from its low level of 1.27 per cent of GDP of the territories
registered in 1977. In 1984, total credit extended to the public amounted
to only 8 per cent of total assets and as little as 10.7 per cent of
deposits. The percentages had therefore steadily declined from their
already low levels of 18.1 and 23.8 per cent, respectively, in 1977 (see
table 19). The low and declining level of these figures contrasts
sharply with the realities of the situation in the territories, where the
financial needs of the productive sectors of the economy are far from
having been met.

98.   Credit to the public from government-earmarked deposits has almost
come to an end. Its share in total credit declined from 43.4 per cent in 1977
to only 1.8 per cent in 1984. On the other hand, balances with branches in
Israel have maintained their high level in proportion to total deposits and
assets. In 1984, these balances amounted to over 80 per cent of total
deposits and 60 per cent of total assets. It can therefore be inferred that
instead of contributing to the financial intermediation process in the
West Bank and the Gaza Strip, the branches of Israeli banks channel funds out
of the territories for investment in Israel itself. Coupled with sizeable
payments by the territories to settle the growing trade deficit with Israel,
this places at the disposal of Israeli money and commercial markets a
significant portion of the foreign exchange which enters the territories in
the form of remittances and support payments.[120] This may be one of the
reasons for the relatively low level of deposits kept by Palestinians in these
branches.

Table 18

Assets and liabilities of Israeli banks' branches in the West Bank and the Gaza Strip, 1977-1984[a]/

(Millions of current shekels)

	1977	1978	1979	1980	1981	1982	1983	1984
ASSETS								
Coins and banknotes	2.6	7.8	10.0	31.0	75.7	137.1	676.3	3,526.2
Balances with branches in Israel	32.0	51.3	95.1	262.7	620.1	1,489.6	3,644.0	26,429.0
Total credit to the public	9.2	14.1	18.0	34.7	54.3	227.7	699.1	3,525.8
From government-earmarked deposits	(4.0)	(6.0)	(6.6)	(4.7)	(3.2)	(9.9)	(13.8)	(66.2)
Other	(5.2)	(8.1)	(11.4)	(30.0)	(51.1)	(217.8)	(685.3)	(3,459.6)
Guarantees and other assets	7.0	10.1	22.0	41.6	132.8	303.8	1,394.0	18,554.2
Total assets	50.8	83.5	145.1	370.0	882.9	2,158.2	6,403.4	44,035.2
Liabilities								
Total deposits of the public	38.6	65.8	116.2	314.6	724.6	1,797.2	4,987.4	32,826.8
In Israeli currency	(34.1)	(49.2)	(63.9)	(127.7)	(213.3)	(527.3)	(1,130.0)	(6,798.3)
In foreign currency	(4.5)	(16.6)	(52.3)	(186.9)	(511.3)	(1,269.9)	(3,857.4)	(26,028.5)
Government-earmarked deposits	3.7	5.4	5.6	5.1	3.2	9.9	13.6	66.2
Guarantees and other liabilities	8.5	12.1	23.2	50.4	155.0	351.0	1,402.4	11,142.2
Total liabilities	50.8	83.5	145.0	370.1	882.8	2,158.2	6,403.4	44,035.2

Sources:

(1) Raphael Meron, Economic Development in Judea-Samaria and the Gaza District, 1970-1980 (Jerusalem, Bank of Israel, 1983), table VI-5, p. 66.

(2) Dan Zakai, Economic Development in Judea-Samaria and Gaza District, 1983-1984 (Jerusalem, Bank of Israel, 1986), table 30, p. 71.

a/ End-of-year figures.

Table 19

Ratio of credit to GDP, bank assets and deposits
1977-1984

Year	Credit to the public (millions of current shekels)	As per cent of GDP	As per cent of bank assets	As per cent of deposits
1977	9.2	1.27	18.1	23.8
1978	14.1	1.12	16.8	21.4
1979	18.0	0.84	12.4	15.5
1980	34.7	0.63	9.4	11.0
1981	54.3	0.48	6.1	7.5
1982	227.7	0.89	10.5	12.6
1983	699.1	1.11	10.9	14.0
1984	3,525.8	1.10	8.0	10.7

Source: Computed from table 18. Figures on GDP are obtained from Israel, Central Bureau of Statistics, Judea, Samaria and Gaza Area Statistics (Jerusalem, C.B.S., 1985), volume XV, Nos. 1 and 2, tables 2 and 9, pp. 164 and 171, and 68 and 75, respectively.

(b) Scope of services

99. Despite their shortcomings, the branches of Israeli banks in the occupied territories are responsible for a number of functions which are considered vital to economic activity in the territories, given the absence of indigenous banking and financial institutions.

(i) Deposit accounts

100. The inhabitants of the territories can maintain deposit accounts in these branches in both Israeli and foreign currencies. In 1984, total deposits accounted for 74.5 per cent of all liabilities. While total deposits show a cumulative annual average increase of 5 per cent in constant prices during the period 1980-1984, they remain low in terms of gross national product and/or gross disposable private income (see table 20). In 1984, total deposits amounted to only 7.5 per cent of national income, as against 29 per cent in 1966.[121]/ Despite a steady growth of deposits in terms of GDP, the level of deposits in Israeli currency has followed a declining trend. In 1984, deposits in Israeli currency amounted to 20.7 per cent of total deposits of the public, as against 88.3 per cent in 1977.

101. The rapid decline and the present low level of deposits in Israeli currency is a manifestation of the continuing and substantial depreciation of its value vis-à-vis the relatively stable currencies, especially the Jordanian dinar. Palestinians in the territories have tried to shield themselves from the effects of accelerated rates of Israeli inflation by minimizing their holdings of and transactions in Israeli currency. Moreover, lack of confidence in Israeli banks, coupled with political instability and preference for the banking system in Amman, are further reasons for the low level of deposits in Israeli currency. In addition to holdings in Jordanian dinars, various types of commercial transactions, salaries and other obligations are

calculated and even paid in dinars.[122]/ Accordingly, bank deposits in
Israeli currency are maintained to the extent that is needed for the
settlement of transactions concluded with or through Israel.[123]/ As may be
expected, cash is deposited in accounts only a short while (usually one day)
before a cheque is to be honoured. The use of cheques between Palestinian and
Israeli businessmen and at times between Palestinian residents themselves has
come to facilitate commercial transactions. Such deposits are much more
important for the inhabitants of the Gaza Strip, who have few links with
Jordan and where the only currency in circulation is that of Israel.[124]/

Table 20

Bank deposits in relation to main economic aggregates
1978-1984

Year	Deposits (millions of current shekels)	As % of GDP	As % of GNP	As % of gross private income from all sources
1977	22.5	3.1	2.3	2.3
1978	65.8	5.3	3.9	3.9
1979	116.2	5.5	3.9	3.8
1980	314.6	5.7	4.2	4.2
1981	724.6	6.5	4.6	4.5
1982	1,797.0	7.1	4.9	4.9
1983	5,235.1 a/	8.4 b/	5.6	5.8
1984	34,180.5 a/	10.7	7.5	7.9

Sources: Computed from Israel Central Bureau of Statistics,
Judea-Samaria and Gaza Area Statistics (Jerusalem, CBS., 1985), vol. XV,
Nos. 1 and 2, pp. 164 and 171, and 68 and 75, respectively, and from
(1) Raphael Meron, Economic Development in Judea-Samaria and the Gaza
District, 1970-1980 (Jerusalem, Bank of Israel, 1983), table VI-5, p. 66, and
(2) Dan Zakai, Economic Development in Judea-Samaria and Gaza District,
1983-1984 (Jerusalem, Bank of Israel, 1986), table 30, p. 71.

a/   Includes IS 247.7 million and IS 1,353.7 million of deposits with
the Bank of Palestine for 1983 and 1984, respectively.

b/   In 1983, bank deposits amounted to 50 per cent of GDP in Egypt,
74 per cent in Jordan, 20 per cent in the Syrian Arab Republic and 26 per cent
in Yemen; computed from ESCWA, "Review of fiscal and monetary issues and
developments in the ECWA region, 1984" (E/ECWA/DPD/85/9), 30 July 1985,
table 7, pp. 40-41, Handbook of International Trade and Development
Statistics, Supplement 1985, (United Nations publication, Sales
No. E/F.85.II.D.12), pp. 435-442.

102. Maintaining deposits in Israeli currency is also claimed to help in
settling various direct and indirect taxes, an obligation which involves the
bulk of businessmen and commercial institutions. All such payments are
effected in Israeli currency, although assessments are usually made in
Jordanian dinars. Converting dinars into Israeli shekels at the market rate
of exchange has enabled dinar holders to earn around 5-15 per cent more in
shekels. Payments to the Government, on the other hand, are made according to
the official exchange rate of the dinar to the shekel.

103. A major form of deposits in Israeli currency consists of the savings schemes available to the public. While some of these schemes are attractive enough to draw customers on purely business grounds, all banks in the occupied territories require those in need of credit facilities to open such accounts and regularly deposit funds in them as a precondition for receiving overdraft facilities. This is viewed by banks as a form of collateral on all credit facilities extended to clients. In addition, a new measure which discourages deposits is a 3 per cent charge on withdrawals.125/

104. As a result of the limited use made of the Israeli currency, the bulk of transactions in the territories are carried out in Jordanian dinars kept either in cash or in banks largely outside the territories and made available through the services of money changers. Bank deposits in foreign currencies have also increased in the territories, presumably consisting almost entirely of deposits in Jordanian dinars. Such deposits are accepted by the branches of Israeli banks in the occupied territories only for safe-keeping purposes, with the depositor incurring a charge. Recipient banks charge depositors a fee of 0.25 per cent on all dinar deposits. This appears to cover the administrative cost involved since 100 per cent liquidity is maintained for these dinar accounts and this prevents banks from earning income on them. Cheques can be drawn on these deposits, but the deposits themselves are not transferable among the banks.

105. Some dinars are, however, also exchanged for Israeli currency and thus serve as a useful source of hard currency for Israel. It is argued that in this sort of situation there is always the possibility that the economic or political situation might change so that the dinars might create a claim on Jordanian reserves, which would no doubt force the Jordanian monetary authorities to place restrictions on convertibility.126/

106. Despite the fee on dinar deposits and the deep political uncertainty surrounding the future of the territories, a number of residents have resorted to these banks for safe-keeping of their surplus dinars. Around 80 per cent of all bank deposits of the general public in 1984 were in foreign currencies, including Jordanian dinars, as against 12 per cent in 1977. The flow of Jordanian dinars into the branches of Israeli banks is precipitated by several factors. In the first place, the increase in bank deposits is due to the scarcity of lucrative investment opportunities open to residents holding small amounts of dinars. Coupled with the deteriorating state of the economy, this has reinforced reticence with regard to either starting new businesses or subscribing to existing ones. The inhabitants have, therefore, been confronted with the choice of either placing their excess dinars in branches of Israeli banks in the territories or channelling them to banks in Jordan. While the bulk of the dinars is handled by the money changers and partly deposited in Jordanian banks, inhabitants have found it practical also to place some of their dinars in branches of Israeli banks operating in the territories to meet their day-to-day needs.

107. Despite the above developments, the overall volume of deposits, both in Israeli and Jordanian currencies, held in branches of Israeli banks remains low in relation to various economic indicators in the territories.

(ii) Credit facilities

108. Israeli bank branches generally follow the traditional banking practice
of safety and liquidity, owing to the lack of an organized money market
coupled with the deteriorating economic situation and the cash habits of the
inhabitants. The banks, therefore, extend short-term loans of up to one year
for commercial purposes and partly as operating capital for agriculture and
industry. Loans exceeding a certain limit are only extended upon the approval
of the military government and are guaranteed by the Israeli Government.

109. Government guarantees for commercial bank loans to residents of the
territories were intended to cover the entire amount of loans which go unpaid
for political reasons and up to 90 per cent of those unpaid for financial
reasons. In practice, however, they will only cover up to a maximum of
50 per cent of the combined total of the latter. The military government
viewed the guarantees as a partial substitute for the underdeveloped banking
system in the territories. It was further argued that an infusion of Israeli
funds was expected to help stem the economic slowdown that had hit the
territories in the late 1970s and early 1980s.[127/] The rate of interest on
loans so extended is negotiated on a case-by-case basis. Early in 1986,
interest charged on loans over $50,000 was about 11-12 per cent. In addition,
a collateral, along with guarantees by three accredited merchants, was also
required.

110. There are no specialized financial institutions geared to meet the
medium-term and/or long-term financial needs in agriculture, industry and
housing. Scarcity of equity and working capital has been a limiting factor,
especially in agriculture and industry. The problem has been further
complicated by rising inflation and the uncertainty of the investment climate.

111. On the whole, two main types of credit facilities are offered by branches
of Israeli banks, namely loans and overdrafts. Advancing loans to borrowers
in agriculture and industry was promoted on a fairly large scale in the early
years of occupation. Funds for this purpose were appropriated by the military
government from earmarked deposits and were administered by banks in
co-operation with local military authorities, as stated above. This was the
main reason why many potential borrowers were openly suspicious of these loans,
which they conceived as tools used in achieving certain political goals, and
no more than half of the funds earmarked for this purpose was actually
dispensed to borrowers. At present, this source of funds for the branches of
Israeli banks in the territories has almost dried up, as noted earlier. Since
the change in Government in 1977, the loan programme has lost its significance.
The rapid deterioration of the Israeli economy itself, during the early 1980s,
provided further justification for the Government's new policy.

112. The second and by far the more common form of credit comprises overdraft
facilities. Under this arrangement, as banks do not use government-earmarked
funds, they are free to exercise their own discretion without having to
consult with the military authorities. The rate of interest charged, in
May 1986, on overdraft accounts ranged between 39 and 50 per cent per annum
calculated on the actual duration of the use of the funds. In addition, a fee
of 8 per cent is charged on the entire value of the overdraft facility.
Security requirements consist mainly of mortgaging funds deposited by clients
into their saving accounts. This form of security has the obvious advantage
of enabling banks to avail themselves of sizeable amounts of time deposits by
incorporating them into their own investment portfolios.

113. An overall evaluation of the role of the branches of Israeli banks, as lending institutions in the territories, reveals the following :

    (a)   Israeli banks have increasingly refrained from advancing term loans to entrepreneurs operating in directly productive areas such as agriculture, industry and housing. They have, however, played a modest role in some service areas, mainly involving firms that operate public transport facilities. Loans in these cases have been extended on attractive terms with respect to both the rate of interest and collaterals;

    (b)   Lending from government-earmarked funds is viewed by Israeli authorities as more of a favour than a purely banking service. Borrowers have been granted loans either for political reasons or because of the nature of their business, such as public transport. The vast majority of eligible borrowers are either unable or not willing to apply for such loans. Moreover, the sources of funds for this type of loans have almost dried up;

    (c)   Branches of Israeli banks have managed to play a role in the external trade sector by advancing overdraft facilities to eligible businessmen on purely business grounds. However, clients interviewed claim that the said service is handled inefficiently and at high cost; and

    (d)   Although Palestinian borrowers may experience difficulties in loan repayments, banks can in such instances resort to the Israeli military authority for compensation against bad debts which carry government guarantees.

(ii) Letters of credit

114. Branches of Israeli banks perform the important function of issuing letters of credit to Palestinian importers. Since the occupied territories procure a sizeable share of their imports from Israel (amounting to 90 per cent in 1984), the volume of imports from the rest of the world is noticeably small. Consequently, the role of Israeli banks in facilitating international trade on behalf of Palestinian businessmen is correspondingly marginal. Nevertheless, that function is crucial to the small number of businesses involved in international trade. This is particularly important as no alternative facility to cater for such a service is available.

115. Opening of letters of credit is hampered more by constraints arising from government regulations than by the banks themselves. Procuring of needed licenses from the Department of Trade and Industry may impede speedy processing of documents by banks and cause problems for Palestinian merchants. Israeli banks charge a commission of 0.5-1.5 per cent on goods imported as a fee for providing the necessary services. This is not viewed as an exorbitant rate by most importers. Nevertheless, Palestinian merchants state that the branches of Israeli banks provide a poor service in arranging the finance of international trade. They quote the banks' failure to arrange proper documents, delays which lead to demurrage costs and inefficient service in operating accounts.[128]/

(iv) Issuing guarantees

116. Branches of Israeli banks issue several forms of guarantees on behalf of Palestinian businessmen and in favour of other firms or official bodies. Guarantees differ markedly in their coverage of financial commitments and hence in the commission charged against each. The "formal" guarantee is the least risky and is usually issued in assurance of a client's observance to an

agreed undertaking. For example, the Jordan Vegetable Oil Company (in Nablus) agrees with a supplier to re-export a certain amount of all the ghee it processes from the crude oil imported across the bridges. The commission charged by banks on such a guarantee amounts to 1.5 per cent.

117. A second form, described as "implementation guarantee", is usually requested by construction firms in connection with projects. Firms undertake to honour the terms of a contract they sign with a third party for the implementation of parts of such projects. The commission in this case goes up to 4 per cent.

118. "Financial guarantees" requested by Palestinian businesses in favour of others in the occupied territories or Israel is the most common type of guarantee, bearing in mind the large volume of trade which is currently being exchanged between Palestinian and Israeli firms. The commission on this type of guarantee amounts to approximately 7 per cent, which is about three times higher than the prevailing rates for similar transactions in Jordan and Israel. Bank officials argue that on this type of service they encounter an unusually high risk arising from the extraordinary political and economic setting which governs trade relations between Israel and the occupied territories.

(v)   Other services

119. Branches of Israeli banks also offer other services which may facilitate business transactions, without necessarily bearing on their role as intermediaries between depositors and borrowers. They act as payment conduits between tax payers and the government. Furthermore, the Government resorts to these branches to pay salaries and pension dues to most of its employees in the territories, as well as to Palestinians working in Israel, though some recipients prefer to receive their payments through post offices.

120. The role of banks in handling shares offered in the stock exchange is common in Israel, and branches of Israeli banks in the territories have, at times, attempted to promote this form of trade within the Palestinian business community. After a brief boom in the late 1970s, trading in stocks suffered from the severe monetary instability in Israel until it almost totally collapsed after the stock exchange crises in Israel in 1983.

121. Although each branch enjoys a monopoly banking business in its own locality, its profitability remains uncertain. Some Israeli sources claim losses or low profitability and draw attention to the closure of several branches during the past 10 years for these reasons. Some complaints of low profitability are understandable due to the fact that on the whole the branches have not been able to attract deposits on a large scale and due to their failure to carry out financial intermediation by making loans to borrowers in the territories.129/ However, some local Palestinian sources assert that not only are these branches profitable, but some of them are more profitable than their counterparts in Israel itself. The claim is based on the fact that the branches operate in a highly favourable situation where they have enjoyed complete monopoly of operation. In particular, they have managed to siphon sizeable amounts of funds from deposits in the territories for use in Israel. In any case, the Israeli authorities have used the Israeli branches' lack of profitability as an argument against permitting Palestinians to operate banks, reasoning that the latter would also be unprofitable.130/

(c) <u>Overall assessment</u>

122. Branches of Israeli banks have failed to restore the pre-1967 level of
banking operations, both in terms of scope and volume. In particular, they
have not been able to play the conventional and fundamental role of serving as
intermediaries between depositors and borrowers which is essential for
mobilizing local financial resources and channelling them to investment
opportunities in the territories. Among the reasons for this are the economic
and political uncertainty associated with military occupation, political
objections to co-operating with the occupying power, the inhabitants'
preference for the healthier and more stable Jordanian currency as against
that of Israel, high interest rates, and the uncommitted attitude of the
Israeli banks with regard to serving the interest of the territories.131/
While the banks have taken advantage of the prevailing situation in the
territories, owing to their monopolistic position, and attracted some
deposits, the bulk of these deposits is channelled to Israel. As a result,
their role as a source of credit to the Palestinian borrowers remains highly
insignificant. Apart from some of the common banking services such as
overdraft facilities, letters of credit and bank guarantees, the Israeli
banks' role in promoting economic growth and development in the territories
has indeed remained minimal.

(d) <u>Other financial ventures</u>

123. Insurance constitutes another important category of financial operations
undertaken by Israeli institutions. Insurance services are rendered on an
extensive scale by a large number of enterprises operating in all towns. A
town of about 20,000 inhabitants is often served by 4-8 insurance offices.
They are mainly involved in car insurance, which is reported to account for
80-85 per cent of all insurance business. Other forms of insurance include
fire, theft, work accidents and medical insurance.

124. Most insurance enterprises operating in the territories are merely
agencies for Israeli firms. There is only one Palestinian insurance company,
namely the Arab Insurance Establishment (AIE) (see Section 3 (c) below).
Insurance services provided by Israeli enterprises do not adequately meet
local needs. Contracts are issued in Hebrew which is not understood by the
vast majority of local clients. In case of accidents, the insured is often
handicapped by the intricate legal details. Premium rates are noticeably
high, especially on cars. A third party car insurance policy costs
around $210, which is 3-4 times higher than in Jordan.

125. Based on a detailed distribution of vehicles according to type and
insurance rates, premium dues on all vehicles in the West Bank and Gaza Strip
are estimated at more than $24 million annually. Premiums on other forms of
insurance are estimated at about $3 million per annum. Israeli affiliated
insurance businesses transmit all premiums to the account of their main
enterprises in Israel. No part of the premiums so collected is invested in
the territories themselves. Similarly, none of the deposits of AIE kept in
branches of Israeli banks in the territories are invested locally.

3. Arab financial institutions and practices

(a) Jordanian banking policy and operation

126. As noted earlier, while all banks and other financial institutions were
closed down by the Israeli authorities in 1967, the Jordanian authorities
decided to retain, in the West Bank, the physical presence of all branches of
the Amman-based commercial banks. The purpose was not only to protect their
legal status but to facilitate some post-occupation contacts between the
inhabitants of the territories and the East Bank with respect to withdrawal of
deposits and maintaining trade and other traditional links. In practice, this
meant ordering all branches of Amman-based banks not to terminate the services
of their staff, to pay their salaries and to maintain formal contacts with
them as much as needed. Some branches were asked by their head offices in
Amman to open their offices periodically in order to answer questions and
process incoming and outgoing correspondence. Furthermore, West Bank offices
were also actively engaged in facilitating the collection of outstanding loans
which became due after the occupation. The rent for the premises of these
branches is paid from Arab banks' funds which were initially confiscated by
Israel in June 1967.

127. In a further move aimed at "supporting steadfastness of the people in the
territories", the Jordanian authorities have also allowed some of the
Jordanian specialized credit institutions (namely the Housing Bank and the
Industrial Development Bank) to manage some funds of the Jordanian-Palestinian
Joint Committee and encouraged the Arab Bank and the Towns and Villages
Development Bank to extend their services to the inhabitants of the West Bank
to the extent possible.

128. After the closure of banks in the West Bank, no significant change took
place in their legal and functional status until 1986, except for the gradual
evolution of services performed by the Arab Bank branch in Nablus, West Bank.
This branch has been operational on a regular daily basis. It has, in effect,
started to perform certain types of banking services. Most importantly, it
has been actively engaged in opening new accounts, but in its sister branches
in Amman. It is claimed that there has been a steady flow of deposits from
the occupied territories to commercial banks in Amman on a sizeable scale of
about $3-6 million per month, much of it through the Arab Bank. It is noted
that the Nablus branch of the Arab Bank still refrains from advancing any form
of loans or credit facilities to inhabitants in the West Bank, in compliance
with Israeli orders.

129. Commercial banks in Jordan generally do not provide any form of credit to
Palestinians residing in the West Bank and the Gaza Strip, except if the
businesses they fund are located outside these occupied territories. However,
should any loan be considered, commercial banks demand full-fledged guarantees
which are all traceable in Jordan (e.g. estate mortgage on real estate located
in Jordan or signatures from 2-3 accredited guarantors). Only very few
residents in the West Bank and Gaza can meet the needed security requirements.

130. The financial implications of the present modus operandi of the Arab Bank
branch in Nablus are obviously significant, both for clients and for the Bank
itself. On the one hand, the bank is now performing the badly needed function
of providing a safe and reasonably remunerative means of attracting savings,
given the marked unattractiveness of the limited alternatives available to
Palestinians in the territories. On the other hand, the bank has found itself

unable to play the other intermediary function of providing credit facilities to borrowers in the occupied territories and invests deposits outside the territories where rates of return are deemed considerably more attractive.

131. Nevertheless, the Arab Bank has been involved in extending long-term loans to municipalities in the West Bank since 1971. The total volume of the loans, which have been guaranteed by the Jordanian Government and were extended to 22 municipalities in the West Bank during the period 1971-1979, has amounted to JD 2.2 million covering 39 development projects for electricity, water, schools, roads and drainage purposes.[132]

132. The Towns and Villages Development Bank has also been extending long-term loans to municipal councils for completion of development projects since the occupation of the territories in 1967. As a government bank, its loans, carrying low interest of 5.5 per cent, have been guaranteed by the Government. Since 1978, government guarantee of loans was made conditional upon co-ordination between the Bank and the municipalities through the Ministry of Occupied Territories Affairs in Amman. Total loans extended to municipalities up to the end of 1984 amounted to JD 609,000, covering 18 development projects.[133]

133. The Housing Bank has also been engaged, as per an agreement with the Jordanian-Palestinian Joint Committee in 1981, in extending loans to West Bank residents for housing construction and repair. The loans have been extended for a period of 15 to 20 years with a 1-2 year grace period secured with the guarantee of a merchant or an employer in the East Bank. A total of 2,150 loans amounting to JD 13.8 million were extended during the period 1981-1985.[134] The resources have been provided by the Joint Committee through the Central Bank of Jordan in support of steadfastness.

134. The Industrial Bank is not engaged in extending loans to West Bank residents, mainly due to the difficulty of appraising loans, monitoring their use and recovering them. However, it has lent money for West Bank projects using funds placed with it by the Jordanian authorities.[135]

135. While the above-mentioned Jordanian banking institutions have been able to provide limited services to the inhabitants of the West Bank, the financial and banking needs of the territories' economy are far from covered. The situation is much more precarious in the Gaza Strip, despite the re-opening of the Bank of Palestine in 1981.

(b)   The experience of the Bank of Palestine

136. Prior to 1967, branches of Arab banks were operating in the Gaza Strip with limited services mainly focused on the financing of trade. There was little willingness to take on risk and engage in the financing of agricultural and industrial development projects.[136]

137. The Bank of Palestine was established in June 1960 with an authorized capital of 500,000 Egyptian pounds (LE). The need to establish a locally based and owned bank arose, in part, from the fact that there were only 2 branches of foreign banks in the Gaza Strip serving 380,800 people, as against 8 banks with 31 branches in the West Bank serving 850,000 residents. The two branches were owned and operated by Jordanian and Egyptian banks, namely the Arab Bank and Bank of Alexandria respectively. The activities of a third bank, Al-Umma, were practically frozen, and the bank was in the process of liquidation.

138. The Bank of Palestine commenced operation in 1961 with an actual paid-up capital of only LE 150,590. By the end of 1966, it had opened two branches, one in Gaza and another in Khan Yunis. A third branch was due to open in June 1967 in Rafah after the completion of its building. Following the occupation of the Gaza Strip in 1967, the building was taken over by a branch of the Israeli bank, Hapoalim Bank.

139. The Bank of Palestine had managed to expand its business until the Israeli occupation. Its services were centred on short-term financing operations covering trade and other services. No funds were made available for medium-term and long-term investments in industry, housing or agriculture. The total size of loans extended remained limited, amounting to LE 0.6 million by the end of 1966. Deposits stood at LE 2.5 million, as against a total equity capital (including reserves) of nearly LE 487,700. The reasons for the Bank's modest performance seem to have stemmed from the competition with well-established banks (Arab Bank and Bank of Alexandria) and from the escalating political uncertainty and confrontation with Israel. Nevertheless, during the period 1961-June 1967, the Bank was able to provide credit facilities in support of foreign trade activities in the Gaza Strip, particularly for the export of citrus fruits and its financing. By June 1967, the paid-up capital of the Bank had reached LE 343,000. The Bank appeared to be making steady progress and could have been of greater service to the Gazan economy had it not been for its closure by the Israeli occupation authorities.[137]/

(i) Post-occupation developments

140. In compliance with Military Order No. 18, which was issued within one day of the Israeli occupation in June 1967, the Bank of Palestine was ordered to close down and cease all its local and foreign operations. Cash assets of nearly LE 100,000 were confiscated from the safe of the main branch in Gaza. Ten years later, and in view of the mounting need for normal banking services, the management of the Bank of Palestine began negotiations with the Israeli authorities in an attempt to re-open the Bank.

141. After long negotiations, an agreement was reached with the Bank of Israel on the re-opening, only to meet the objection of the Ministry of Defence which considered the name of the bank provocative and a security hazard. It was not until the intervention of the Supreme Court of Israel that the issue was settled and the bank was allowed to carry the name it had prior to occupation.[138]/ While the permission granted was independent of Israeli banking legislation, in practice the bank has been subject to full supervision and control by the Bank of Israel through the "Examiner of Banks", as is the case with all Israeli banks. In addition, the Bank has been in a disadvantageous position as its activities are liable to scrutiny under the strict control of the local military administration.

142. Essentially, the agreement permitted the Bank of Palestine to render "normal banking services" from its headquarters in Gaza City, with a commitment also to subsequently consider the opening of branches in the future in Khan Yunis and Rafah. Despite repeated requests, none has been permitted so far. Although the Israeli military authorities in Gaza did "in principle" approve in June 1986 the opening of the first branch of the Bank of Palestine in Khan Yunis, the final approval of the Bank of Israel is still pending. The decision to open the branch was described as "a gesture of flexibility to raise the quality of life in the territories".[139]/ The branch will

benefit 100,000 residents of Khan Yunis who in the past year have had to make a round trip of 45 kilometers to Gaza City to deal with the Headquarters of the Bank of Palestine. The Israeli Bank Leumi closed its branch in Khan Yunis, allegedly after failure to make a profit.[140/]

143. While the Bank's statements of accounts (balance sheet and profit and loss) are presented in Egyptian pounds, all its dealings are conducted in Israeli shekels. Moreover, customers' loan repayments are indexed to the US dollar. The Bank has been allowed to continue maintaining its pre-1967 accounts in Egyptian pounds. However, transactions with these accounts, including withdrawals, can only be carried out in Israeli shekels. An appeal to allow it to deal in foreign exchange, like the branches of Israeli banks, has not been acted upon by the Israeli authorities for the last four years. The bank is not permitted to release its financial reports before these are scrutinized and approved by the Examiner of Banks, who has assumed full responsibility, as the appointed staff of the military government, for the supervision of this and other banks in the territories.

144. Apparently, the inability of the bank to act as an "authorized dealer" in foreign exchange, including Jordanian dinars, has been a major constraint adversely affecting the direction and size of its operations and preventing it from effectively contributing to the growth and development of the local economy, especially in the context of the significance of trade between the Gaza Strip, Jordan and other countries.

(ii) Appraisal of progress

145. The opening of the Bank of Palestine's main office in Gaza City in 1981 coincided with a worsening of economic conditions in both the Gaza Strip and Israel. Inflation was surging at unprecedentedly high rates. The exchange value of the Israeli shekel against other currencies (especially the dinar and the dollar) was sharply depreciating, with monetary and fiscal policies unable to check its further deterioration. Amidst these unfavourable developments, the bank has continued its fight for survival. However, the nature and volume of its operations remain noticeably modest.

146. An analysis of the balance sheet (table 21) reveals that total assets at the end of 1984 were LE 4.68 million, of which there were LE 1.7 million in loans and discounted bills, and LE 2.25 million in cash. Equity capital amounted to LE 1.25 million, of which LE 0.5 million was in share capital. Total deposits and client accounts amounted to LE 3.23 million, 4 per cent higher than the previous year. The number of shareholders at the end of 1984 was 1,150 persons. The ratio of credit to total deposits was low, resulting in a high liquidity ratio compared to commercial banking standards prevailing in Jordan (i.e. 70 per cent as against 30-40 per cent).

147. The limited volume of business handled by the Bank of Palestine is manifested in the noticeably narrow range of services it offers. Its inability to deal in foreign exchange has made it difficult to attract a substantial volume of deposits, especially as depositors are able to earn far more attractive real rates of interest in Jordanian, foreign and even Israeli banks. Suspicion surrounding the real intention of Israeli authorities regarding the future of the Bank has further discouraged depositors. In an effort to promote deposits, the Bank's management agreed reluctantly to index time deposits to the United States dollar, but it then offered an interest rate of about 5 per cent, which is generally considered unattractive given the relatively higher rates of return available on other options.

Table 21

Bank of Palestine - balance sheet
(Egyptian pounds)

	1961	1966	1978	1979	1980	1983	1984
Assets							
Cash and balances with other banks	208,236	2,253,581	1,306,168	1,342,558	1,441,275	2,569,678	2,250,104
Loans, bills discounted, other credit facilities	118,173	730,736	1,034,960	1,006,548	947,999	1,305,580	1,700,730
Fixed assets	4,700	7,328	57,926	58,439	63,385	324,061	525,679
Other assets	100,916	1,197,525	603,286	603,279	538,087	406,267	201,342
Total assets	432,025	4,189,170	3,002,140	3,010,824	2,990,746	4,605,586	4,677,855
Liabilities							
Capital	150,590	343,000	343,000	343,000	343,000	500,000	500,000
Reserves	-	125,856	173,909	173,909	173,909	605,696	745,760
Deposits	173,105	2,434,737	1,673,975	1,633,663	1,616,404	3,093,623	3,230,753
Undistributed profits	7,664	58,845	211,007	259,010	321,383	-	-
Other liabilities	100,666	1,226,732	601,249	601,242	536,050	406,267	201,342
Total liabilities	432,025	4,189,170	3,002,140	3,010,824	2,990,746	4,605,586	4,677,855

Source: (1) Bank of Palestine in Twenty Years, Gaza, 1980, pp. 22-24; (2) Jalal Dawoud, "Bank of Palestine in Gaza Strip", Samed, No. 18, 1980, p. 12; and, (3) Report of the Board of Directors of the Bank of Palestine for 1984.

148. The Bank's non-involvement in foreign currency dealings has also prevented it from promoting the foreign trade of Gaza. This was coupled with the restrictions imposed by Israeli authorities on local business firms to have direct contacts with the rest of the world.

149. Lending operations and overdraft facilities, covering trade, agriculture and industry, have also remained limited. The Bank extends modest loans of very short duration, rarely exceeding 10 months. Some loans are renewed for another term, thus giving the borrower more time for repayment. Loans are guaranteed mostly by three qualified guarantors, as real estate mortgage is viewed by Palestinian residents with deep suspicion in view of the Israeli authorities' continued encroachment on Arab land through confiscation. Nevertheless, bad debts and defaults are few in number and have posed no serious problems for the Bank. Interest charged on loans is 13 per cent, which is about half of the rate charged by Israeli banks and a little higher than the interest paid on funds placed with the Bank of Israel. Despite the interest rates, the Bank was able to make an attractive margin of profit in view of the low rates of interest paid on deposits and the low opportunity cost for local investments or placement with the Bank of Israel.

150. In trying to demonstrate its proclaimed concern for local economic development, the Bank of Palestine has initiated a lending scheme mainly aimed at reviving the ailing citrus industry and at creating jobs for unemployed graduates. As regards the citrus industry, the Bank has proposed to offer loans to owners of medium and large groves (minimum area of 10 dunums) through the Union of Citrus Growers in the Gaza Strip, which acts as an intermediary between its members and the Bank. The loan size is $100 per dunum and interest charged is 13 per cent.

151. Projects aimed at employment generation include a range of farming activities. By May 1985, the Bank had extended loans to the following projects:

		No. of owners	Loan ($US)
1.	Modern rabbit farm	2	12,000
2.	Tree seedling nursery	2	5,000
3.	Sheep farm	1	10,000
4.	Bee project	2	10,000
5.	Bee project	1	3,400

152. In 1986, the Bank of Palestine developed its operations along two major lines. Firstly, it has come to an agreement with a United States private voluntary organization, the Community Development Foundation (CDF) to act as an intermediary in channelling and administering a loan fund of $0.5 million earmarked by CDF for individual borrowers. This is equivalent to approximately one third of all lending facilities made available by the Bank as at the end of 1984. Secondly, it has financed the purchase of 48 Italian orchard-type tractors through a loan advanced by an Italian bank. Tractors will be resold to individual farmers who have already paid a first instalment of $1,000 in cash out of a total of $6,900. Again, interest is charged at the rate of 13 per cent. These new lines of activity have been financed from external sources.

153. The experience of the Bank of Palestine, since its reopening in 1981, reveals the following:

(a) The Bank is confronted with numerous constraints that limit its operations. It is not allowed to deal in foreign exchange. It has had no hedge against the continued devaluation of the Israeli currency. It competes with more than six branches of Israeli banks in the Strip which enjoy the support of their head offices with regard to risk. It is subject to income tax at the rate of 37.5 per cent instead of the 25 per cent applicable according to the Egyptian income tax law prevailing prior to Israeli occupation - the dispute has reached the Supreme Court of Israel. It does not have the final say in approving investment projects, regardless of their feasibility, as a decision on this issue continues to rest with the Israeli military authorities. The Bank is also not allowed to open new branches and thus extend its operations to new areas; [141]/

(b) As a result, the Bank has not been able to intermediate effectively in the financial market of the Gaza Strip. It has not yet succeeded in mobilizing available resources, however small, and allocating them to needy and priority areas, and it has thus not contributed to an increase in output and income. While the ratio of its credit to deposits is generally higher than those of the branches of Israeli banks operating in the territories, it is still low for a commercial bank. This partly reflects management's policies aimed at maintaining a greater degree of liquidity than is needed and partly indicates the overall economic and political uncertainty surrounding the operation of the Bank in addition to the constraints enumerated above;

(c) The capital of the Bank remains small. Attempts at increasing it threefold have been obstructed by the Bank of Israel. While it is certain that a much larger capital would enable the Bank to further expand the scope of its services to a wider area, the viability of such a move remains questionable given the Bank's inability to exploit its relatively high cash holdings and reserves;

(d) The role of the Bank as an intermediary between depositors and borrowers will continue to be insignificant as long as its ability to mobilize savings and external loans remains limited. In order to attract more deposits, the Bank may have to reconsider the structure of its rates of interest. It should consider offering a real rate of interest which is higher than the rate of inflation and try more actively to promote its credit and investment operations which, obviously, may entail assuming higher risks and further strengthening its technical capabilities in credit management;

(e) In view of the prevailing constraints and the wide areas of disagreement, relations between the management of the Bank and Israeli authorities have not been conducive to enhancing the role of the Bank in the process of financial resource mobilization, allocation and management. This has added to the difficulties confronting the Bank and impeded its normal functioning. A satisfactory resolution of these disagreements and the entrusting of full authority and support to the Bank in legitimate areas of its operations, perhaps through the mediation of an international mechanism such as the International Monetary Fund, could enable the bank to play the role initially assigned to it and achieve its declared objectives.

(c) Other institutional sources

154. A variety of establishments are engaged in financial operations in the territories to help fill the gap created by the non-existence of appropriate financial institutions and by an inadequate and undeveloped banking system. The nature and scope of their operations are discussed below.

(i) Arab Development and Credit Company

155. The company was established in 1985, with financial intermediation intended to constitute a major part of its business through the accepting and extending of loans. Although established in Jerusalem under Israeli laws, the company is allowed to operate within the occupied territories under the supervision of the Israeli military authorities. It has a limited capital of 15 shares, each having a nominal value of 1,000 Israeli shekels, with restrictions on their transferability and increases in their number.142/ Undoubtedly, its ability to provide investment finance will depend on the extent to which the company is able to enlarge its capital and engage in financial intermediation, especially that involving external sources of finance, both Arab and non-Arab.

(ii) Arab Insurance Establishment (AIE)

156. There is only one Arab insurance facility, namely the Arab Insurance Establishment, involved in general insurance activities, with reinsurance secured in London. It undertakes about half of all insurance business in the West Bank and Gaza Strip and has also been permitted to operate in East Jerusalem since the mid-1970s. The Establishment is governed by the Jordan Insurance Law of 1965, which requires all firms to keep a minimum of 40 per cent liquidity. Due to low returns on most common forms of investment in the territories, AIE keeps an even higher rate of liquidity in the form of time deposits, mostly in branches of Israeli banks. AIE has also allocated part of its funds to some local investment projects by subscribing to major share-holding firms in the West Bank, despite the fact that such investments are not lucrative, even when compared with time deposits held in branches of Israeli banks. A relatively small part of its resources is used in lending for commercial and construction purposes. Analysis of AIE's 1984 balance sheet reveals that 80 per cent of all assets ($1.25 million) is in the form of time deposits, 0.003 per cent in shares, and 9.4 per cent in loans and discounted bills.

(iii) Co-operatives

157. By the end of 1966 there were 238 co-operative societies in the West Bank, with a total of 14,377 members and share capital of $683,000. The total volume of loans made to members was $1.6 million, i.e. around $114 per member.143/ Of all registered co-operatives, there were no more than 50 active societies, with the rest remaining inactive and awaiting official liquidation. On the whole, this suggests a rather modest role for these co-operatives, especially in the area of agriculture, which was supposed to be their top priority. In the Gaza Strip, on the other hand, there were 17 co-operatives involving 2,150 members in existence prior to 1967.

158. The co-operative movement remained relatively dormant for 10 years after occupation, but it was vigorously reactivated after 1978 following the influx of funds from the Jordanian-Palestinian Joint Committee and from certain private voluntary organizations, especially, American Near East Refugee Aid (ANERA). Both the Joint Committee and ANERA have designated co-operative societies as their major conduit for channelling funds to desired projects (these activities are discussed at greater length in chapter IV, below).

159. By the end of 1985, there were in the West Bank around 30 active agricultural co-operatives and 80 non-agricultural societies, with the most important of the latter (24 societies) engaged in housing. In the Gaza Strip there were four co-operatives, all engaged in agriculture, two of which were closely linked to an Israeli agricultural exporting monopoly (Agrexco).

(a) Resource base

160. The financial resources of these co-operatives were raised essentially from four sources: the Joint Committee, the Jordanian Co-operatives Organization, ANERA, and equity capital subscribed by members. The total amount of aid advanced by ANERA to co-operative societies, up to the end of 1983, is estimated at $22.3 million. By the end of 1984, the Joint Committee had channelled a total of $64 million through these co-operatives, with the bulk (around $40 million) going to housing, followed by agriculture, electricity and other areas. The Jordanian Co-operatives Organization made available JD 1.2 million benefiting 37 agricultural co-operatives.

161. As for equity capital, the amount of resources raised is surprisingly low. For example, a regional marketing co-operative requires its members to subscribe to $250 worth of shares, which adds up to $175,000 for a relatively large marketing co-operative society involving 700 members. Such a co-operative society is likely to have received a grant of about $200,000 to $300,000 from ANERA and around $800,000 in loans from the Joint Committee. As such, the equity capital in the average-size co-operative society is estimated to be in the range of 10-20 per cent of its total available resources.

(b) Services rendered

162. The following three main types of loans are offered by co-operatives using funds procured from the Joint Committee and ANERA:

(a) Housing loans, whereby each borrower is provided with a loan of $17,000 with a view to assisting in the construction of a private house. On average, this covers around 35 per cent of total construction expenses and the rest is provided from private sources;

(b) Loans for the purchase of machinery and equipment to be used in providing services needed by members. This includes such items as agricultural machinery, olive oil presses, oil tinning plants, and soap manufacturing machinery;

(c) Loans for the construction and installation of irrigation canals and facilities, and the opening of roads.

163. In addition to the above-mentioned services, some co-operatives, specifically those described as "regional marketing societies", were being asked by the Joint Committee to extend to their members loans in cash ranging from $1,400 to $2,000 per borrower at an interest rate of 2 per cent. It is estimated that about 2,000 members have received such loans. Since loan security requirements are too lenient (two guarantors from among other members) and uncertainty surrounds the nature of the loans extended, the rate of repayment is rather low, ranging between 30 and 50 per cent of outstanding loans in 1986.

(c)   Overall assessment

164. Co-operative societies have not played their role aimed at meeting the pressing needs of their members for medium and long-term loans. On the other hand, they have provided their members with seasonal loans, meeting about 30-50 per cent of members' needs. The number of farmers who have received such loans is around 10 per cent of all eligible borrowers.

165. Housing co-operatives have succeeded in starting construction work on a large number of houses. However, due to a demand for high-standard housing and because of the relatively low share of loans in the total cost of the house, the vast majority of houses take many years to complete and are completed only after causing painful stress and inconvenience to the bulk of borrowers. Nevertheless, housing projects have been among the most successful achievements of the co-operative movement and the Joint Committee.

166. In view of the traditional and political orientation of management, most co-operative societies are in need of qualified cadres capable of conducting their businesses with technical and managerial efficiency. Poor management has clearly reflected on the performance of most co-operatives, preventing them from achieving their proclaimed objectives, especially in the area of agricultural marketing, where their services do not go beyond issuing certificates of local origin for goods to be shipped to Jordan.

167. The repayment record of borrowers from co-operatives is mixed. Repayment of housing loans given to government employees has been fairly easy, since instalment dues have been deducted at source directly from salaries paid by employers in Amman. The situation has been much more difficult in the case of less reliable borrowers. The repayment record of individual borrowers in marketing co-operatives has been generally low (30-50 per cent), mostly because of inadequate safeguards and collateral arrangements. The repayment record of co-operatives themselves to the Joint Committee, has been similar due to difficulties in management and the lack of adequate and reliable guarantees on loans received.

(iv) Dealers in farm supplies

168. Dealers in farm supplies have played a major role in meeting the needs of most commercial farm owners for seasonal credit facilities. This is the case, for instance, in such branches as vegetable, poultry and sheep-raising projects. This source of credit is characterized by relatively simple transactions and great effectiveness in meeting desired needs, whether in terms of quality of inputs or volume of credit advanced.

169. The role of farm-supply dealers had always been crucial in meeting short-term credit requirements of farmers in the West Bank, and to a lesser extent in Gaza Strip. This is evidenced, for example, by the fact that by June 1967 two poultry feedmills had provided about $1 million in loans in the West Bank, which was roughly equivalent to all loans advanced by agricultural co-operatives to some 8,951 member farmers.

170. The credit role of agricultural companies which continued to operate even after occupation became more important. However, the situation took a sharp turn after the mid-1970s because of galloping inflation and the resulting fast and unpredictable devaluation in the Israeli currency. This has forced all sellers to minimize the duration of credit and insist on cash payment. In many cases when lending is deemed risky, transactions are tied to the Jordan dinar at the prevailing exchange rate at the time of sale. While the role of agricultural dealers has sharply declined in absolute terms, they still play a crucial role in the area of seasonal credit and on a scale which is much more significant than that performed by co-operative societies.

(v) Rural credit

171. Prior to Israeli occupation, rural credit in the territories had been supplied by different specialized Jordanian institutions, each with a defined frame of operation. Medium and long-term credit needs in the West Bank were handled by the Jordanian Agricultural Credit Corporation (ACC) through its district offices. It charged an interest of 6 per cent on loans and insisted on real estate as the mortgage. The volume of outstanding ACC loans on the eve of occupation amounted to JD 1.7 million.[144]/ Production loans for seasonal purposes, on the other hand, were handled by the Jordan Central Co-operative Union (JCCU) through its member co-operatives, which, in turn, advanced loans only to their members (around 10 per cent of all farmers) at an interest rate of 9 per cent. By June 1967, loans extended by the co-operatives to their members amounted to JD 457,000.[145]/

172. In the Gaza Strip, the major sources of rural credit prior to occupation were the three branches of the Agricultural Credit Bank in Gaza City, Khan Yunis and Rafah. Credit was extended both in cash and in kind on concessional terms, by virtue of the financial subsidy schemes sponsored by the Egyptian Government. Furthermore, there were 17 co-operatives in the Strip which provided some form of credit services. However, no information is available on the volume of credit advanced by these institutions.

173. In addition to the institutional sources of rural credit, farmers in the occupied territories also had access to other sources of credit for seasonal and short-term purposes. Most importantly, they were able to procure loans from suppliers of production inputs and from marketing middlemen.

(a) Post-occupation developments

174. The rural credit situation underwent a sharp transformation in the wake of Israeli occupation in June 1967. As indicated earlier, the Government of Jordan had to close all West Bank ACC branches and ordered a freeze on the lending operation of JCCU branches in view of Israeli conditions.

175. Sources of rural credit, during the first 6-8 years of occupation, consisted primarily of suppliers of production requisites and, to a much lesser extent, marketing middlemen. By the late 1970s, rural credit had witnessed three major structural transformations. Firstly, farmers displayed a growing trend toward scaling down their long-term investments to the bare minimum because of erratic fluctuations in profitability and the noticeably insecure political environment, especially following the Likud Party's accession to power in 1977. Yet it should be emphasized that had there been credit available on concessional terms, like that of ACC and JCCU, many farmers in the territories would have been encouraged to apply for it, as that would have made the marginal rate of return of their enterprises markedly more attractive. Secondly, the second part of the 1970s witnessed the emergence of a large number of "private voluntary organizations" (PVOs), many of which were involved in providing financial aid to rural and agricultural projects. However, until early 1986, none of these PVOs was involved in advancing loans for production and rural development purposes. They all resorted instead to giving grants to "eligible" beneficiaries, as prescribed in their policy criteria (see chapter IV on this issue).

176. Thirdly, a major development took place in 1978 when the Arab Summit, held in Baghdad, decided to establish the Jordanian-Palestinian Joint Committee and proclaimed it as the main conduit for channelling Arab aid to residents of the occupied territories (see chapter IV).

(b) Rural credit at present

177. With the non-involvement of the branches of Israeli banks in rural finance and development and the subsequent halt in payments through the Joint Committee, potential sources of rural finance are, therefore, confined to the following:

(a) Suppliers of production inputs, who have been encouraged by the stability in the Israeli currency since mid-1985 to resume their credit services to their customers. While not yet operating at the pre-1967 level, agricultural dealers remain by far the most important source of seasonal and short-term finance in the territories. No interest is charged on this kind of loan, but the price of inputs supplied is usually set at a level which covers the interest on the actual value of such goods. Quite often the rate of such "quasi" interest is negotiated by sellers and buyers in advance at the time of sale. Delays in the supplier recovering his loan leads to an interest charge which may be as high as 30 per cent per annum on the loans;[146]/

(b) Marketing middlemen, who play an important credit function in the Jordan Valley, which is the major production area for vegetable crops in the West Bank. Again, no interest is charged on loans made to the borrowing farmer. Lenders are able to earn noticeably high rates of return by charging higher prices on inputs sold to farmers and through the commission they accrue on the sale of their clients' produce. Apart from close personal knowledge of their borrowers gathered over a number of years, the only guarantee that middlemen require is to bind borrowers to sell their produce through the middlemen's wholesale shops in the markets of Nablus or Amman;

(c) One European based PVO, which initiated its own lending scheme in 1986, giving priority to unemployed college graduates who are interested in initiating new businesses in the area of agriculture, mainly in animal production. The scheme has recently also been extended into the industrial sector with a view to promoting small-scale industrial projects, including workshops. The duration of loans is limited to a maximum of five years, with a grace period ranging from one to two years depending on the nature of the project, and loans have to be guaranteed by a solvent guarantor. A service fee of 2 per cent is charged on the total value of the loan and deducted from the first instalment. An interest of 4 per cent per year is charged on the outstanding balance starting after the grace period.

(d) Some private voluntary organizations, which have already approved plans to provide credit for agricultural and rural development purposes. They include the Community Development Foundation and the Agricultural Development Credit Corporation (a Palestinian, Jerusalem-based institution). However, neither had commenced its operations by August 1986.

178. While PVOs have yet to play a more active role in the overall area of agricultural production, they have succeeded in becoming a major donor for financing a wide range of rural development projects, such as road construction, building and equipping village clinics, drinking water projects, and health education. In fact, following the near total freeze of the Joint Committee's operations during the last two years, and in view of Israel's reluctance and disinterest in allocating any of its own resources, PVOs have recently become the only available source of funding for such purposes. It should be pointed out, however, that PVOs' activities are largely grant-oriented. As a result, they cannot replace the purely institutional and/or individual sources of business finance.

(d) Money changers

179. Prior to 1967, money changers were allowed to operate in both Jordan and the West Bank. However, their number increased sharply in the West Bank after Israeli occupation and the closure of banks and other financial institutions. Their business now encompasses various kinds of services. They have come to play a significant role in the functioning of the monetary sector in the occupied territories.

180. A number of factors are behind the success of the money changers and their contribution to the economy of the territories, especially in the West Bank (including East Jerusalem). The absence of national banking institutions created an important gap in the monetary and financial transactions of the territories, which money changers were able to fill to some extent with commendable efficiency. The recognition by the Israeli occupation authorities of two currencies as legal tender in the West Bank, namely the Jordanian dinar and the Israeli shekel, made money exchange a daily affair. This was intensified by the continued depreciation of the Israeli currency, a fact that forced Palestinians in the territories to hedge against a weak currency by preferring more stable currencies, namely the United States dollar and the Jordanian dinar. Arab financial support, including payments by the Jordanian Government to employees of public institutions, and Palestinian workers' remittances were largely transferred to the territories through money changers and/or by persons crossing the bridges. There are no direct banking

operations between the territories and the Arab countries. In addition to these factors, dealing with money changers would have had certain advantages over banking institutions even if Arab banks had still been operating in the territories. They are more flexible and speedy and offer exchange rates which are usually closer to the regional and international market rates.

181. The number of money changers, who are mostly not licensed, rose sharply in the West Bank to reach 196 in April 1986, as shown in table 22. Prior to 1967, their total number was 42. Although Israeli authorities do not consider the Jordanian dinar as legal tender in East Jerusalem, it is often used by residents and money changers there. A similar situation exists in the Gaza Strip, but to a smaller extent as Israeli policy prohibits money changers from operating in the Gaza Strip and because of the fact that the Strip is on a single currency standard. Nevertheless, there are money changers who perform the same types of services as are rendered by money changers in the West Bank. In addition, there are numerous peddlers who engage in money-changing activities.

Table 22

Distribution of money changers by localities in the West Bank
April 1986

Towns	Number of money changers
Nablus	64
Jerusalem	34
Ramallah	22
Bethlehem & Bet Sahour	22
Jenin	16
Tulkarm	15
Qalqilia	14
Hebron	7
Jericho	2
Total	196

Source: field survey.

(i) Functions of money changers

182. Money changers differ widely in the nature and scope of their service, depending on several factors: whether they were established prior to 1967 or after; whether they have branches in Jordan and other Arab countries; whether located in the West Bank, Jerusalem, or Gaza; their size; and personal relationships. In most cases, money changers perform a wide range of activities including currency exchange, money transfers, clearing of accounts, accepting deposits, extending loans, and managing investment portfolios. The first three functions are more common, while the rest are confined to large money changers and remain relatively modest.147/

183. The basic function which all money changers perform is exchanging currencies. The exchange of Jordanian dinars and Israeli shekels is requested routinely by practically all categories of inhabitants. Merchants and workers who receive their wages in shekels prefer to exchange their excess holdings of Israeli currency into Jordanian dinars for fear of continuous and, at times, even immediate depreciation. On the other hand, merchants change their dinars to shekels only shortly before they pay for goods they purchase from Israeli suppliers and/or settle an obligation. Even ordinary citizens try to preserve the purchasing power of their income by exchanging their dinars to shekels gradually and in pace with their family expenditures. While rendering this service, money changers earn a narrow spread of 0.6 - 1 per cent. They set their own exchange rates bearing in mind market conditions both locally and abroad to the extent that contacts with external markets provide the necessary information, even if there is some time lag.

184. In addition to the dinar-shekel exchange transactions, money changers are also deeply involved in unofficially handling other currencies, most importantly the United States dollar, the Saudi Arabian riyal, the Kuwaiti dinar, the pound Sterling, and other Arab currencies received in the form of remittances from relatives working abroad. United States dollars are circulated on a considerable scale, often involving Israeli citizens. Israeli military and monetary authorities display some degree of tolerance of this activity because of its net positive effect on the Israeli economy.

185. The transfer of money to and from the occupied territories is another major function which big money changers perform efficiently on an extensive scale. The absence of an adequate banking system has thus given rise to money changers performing a function which is otherwise a typical banking operation. Given the undesirable circumstances prevailing in the territories, big money changers with branch offices and correspondent arrangements in Jordan and the Gulf States transfer remittances fairly efficiently. In addition to charging a fee of about 1 per cent, money changers also benefit by holding the money in their accounts for several days (maybe weeks) and from the spread that can accrue while exchanging currencies during the process of transfer.

186. Transfer of money from the territories to residents abroad is also efficiently managed, whether to recipients in Arab countries or to Europe and North America. That was a vital function for a long time when parents were transferring stipend allowances to their children studying abroad, but with the recent proliferation of local universities, the demand for this service has markedly declined.

187. Money changers also render two other types of services which normally constitute the basic intermediary function of banks and other financial institutions. Firstly, they extend loans to borrowers whom they know well through the course of their business. Loans are given mostly for short periods of less than four months and at interest rates which vary considerably from one borrower to another, ranging from zero to 40 per cent if computed on an annual basis. Money changers may advance interest-free loans to some of their clients as a bonus on what is viewed by them as a more important type of business.

188. The resource base available to large money changers is derived basically from their other major function of accepting deposits from residents and institutional entities. In the absence of an adequate banking system in the territories and the refusal of the branches of Israeli commercial banks to accept interest bearing deposits in Jordanian dinars, which is in fact legal tender in the West Bank, the inhabitants have been pushed into dealing with the money changers. Due to the non-existence of an indigenous central monetary authority, such operations of money changers, while beneficial, remain quite vulnerable in the long run. About half of deposits with money changers are placed against interest, and the other half is entrusted to money changers interest free, mainly for religious reasons pertaining to interest charges. The incentive to resort to money changers for the holding of cash surpluses is also explained by other hazards such as theft. Money changers have learned, as early bankers did, that depositors do not all withdraw their total deposits at one time. Thus, large money changers provide an accounts clearing service to their customers. They only move across the bridges the net balance between cheques cashed and money deposited.

189. Cashing of bank cheques drawn by merchants on their accounts in Jordanian banks is another important service which money changers extend to their trusted clients. This is viewed as an important service in the light of the difficulty and high cost involved in commuting to and from Amman. Money changers charge a commission of 0.5 - 2 per cent on such services.

190. There are a few examples of large money changers also performing other functions on a selective basis, namely investment on behalf of others in shares in the Amman financial market. In fact, it is maintained that the flow of financial resources from the West Bank into Amman contributed to the development and expansion of the Amman Stock Exchange. The stability of the Jordanian dinar and the growth of the Jordanian economy evidently contributed to this phenomenon.[148]/ Some money changers have even subscribed to the capital of new firms. This development is likely to have been further stimulated by the decision of the Jordanian authorities to lift most of the major restrictions on investment by non-Jordanian Arabs in an attempt to attract more capital and promote inter-Arab economic co-operation. Such investment will be eligible for the various tax concessions available to locals.[149]/ On a few occasions, a money changer has also guaranteed clients vis-à-vis a third lender.

(ii) Evaluation

191. Given the lack of an adequate banking system and the severe financial problems encountered by the inhabitants of the territories following Israeli occupation, money changers have managed to extend a number of vital services to residents and institutions in these territories. The services they render have greatly helped in alleviating some of the numerous inconveniences which have emerged in the wake of Israeli occupation and the closure of Arab banks. However, their role in financial intermediation remains basically limited in scope, with credit facilities confined to "first aid" lending in the services sector. Their role in financing industry has been virtually nil, and in agriculture and the housing sectors they play no role at all. In fact, in view of the very nature of their operations and status, money changers are

basically ill-suited for financial intermediation even if they were somehow allowed to accept money for safe keeping and extend short-term credit to people.

192. The dealings of private money lenders have always remained part of the operation of the informal monetary sector. In the economy of the West Bank and Gaza Strip, which is void of a national banking system, the operation of the informal monetary sector has indeed acquired an institutional character where money changers are obliged to act as banks. This, however, has taken place in the absence of the requisite laws and regulations and an indigenous central authority concerned with protecting the parties concerned and regulating monetary policy in the interest of economic objectives. As a result, there is always the danger of insolvency if it is necessary to honour obligations under unpredictable circumstances. The recent collapse of a few money changers in Amman is a clear sign of this. Fear was also expressed that the collapse of the money changers in Amman, who carried on business with their counterparts in the West Bank and who provided loans at a 16 per cent interest rate to their clients, might cause heavy losses to West Bank residents and an undisclosed number of Israelis, all of whom use West Bank money changers as surrogate banks.150/ In view of the risks involved, financial intermediation, on a very small scale, is largely confined to a few large money changers. However, their ability to mobilize domestic savings as an element in economic development is severely limited by the risky environment.151/

193. In the area of foreign exchange, the money changers' business is not confined to exchanges of dinars and shekels alone. Money changers have equally found the scope of their operations extended to include also the exchange of other desirable currencies. The state of the Israeli shekel and inflation has further encouraged dealings in such currencies as a lucrative source of income. However, this has always entailed high risks in view of Israeli prohibitions. Transfer of money across the bridges has always been difficult, risky and expensive. Problems with tax authorities have been chronic.152/ Despite these difficulties, most well established money changers have been able to earn high returns on their business. Newcomers to the business, however, provide a considerably narrower range of services and their volume of business is much smaller, hence depressing their income to barely acceptable levels. Nevertheless, owing to lack of other opportunities and the political and economic uncertainties prevailing in the territories, dealings in foreign exchange have attracted a sizeable number of businessmen whose business outlook has been increasingly tuned to making fast and sizeable profits from such dealings. The shrinking trend in the output of the productive sectors of the economy (agriculture and industry) creates a need for measures to enhance the development of the entrepreneurial class in the territories.

194. The illegal and undocumented nature of the greater part of the moneychanging business has undermined the potential of both money changers and their clients to pursue legal means in settling business disputes. This situation has given rise to numerous incidents of fraud involving substantial losses, with victims not being able to resort to legal action.

4.   Attempts at re-opening banks

195. Following the occupation of the territories, attempts were made to
re-open the local banks both in the West Bank and Gaza Strip. The Israeli
authorities demanded that the banks concerned should operate under the
supervision of the Central Bank of Israel - a demand considered to be contrary
to the laws and regulations prevailing in the territories when occupied.
In 1973, the negotiations, which also involved the International Monetary
Fund, came to an end without any agreement. However, the two branches of
foreign banks, namely the Ottoman Bank and the British Bank of the Middle
East, were allowed to re-open, but both refused to do so.

196. By the mid-1970s, a new round of negotiations had begun, but the
following stumbling blocks remained:

      (a) Israeli authorities would permit the opening of all branches except
those in East Jerusalem, and this had serious political implications
unacceptable to the Arab Bank;

      (b) Legal reserves of over 70 per cent were to be kept at the Bank of
Israel (in Jordanian dinars) at no interest;

      (c) Deposits which were held in banks outside the country would have to
be transferred back to local branches;

      (d) Re-opened banks would be asked to generate more equity capital so
that they could maintain their finances on an autonomous basis independent of
their main offices in Amman.

197. The third round of re-opening negotiations took place during the
period 1982-1985 again involving only the Arab Bank. A tentative agreement
was reached in late 1985 to re-open the Arab Bank in Nablus, and all other
differences were settled. However, the Israeli authorities have still not
responded positively to this move, and most knowledgeable local experts are
skeptical of any positive outcome on this issue. In view of the unsuccessful
efforts to re-open local banks and the continued need for regular banking
services in the territories, attempts have been made in recent years to open
new banking institutions in the West Bank.

198. In 1984, a group of prominent West Bank businessmen began an intensive
dialogue with the Israeli authorities in an effort to license a new bank to be
based in Nablus, with more branches to be opened later in other cities. The
request was considered by the Israeli authorities. The Central Bank of
Jordan, however, demanded that the licensing of the proposed bank should be
accompanied by a pledge from Israel to open the other branches which were more
advantageously placed compared to any new bank in terms of capital, experience
in the territories, know how, and ability to mobilize external resources.
Moreover, it did not accept that the Bank of Israel should oversee the
operation of the bank, maintaining that it must be governed in accordance with
the prevailing laws in the territories. Meanwhile, the Supreme Economic
Committee in Jordan called for the opening of all banks in the West Bank in
accordance with international law and subject to the Jordanian rules and
regulations prevailing in that territory. The attempt to establish a new
bank failed.

199. In January 1986, another request was submitted to the Israeli authorities to establish a financial institution under the name of the "Arab Finance House" (AFH). The founding shareholders consisted of 20 businessmen spearheaded by the largest moneychanging offices in the Middle East. Unlike the bank initiative mentioned above, the founders of AFH were able to procure a license from Jordan, but for a financial institution (lending bank) aimed at promoting economic development for local Palestinians.

200. After lengthy negotiations with Israeli authorities, a tentative agreement was reached along the following lines:

(a) The starting share capital would be $5 million, half of which was to be subscribed to by the main founders (no more than 20);

(b) AFH would be liable to inspection and supervision by the "civil administration" and not by the Bank of Israel;

(c) AFH could retain its dinar reserves abroad, and not in the Bank of Israel, provided that it produced acceptable guarantees that the volume of its reserves conformed with required criteria;

(d) AFH would be allowed to handle Israeli and Jordanian currencies. The handling of foreign currencies, on the other hand, would be prohibited until AFH obtained a license as an "authorized dealer";

(e) AFH would be permitted to perform functions very close to normal banking operations and to open branches in a number of locations, except in Gaza Strip and Jerusalem.

201. By April 1986, the negotiations had come close to completion and the founders were awaiting a response from the Israeli officials concerned. The approval of the Israeli authorities was still pending at the end of 1986. In the meantime, the move began to lose momentum.

202. In yet another attempt, supported by United States Government mediation, the Israeli authorities agreed to a request to re-open the branch of the Jordan-based Cairo-Amman Bank in Nablus.[153]/ To that effect, an understanding was subsequently reached in London, late in 1986, between the Central Banks of Jordan and Israel. Certain unresolved issues, such as the securing of international guarantors, the availability of the bank's services to Palestinians of East Jerusalem and the inhabitants of Gaza, and dealing in foreign exchange, delayed the opening of the branch. It is the first Arab bank to open in the West Bank since 1967 and follows the re-opening of the Bank of Palestine in Gaza in 1981.

203. The branch, which finally opened at the end of 1986, will operate in accordance with the Jordanian law in force in the territories, as amended by Israel. It will operate under the parallel supervision of Jordan and Israel, with Jordan supervising transactions in dinars and monetary transfers to Jordan allowing dinars to be kept at the Central Bank of Jordan, and Israel looking after transactions in shekels and other currencies.

204. The Egyptian Government owns 12 per cent of the bank's shares, Jordanian public institutions such as the Pension Fund hold 10 per cent, and the rest is held by Jordanians. One source estimated that there is up to $250 million in uninvested Palestinian savings which could be deposited in the bank and used also to launch industries in the West Bank.154/ The bank is expected to serve businessmen in both the West Bank and Gaza Strip and hopes to open branches in other West Bank cities if proved to be successful. The opening of the branch is no doubt a positive development giving rise to expectations for the opening of other Arab and local banks which were operating in the territories before 1967. However, the nature of the arrangement governing the operation of the bank poses a number of questions with regard to possible effects on small financial businesses, the unwillingness of individuals to disclose all financial operations to the Israeli authorities and the influence of these authorities on the direction and size of loans.155/

205. The success of the bank obviously depends on the volume of its capital and its ability to attract the savings of individuals and institutions and to effectively allocate resources to borrowers in various needy economic sectors of the occupied territories, especially commerce, agriculture and industry. The involvement of both the Jordanian and the Egyptian Government and the high standing of the bank itself (being the second largest bank in Jordan, with 14 branches throughout the country) should enable it to secure funds from outside at existing market rates of interest and to extend to borrowers loans at rates lower than the prevailing rates of interest in the territories. Such an effort should equally help bring down the level of interest rates and make the element of de facto subsidy highly concentrated and cost-diffused. It is equally, if not more, important to develop an adequate technical cadre capable of designing feasible programmes for the mobilization, allocation and management of financial resources. Above all, the success of the bank in serving the economy of the territories will depend on the manner in which the occupation authorities treat the bank regarding the nature and scope of its activities and the legal framework within which it expects to operate.

C. A general assessment of the monetary sector and its prospects

206. The closure of the branches of Arab and non-Arab banks since the occupation of the West Bank and Gaza Strip has left the territories with virtually no banking and financial system to meet their immediate needs and contribute to their economic development. An economy void of such vital facilities and deprived of an indigenous central authority and its requisite institutions can never expect to accumulate adequate amounts of resources to be channelled into productive sectors to promote growth and development. This presents a striking contrast with the situation in Israel where the short, medium and long-term financial needs of the public are met by commercial banks and other specialized financial institutions established to serve agriculture, industry, housing, tourism and shipping. These institutions are either fully government-owned or owned jointly by the banks and the government. Government development funds are channeled through both commercial and specialized financial institutions.

207. While foreign sources of finance have helped to alleviate the hardship encountered, they are only expected to supplement national efforts to mobilize domestic resources and not to replace them. Besides, grants aside, loans and private foreign investments which are usually governed by a myriad of

conditions, cannot be considered under the present situation in the territories. Despite the efforts made to establish alternative arrangements, the facilities so created remain inadequate in terms of resources, outlook and technical capabilities. They have, at best, tried to accommodate the minimum immediate needs of the economy under the constraints of occupation.

208. The branches of Israeli banks and other financial institutions have not been able to fill the gap by effectively carrying out financial intermediation and rendering other banking and related services to the inhabitants of the territories. In the 20 years of their existence, these branches have managed to steer away from the mainstream of Palestinian economic development efforts, while siphoning resources out of the territories by holding large balances in banks within Israel itself. The volume of their credit in the territories remains negligible. Their role in contributing to the development of the territories has been equally nil. The resentment of the population of the territories towards dealings with the institutions of the occupying power, coupled with the steadily declining value of the Israeli currency, partly explains the non-involvement of these branches in the economy of the territories.

209. The Bank of Palestine has equally been unable to engage in active financial intermediation, largely due to the constraints imposed on its operations. Its capital, geographic coverage and range of services to the public in the Gaza Strip have remained negligible since its re-opening in 1981. It has no national central authority to look to for support and guidance in carrying out its mission. As a result, its management has been forced to follow a rather conservative line of policy in its operations.

210. The indigenous informal facilities that have emerged in the resulting vacuum comprise a set of fragile and fragmented arrangements incapable of filling the gap and meeting the mounting needs of the territories' economy. The dual, if not triple, currency standard has in effect caused money changers to multiply in number and to engage in the business of exchanging one currency against another with the intention of earning profits in the process. They are hardly able to intermediate between borrowers and lenders on a large scale. The major part of their business consists of exchanging mainly Israeli and Jordanian currencies which accrue to the inhabitants of the territories from their employment in Israel and Arab countries and from the transfer of resources from Jordan and other Arab and non-Arab Governments and organizations.

211. So far, these money changers have been operating under somewhat favourable conditions, particularly since 1974 when the region as a whole benefited from an unprecedentedly high level of financial resources resulting from a series of changes in the price of oil. The current relative stability of the Israeli currency, coupled with high real rates of interest, the recent decline in the international value of the United States dollar and, most importantly, the fall in the volume of remittances and transfers do not augur well for the continuation of this important segment of the financial sector. These factors undermine its role of serving the economy of the territories even at the economy's present level, let alone meeting its long-term development needs. The recent move of the Israeli authorities to regulate the activities of money changers and the payment of their taxes is likely to add to the difficulties which will be encountered by these money changers.

212. The economy of the territories is in a more precarious situation now than at any time during the 20 years of their occupation. Indeed, over the past few years there has been no marked improvement, and perhaps no improvement at all, in living conditions in the territories. To judge from the realities on the spot, the situation, if anything, has deteriorated - in part, it is true, because of the general recession in the Israeli economy and the drop in the price of oil, which has meant less money reaching the territories from Palestinian workers, as well as from official and private transfers. Bold measures are needed to remedy the situation.156/

213. The present financial system in the territories calls for drastic changes in the institutional structure of finance, with emphasis on a reorientation in the nature and scope of its operation. New indigenous facilities are needed to replace the very fragile and vulnerable arrangements, to appeal to a wider public, and to provide a variety of interrelated financial services that meet the needs of the economy. Above all, the new facilities should be able to actively and adequately engage in financial intermediation with a view to mobilizing personal savings and allocating them to needy areas. An adequate institutional source of finance and the existence of a central monetary authority to design and co-ordinate appropriate instruments of monetary policy within the frame of overall economic objectives are among the pressing requisites for initiating and enhancing economic development activities in the territories.

214. The re-opening of one branch of an Arab bank (i.e. the Cairo-Amman Bank) is no doubt a move in the right direction. It should in principle be able to provide the foundation for the provision of services which neither the Israeli banks nor the money changers have been able to satisfactorily extend in view of their inherant limitations relating to the problem of legitimacy, poor service, high cost, lack of expertise and risk. However, this new move leaves much to be desired if it is intended to prepare the grounds for, and create the foundation of, an institutional approach to meeting the bulk of the financial requirements of the territories.

215. To begin with, the resources of the branch should be augmented through external contributions until it succeeds in mobilizing savings within the economy. The Central Bank of Jordan should be able to serve not only as a repository of reserves but also as the lender of last resort in order to enable the branch to take calculated risks and compete with established foreign institutions which enjoy the support of their Governments and parent organizations.

216. An adequate scheme of extending and monitoring credit needs to be developed to ensure prompt repayment of principal and interest. Similarly, a range of incentives is needed to help mobilize personal savings over a wider geographical area. As experience has shown in many developed and developing countries,157/ it is the savings of the non-corporate sector that provide a significant source of finance in the economy. In the context of the territories, this is of crucial importance, given the virtual non-existence of savings from the government and corporate sectors. In view of this and the fact that personal savings have always found their way into other places for other purposes, the incentives need to be attractive enough to bring about a change in attitude and decision. These incentives could consist of different deposit schemes with varying rates of interest and other features aimed at increasing their appeal to different categories of savers over a wider geographical area.

217. It is equally necessary for the new bank and future financial institutions to establish close links with existing formal and informal facilities such as the co-operatives, insurance companies and even money changers with a view to mobilizing greater savings and channelling them over a wider area. It is important for the bank to avoid developing an urban bias in its operation whether directed to trade and/or industry. If it is not possible to provide credit to all sectors and categories of borrowers, it could at least follow a selective approach geared to serving priority areas and projects. Such an approach is likely to prove more effective, since limitations on credit tend to affect economic decisions more than does the rate of interest. This is of particular importance to attempts aimed at supporting small entrepreneurs whose sources of finance are limited. In the meantime, the bank should be allowed to widen and deepen the geographical and functional scope of its business. It is particularly important for this bank and other subsequent financial institutions to establish organic links with co-operatives, as the latter are in a better position to tap much of the potential savings from rural areas which are not usually mobilized in view of the high transaction cost of acquiring, and lack of familiarity with, instruments of deposit. They are also in a better position to identify and serve promising borrowers and projects than the bank would be under the present circumstances. This outlook is conducive to promoting complementarity between banking services and services offered by co-operatives, thus creating the basis for a multi-functional facility in the territories. It will further contribute to the development of producers' and marketing co-operatives, thus enabling farmers to benefit also from the advantages of economies of scale in the handling of inputs, outputs and marketing.[158]/ Special emphasis should be placed on those co-operatives which serve rural areas. The bank's relations with money changers is equally important and should be developed so as to bring them closer to the norms of the organized part of the financial market, however small it is at present.

218. Furthermore, it is necessary to establish a realistic structure of interest rates, making the real rate of return on bank deposits attractive to personal savings, given the political uncertainty prevailing in the territories and the alternative sources of investment available both within and outside the territories, especially in unproductive and speculative ventures.

219. The success of the new branch would largely depend on the extent to which it is able to develop an adequate and qualified technical and managerial cadre capable of evaluating the economic and financial viability of projects proposed by entrepreneurs. Such a cadre would equally be in a position to provide entrepreneurial and managerial as well as technical guidance to co-operatives and to co-ordinate their activities in channelling resources to their members.

220. Finally, an appropriate legal frame of reference needs to be agreed upon if the newly re-opened branch of the Cairo-Amman Bank is to function smoothly and achieve its objectives. Such a legal framework is needed following the suspension of the administrative and legal structures of the territories upon Israeli occupation. It is specially necessary to provide the basis for contractual dealings involving the bank and the inhabitants of the territories. Similarly, the role of the Central Bank of Jordan needs to be specified, in line with Jordanian law, in rendering supervision, in serving as the lender-of-last-resort, and in exercising some of the orthodox functions of

the central bank, namely in respect of the legal reserve ratio, the discount
rate and the use of moral suasion. The exercise of authority over these is
crucial if the central bank has to indirectly regulate the direction and
volume of credit and the supply of Jordanian dinars in the territories.

221. The fact that the newly re-opened branch is allowed to keep its reserves
with its head office in Amman and to operate under the supervision of the
Central Bank of Jordan for the operation of its Department dealing in
Jordanian dinars should enable the Central Bank of Jordan to exercise its
authority over these issues.159/

222. There is no central monetary authority in the territories to regulate,
inter alia, the supply of and demand for Israeli shekels and/or Jordanian
dinars. In the absence of such an authority, the supply of and demand for
money is largely determined by the capital flows into and out of the
territories. The stock of money, therefore, generally tends to adjust itself
through these movements, thus reflecting a combination of the transaction,
precautionary and speculative motives behind the demand for money and the role
of outside sources over its supply. It hardly reflects the level of domestic
output and income. The dual and often triple currency standard imposed on the
territories has continued to exacerbate the situation. With the re-opening of
the Cairo-Amman Bank, the ground is prepared for the Central Bank of Jordan to
exercise supervision and control over the volume of, at least, one of these
currencies, namely the Jordanian dinar. However, this will not be enough for
designing and using instruments of monetary policy to regulate the economy as
a whole. Close co-ordination with the monetary authority of Israel will be
needed to render the use of monetary instruments more effective for economic
management in the territories. Such an arrangement is technically cumbersome
and politically undesirable, given the prevailing circumstances. Moreover, it
cannot be a substitute for an autonomous indigenous body whose sphere of
responsibility for economic management is indivisible.

223. The present financial system has failed to meet the development finance
needs of the Palestinian economy. The volume of capital formation and the
share of the financial system in it during the past 20 years clearly bears
witness to this fact. The resources that have provided impetus for the growth
and development of the Palestinian economy have been supplied almost entirely
from external sources, be they remittances from Palestinians employed abroad
or transfers of public and private bodies. The existing financial system in
the territories has hardly played any role in this, except by serving as an
intermediary. The lack of an indigenous central authority devoted to
development has added to the problem, as has the dual or triple currency
standard, over the operation of which the authority of no single regulatory
body prevails.

224. As a result, the short-term as well as the medium-term and long-term
financial needs of such crucial sectors as agriculture, industry, tourism and
housing are unattended. The position of small farmers and industrialists is
particularly precarious, as they have had to rely on small personal savings or
resort to other sources of finance at exhorbitant costs, with adverse effects
on their output and even the very existence of their establishments. It is
necessary to restore the economic viability of the territories and ensure the
basis for their self-sustained growth and development. Among other things,
specialized financial facilities are needed to support private initiative in
productive areas and encourage entrepreneurs to embark on viable projects

aimed at increasing agricultural and industrial output, promoting exports and improving the balance of payments of the territories, despite the prevailing political uncertainties and constraints of occupation.

225. Indigenous efforts to establish an Arab finance house or lending institution deserve full support, as they promise the creation of a nucleus of long-term financing arrangements. In addition to mobilizing domestic resources, such an institution can also attract external capital for investment in the vital sectors of the Palestinian economy. Multilateral and bilateral sources could provide it with funds on concessional terms, if not on an interest-free or grant basis, which could be crucial in the initial stage of its operation. Subject to its success, the company could also solicit the support of such regional finance institutions as the Arab Fund for Economic and Social Development. It would be necessary for the company to diversify its sources of funds if it is to avoid going through the experience of the Arab Development and Credit Company. In addition to its initial paid-up capital and the funds placed at its disposal from various multilateral and bilateral sources, the proposed facility could also be allowed to raise more funds from the market, local and external, and issue bonds, if necessary. This becomes important if the new facility cannot by law or otherwise attract deposits. Low rates of return coupled with high rates of inflation have been among the factors rendering deposits less attractive, judging by the experience of the branches of Israeli banks and the Bank of Palestine.

226. In view of the nature of its fields of operation, it is important that the new facility not be viewed as a profit-making undertaking from the very outset. However, despite some government budgetary allocations or a credit line to give it initial support, its loan policies and programmes should reflect economic considerations. It must aim at a rate of return on capital which is comparable to alternative uses. In other words, the opportunity cost of capital should always guide loan policies.

227. Once established, the proposed facility should concentrate on helping small-scale enterprises, whether in agriculture or industry, until separate financial institutions can be created for each sector. It would be preferable to aim at creating separate institutions for the agricultural, industrial, housing and construction sectors. While this would make the task of the proposed facility difficult and costly, it is the appropriate way of financing the territories' businesses, which are small and privately owned. Moreover, less emphasis should be placed on collateral, which has always been difficult to secure due to the mounting constraints confronting real estate resulting from continued occupation and land confiscation. More attention needs to be given to the merit of proposals, the personal qualities of borrowers, potential cash flows and other related factors. The proposed facility, once established, will find itself obliged also to help borrowers develop a spaced schedule of repayment from their earnings. It would also be rewarding to engage co-operatives to act as intermediaries for sub-loans of funds to small enterprises for working capital and term loans.

228. Whether loans are extended to small or big businesses, it would also be necessary for the proposed facility to develop technical capabilities not only for evaluating loan requests but also for helping entrepreneurs in the formulation and valuation of project proposals. In this, the use of technical assistance services available from various multilateral sources would be appropriate.

Chapter III

FISCAL DETERMINANTS

Introduction

229. Growth, stabilization and the distribution objectives of public policy
have been preoccupying economists and planners in an increasing number of
countries since the 1950s. The role entrusted to public finance in this
process has increasingly gained acceptance in both developed and developing
countries. Annual Government budgets have assumed growing importance as the
most effective instrument of fiscal policy aimed at affecting the level of
income and demand, influencing economic activity, redistributing wealth and
mitigating inflationary pressure. This role became crucial in situations where
the Government budget also served as the instrument for the implementation of
socio-economic development plans and programmes. In fact, the Government
budget under these circumstances has provided a broad frame of reference for
policy measures and their co-ordination in various areas, especially when
complementary instruments of economic policy such as those in the monetary and
other related sectors have been lacking. Many developing economies have been
characterized by this phenomenon in the process of their development. The
situation in the occupied Palestinian territories represents an exception to
this pattern, as public finance has served only a marginal role, if any. The
purpose of this chapter is to examine briefly the extent to which instruments
of fiscal policy have promoted efforts aimed at improving the performance of
the Palestinian economy in the occupied territories during the 20 years of
their occupation by Israel.

A.   Pre-1967 situation

230. The fiscal system applicable in Palestine, prior to the First World War,
was that obtaining generally throughout the Ottoman Empire, with parts
directly controlled by the Ministry of Finance at Constantinople and parts
administered at district level from Beirut. Government expenditures were
largely concentrated on maintaining law and order and providing some other
public administration services. Traditional taxes on movable and immovable
property, customs duties and excises constituted the main sources of
Government revenues.[160]/

231. With the occupation of Palestine by the British Expeditionary Forces, the
military administration assumed responsibility over matters related to public
administration and reinstated, in February 1918, all the taxes that had been
in force under the Ottoman Government. Subsequently, a number of changes were
introduced in the tax system, including the "in-kind" assessment of tax on
crops at the village level with provision for appeal within six days to the
Military Governor of the district.[161]/

232. In 1920, a civil administration was set up under the Foreign Office in
London and took over the Government of the country from the military
administration. Several changes and reforms were introduced in the fiscal
system. These included the reduction or elimination of one or more taxes, the
modification of assessment and collection methods, and the substitution of new
taxes for old ones, all aimed at rationalizing the tax system from the point
of view of generating more revenue, facilitating its administration,

especially assessment and collection procedures and practices, and ensuring
equality. The introduction of a tax on the income of individuals in 1942, and
on company profits in 1945 also reflected these considerations. Nevertheless,
the tax system remained regressive in its burden, as it relied largely on
property and consumption taxes at flat or proportional rates.

233. The budgetary process was not based on expenditure considerations
determining the level of revenues to be raised. In fact, the size of estimated
revenues determined the level of Government expenditures. The order of
precedence followed a fiscal outlook which was based on the need to continue
necessary services. Proposals for new services deemed necessary or desirable
were liable to be eliminated so as to produce a balanced budget with a margin
of safety, allowing for conditions which would have vitiated the
forecast.162/ This policy resulted in budgetary surpluses in many years
during the period 1920-1947.163/ Nevertheless, Government expenditures on
developmental and economic services represented 33 per cent of total
expenditures in 1936/37.164/ As the Government of Palestine did not have
money-creating power, its revenues from local sources were supplemented by
advances from the Crown Agents and the Joint Colonial Fund or grants-in-aid
from the British Government. The Colonial Development Fund also extended
grants aimed at developing export trade with the United Kingdom and
particularly at carrying out various water works.165/ Only the central
Government in Palestine also resorted to borrowing to a small extent from the
public at home and abroad. The debt burden was therefore slight at all
times.166/ The budget of the central Government was supplemented by
"special" budgets, such as the budget of the Palestine Railways, local and
municipal budgets and the "Jewish budget".167/

234. Upon the establishment of the State of Israel, the West Bank was
subsequently subjected to Jordanian and Palestinian fiscal legislation. In the
Gaza Strip both Palestinian and Egyptian legislation provided the basis for
the operation of the fiscal system.

B.   Post-1967 situation

235. While it is claimed that fiscal laws and regulations prevailing in the
West Bank and Gaza Strip prior to their occupation by Israel in 1967 are still
in force, a wide range of Israeli military orders and proclamations have
created a different situation. The tax system alone has been the subject of
more than 177 military orders and proclamations (including amendments), all
aimed at increasing Government revenues in order to meet expenditures by the
occupation authorities. As a result, a colonial pattern of public finance has
emerged, whereby revenues and expenditures are more or less balanced.

236. The Israeli authorities do not publish or provide comprehensive data on
total Government revenues in the occupied territories. As in the monetary
sector, Government finance statistics remain fragmented and inadequately
reported, appearing partly in national accounts, partly in the balance of
payments and to a small extent in monetary statistics. This shortcoming is
particularly apparent regarding the public finances of the Gaza Strip. As a
result, a thorough analysis of the impact of changes introduced in the fiscal
system of the territories through military orders and proclamations on various
aspects of the economy is rendered difficult. Similarly, the extent to which

Government expenditures are financed through local and other sources of
revenues is also unclear, as no data are published on deficit financing. In
the light of these deficiencies, public finance statistics available on the
territories should be treated with caution.

1. Government expenditures

237. Figures for Israeli Government expenditures, both current and
developmental, in the territories are presented in tables 23, 24, 25 and 26,
covering the period 1984-1986. Although the data fail to provide the trends
and developments in Government expenditures, their order of magnitude is
indeed revealing in every respect.

238. A brief examination of these figures clearly indicates that the total
expenditures of the Israeli military Government fall short of providing the
minimum level of basic Government services to a growing population, meeting
present investment requirements and creating an adequate infrastructural basis
for sustained growth and development. The level of Government expenditures in
real terms is overstated by these figures in view of rapid increases in
prices. The nominal figures adjusted to take account of price rises indicate
little, if any, increase in certain areas. In fact, Government expenditures
have declined in real terms during the inflationary period and have not been
able to maintain the previously existing level of Government services to the
inhabitants. Natural increases in population and return migration have further
reduced the per capita value of these services.

239. Total expenditures of the Israeli military Government in 1984 amounted to
only 12.8 per cent of the GNP of the territories, or $US 128 per capita,
representing one of the lowest levels of Government outlays among developing
economies. By comparison, in 1982 Government expenditures amounted to
79 per cent of GNP in Israel, 48 per cent in Egypt, 47 per cent in Jordan,
46 per cent in Yemen, and 38 per cent in the Syrian Arab Republic.[168]/ In
none of these countries, has the Government budget followed an approach
whereby expenditures and revenues are balanced. In addition to sizeable
external budgetary support, deficit financing has allowed increases in
Government expenditures. This pattern has largely emerged as a result of the
particular importance attached to public expenditures at the early stages of
development. It is widely accepted that various infrastructural facilities
having external benefits must be publicly provided by either the central or
local Government or both and must be financed through the budget but not
necessarily produced by the public sector.[169]/

240. The Government budget has often served as a mechanism for channelling
resources into the economy for this purpose using the public and private
sectors, both directly and through a range of financial institutions. The
significant role of the private sector has been increasingly recognized in
developing economies where entrepreneurial capabilities have been able to
demonstrate their vital contribution to the process of growth and development.
Not much of this widely accepted approach to development and the crucial role
that the Government budget (central or local) has played in this process has
been discernable in the occupied territories, especially during the past
20 years.

Table 23

Israeli Government current expenditures in the West Bank, 1984-1986
(Thousands of new Israeli shekels (NIS) and percentages)a/

Item	1984 (actual)		1985 (budget)		1986 (budget)	
	(NIS)	(%)	(NIS)	(%)	(NIS)	(%)
Civil Administration	251	0.1	1,048	1.6	5,308	3.4
Statistics	101	0.3	198	0.3	538	0.3
Finance	1,355	3.9	5,306	8.1	12,166	7.8
Customs	541	1.6	932	1.4	2,158	1.4
Tax	1,364	4.0	2,648	4.0	5,792	3.7
Interior	1,151	3.3	2,968	4.5	6,911	4.4
Justice	366	1.1	545	0.8	1,406	0.9
Land	75	0.2	152	0.2	320	0.2
Assessment	14	0.0	27	0.0	60	0.0
Education	16,119	46.9	27,331	41.6	55,876	35.8
Archeology	93	0.3	187	0.3	445	0.3
Religion	26	0.1	57	0.1	126	0.1
Labour	480	1.4	808	1.2	1,295	0.8
Employment	111	0.3	217	0.3	1,003	0.6
Health	6,101	17.8	10,873	16.6	31,149	19.9
Welfare	1,308	3.8	2,746	4.2	6,443	4.1
Housing	53	0.1	83	0.1	156	0.1
Public works	1,065	3.1	2,614	4.0	6,546	4.2
Surveying	42	0.1	95	1.4	205	0.1
Agriculture	692	2.0	1,171	1.8	2,586	0.1
Water expenditure	1,331	3.9	2,400	3.6	8,400	5.4
Natural reserves	20	0.1	41	0.1	240	0.2
Industry and trade	282	0.8	441	0.7	919	0.6
Quarries	8	0.0	14	0.0	33	0.0
Tourism	23	0.1	37	0.1	80	0.1
Energy	23	0.1	34	0.1	76	0.0
Transportation	163	0.5	413	0.6	888	0.6
Postal services	504	1.5	1,023	1.6	2,419	1.4
Telecommunications	394	1.1	741	1.1	1,619	1.0
State & absentee property	289	0.8	464	0.7	1,021	0.6
Totalb/	34,345	100.0	65,614	100.0	156,184	100.0

Source: Israel, Budget for 1986/1987, Jerusalem, 1986.

a/ The period average exchange rates for the NIS were as follows:
in 1984, $1 = NIS 0.293; in 1985, $1 = NIS 1.179; in 1986, $1 = NIS 1.488.

b/ Percentage points are rounded for ease of computation. The total
expenditure figures in NIS, which are the sum of the various expenditure
items, differ slightly from those officially reported.

Table 24

Israeli Government current expenditures in the Gaza Strip, 1984-1986
(Thousands of new Israeli schekels (NIS) and percentages)a/

Item	1984 (actual) (NIS)	(%)	1985 (budget) (NIS)	(%)	1986 (budget) (NIS)	(%)
Civil Administration	215	1.4	562	1.8	940	1.4
Statistics	76	0.5	137	0.4	308	0.4
Finance	513	3.4	1,631	5.2	3,550	5.2
Interior	310	2.0	689	2.2	1,563	2.3
Justice	384	2.5	806	2.6	1,690	2.5
Education	5,293	35.1	10,325	33.1	22,411	32.8
Religion	97	0.6	201	0.6	422	0.6
Energy	12	0.1	28	0.1	60	0.1
Labour	304	2.0	623	2.0	1,335	1.9
Health	5,619	37.3	10,893	35.0	24,003	35.2
Welfare	948	6.3	2,548	8.2	5,518	8.1
Agriculture	363	2.4	769	2.5	1,620	2.4
Trade & industry	47	0.3	98	0.3	206	0.3
Transportation	105	0.7	224	0.7	517	0.8
Public works & surveying	107	0.7	266	0.8	570	0.8
Communications	595	3.9	1,175	3.8	663	1.0
State & absentee property	85	0.6	170	0.5	358	0.5
Refugees' rehabilitation	-	-	-	-	250	0.4
Reserve for wages & purchases	-	-	-	-	2,264	3.3
Totalb/	15,073	100.0	31,145	100.0	68,248	100.0

Source: Israel, Budget for 1986/1987, Jerusalem, 1986.

a/   The period average exchange rates for the NIS were as follows: in 1984, $1 = NIS 0.293; in 1985, $1 = NIS 1.179; in 1986, $1 = NIS 1.488.

b/   Percentage points are rounded for ease of computation.

Table 25

Israeli Government development expenditures in the West Bank, 1984-1986
(Thousands of new Israeli shekels (NIS) and percentages)[a]

Item	1984 (actual)		1985 (budget)		1986 (budget)	
	(NIS)	(%)	(NIS)	(%)	(NIS)	(%)
Development of water resources	535	9.8	2,200	12.6	4,700	11.1
Loans and grants to local authorities	1,634	29.9	3,500	20.1	8,700	20.5
School buildings	266	4.9	1,200	6.9	3,200	7.5
Development of post offices	10	0.2	75	0.4	100	0.2
Electric grids	668	12.2	1,400	8.0	2,600	6.1
Telephones	556	10.2	1,800	10.3	4,900	11.6
Roads	563	10.3	2,800	16.1	6,100	14.4
Health	634	11.6	2,490	14.3	9,540	22.5
Civil administration	6	0.1	520	3.0	400	0.9
Archeology	58	1.0	108	0.6	280	0.7
Natural reserves	20	0.4	16	0.1	20	0.0
National parks	40	0.8	20	0.1	35	0.1
Bedouin settlement	55	1.0	120	0.7	140	0.3
Quarries	-	-	60	0.3	-	-
Buses	8	0.1	170	1.0	300	0.7
Industry & agriculture	405	7.4	60	0.3	100	0.2
Reserve for inflation	-	-	845	4.9	1,270	3.0
Non-recurring items	13	0.2	-	-	-	-
Total[b]	5,471	100.0	17,384	100.0	42,385	100.0

Source: Israel, Budget for 1986/1987, Jerusalem, 1986.

a/ The period average exchange rates for the NIS were as follows: in 1984, $1 = NIS 0.293; in 1985, $1 = NIS 1.179; in 1986, $1 = NIS 1.488.

b/ Percentage points are rounded for ease of computation.

Table 26

Israeli Government development expenditures in the Gaza Strip, 1984-1986
(Thousands of new Israeli shekels (NIS) and percentages)a/

Item	1984 (actual)		1985 (budget)		1986 (budget)	
	(NIS)	(%)	(NIS)	(%)	(NIS)	(%)
Miscellaneous	116	3.7	199	3.8	1,076	8.9
Loans & grants to local authorities	1,473	47.1	2,546	49.3	5,572	46.3
Welfare	-	-	40	0.8	101	0.8
Agriculture	10	0.3	52	1.0	82	0.7
Schools	400	12.8	1,248	24.2	2,029	16.9
Health	572	18.3	606	11.7	2,074	17.2
Planning	4	0.1	4	0.1	632	5.2
Telephones	425	13.6	210	4.1	106	0.9
Reserve	-	-	258	5.0	348	2.9
Roads	102	3.3	-	-	-	-
Vocational training	23	-	-	-	-	-
Totalb/	3,125	100.0	5,163	100.0	12,020	100.0

Source: Israel, Budget for 1986/1987, Jerusalem, 1986.

a/   The period average exchange rates for the NIS were as follows:
in 1984, $1 = NIS 0.293; in 1985, $1 = NIS 1.179; in 1986, $1 = NIS 1.488.

b/   Percentage points are rounded for ease of computation. The total
expenditure figures in NIS, which are the sum of the various expenditure
items, differ slightly from those officially reported.

241. Current expenditures amounted to almost 69 per cent of total Government
outlays in 1984. Only a few items under this category of expenditures are of
direct relevance to the Palestinian population in providing a minimum level of
public services. They include education, health, welfare, public works, postal
services and telecommunications. However, much of each allocation covers
salaries and other expenses. The level and standard of services provided in
some of these areas leave much to be desired, as can be seen from the
prevailing conditions in these areas.

242. In the area of education, for example, much of the allocation covers the
salaries of teachers in public schools and Government employees serving this
sector. While there are five universities in the territories, their activities
are severely constrained by lack of financial resources, as contributions from
the various Arab sources have declined and the occupation authorities have
imposed restrictions limiting the freedom to design curricula. Financial
constraints have forced some universities, such as the Bir Zeit University, to
obtain loans from the Higher Council of Education, a body grouping local
universities, to pay their salaries. The absence of a central authority to
plan, co-ordinate and execute programmes involving several universities has
been an impeding factor. As a result, the curricula often duplicate

themselves, with the universities largely concentrating on humanities and not on applied sciences, except for one which has a faculty in engineering and another in medicine. As a result, the qualifications of around 20,000 graduates do not enable them to find suitable jobs.

243. In the area of vocational training, despite the fact that there are around 27 centres which have graduated some 52,000 trainees, the training provided is essentially for semi-skilled employment in Israel, for example in construction, mechanics, plumbing, weaving and clerical functions. Many of the trainees cannot find work in the territories when they complete their training. They either go to Israel for work or emigrate to other Arab countries.170/

244. With respect to health, there are indications that the level and standard of medical services are very poor, with the number of hospitals and the number of beds remaining the same. In fact, with the closure of the "Hospice" Government hospital, in 1985, the situation has further deteriorated. On the whole, the Israeli Government budget provides for a total of 34,500 free hospital days for the entire population of the territories, allocable upon the approval of the military Government. This means that every 37 persons of the population of the territories can benefit from one free hospital day per year. For a large percentage of population which is not covered by health insurance schemes, hospitalization beyond these days requires self-financing. 171/ The area of pharmaceuticals is severely handicapped by lack of research and control in respect of the development and production of medicine. The result has been increasing hazards to health, under-utilization of production capacity in pharmaceutical firms and an increasing drain on foreign exchange for imports from Israel and elsewhere owing to lack of confidence in local output.172/

245. Of the remaining items, much of the allocations cover the operations of the military Government and civil administration. Increases shown in subsequent years (1985 and 1986) for Government expenditures, both current and capital, should be viewed against the rising rate of inflation and the continuous depreciation of the Israeli currency. Moreover, these figures are budget estimates. The level of actual outlays remains to be seen.

246. Capital or development expenditures involving water resources, electricity grids, telephones, roads, civil administration and archeology are at least partly aimed at contributing to the construction and/or improvement of Israeli settlements and meeting the needs of the military administration. Loans and grants to local Palestinian authorities constitute an important item under this category of Government outlays, the aim being to boost the meagre resources of these authorities for the provision of vital social services at the municipal level. Overall, actual development expenditures under this crucial category of Government outlays amounted to as little as 1.9 per cent of the GNP of the territories in 1984. By contrast and as noted earlier, the size of Government expenditures on the development of Israeli settlements in the territories is striking.173/ Coupled with restrictions on private investment, lack of a full fledged banking system, and policies aimed at expanding Israeli settlements and increasing the economic dependence of the territories on the Israeli economy, the low level of capital outlays has not been able to contribute to capital formation or growth in employment, output and income in the Palestinian economy.

247. The assistance of the international community, covering a wide range of activities and carried out independently of the Israeli Government, has supplemented the meagre Israeli budgetary outlays in the territories. This assistance includes involvement in the creation of an adequate physical and human infrastructure relating, for example, to the supply of water and electricity and the provision of sewage facilities, which are all obligations of the Government. While such assistance is welcome since it fills a gap, its magnitude and nature ought to be carefully studied.[174]/ It is important to ensure that external assistance does not relieve the occupying authorities of their obligations and/or increasingly lead the people under occupation to over-rely on outside assistance and support in respect of activities that they could probably undertake themselves. Accordingly, every effort is needed to encourage and enable the inhabitants of the territories to increasingly assume direct responsiblity for the development of their economy. Above all, it is necessary to create the relevant indigenous institutional facilities and an environment which will assist the inhabitants in designing their future path of development and in mobilizing and managing their human and material resources within a sound set of priorities. External assistance under these conditions will have a more purposeful impact and will effectively contribute to local efforts.

2. Government revenues

248. The national income accounts of the territories reveal two major sources of Israeli Government revenues, namely "income tax and transfers to the Government" and "net indirect taxes on domestic production". No definition is given as to the composition of these categories. A major source of Government revenues, i.e. taxes on international trade or transactions effected directly or through Israel, is omitted altogether from these categories. Similarly, they exclude social security contributions and a number of other tax and non-tax sources of Government revenues. As a result, total actual tax and non-tax revenues of the Israeli Government from the territories are only partially reflected in the two aforementioned categories. Despite these limitations, Israeli Government revenues from these two sources amounted to 12 per cent of the territories' GNP in 1984 which is comparable with performance in a number of countries.[175]/

249. According to available statistics, the Israeli Government budget for the occupied territories produced a relatively small surplus in the West Bank and a deficit in the Gaza Strip in 1984 (see table 27). The final picture will be different if revenues from other sources, as indicated above, are also included. Revenues from taxes on the wages of Palestinians working in Israel, customs duties collected by Israeli authorities on the territories' imports through Israel and Jordan, the hidden value added tax charged on all Israeli exports to the territories in lieu of customs duties chargeable by the territories, fees on permits for crossing the bridges into Jordan, and a number of other levies can roughly be estimated at over $150 million in 1984. Including this sum in the Israeli Government budget for the territories will result in an overall surplus - a development which is contrary to the pressing need to improve the economic and social situation of the Palestinian people. It should be noted, however, that these calculations do not cover the direct and indirect benefits that accrue to the economy of Israel from the activities of Israeli settlers in the occupied territories.

Table 27

Estimates of government expenditures and revenues in the occupied Palestinian territories, 1984

(Millions of Israeli shekels and percentages)

	Current expenditures (as % of GNP)	Development expenditures (as % of GNP)	Total expenditures (1) (as % of GNP)	Income tax transfers to the Govt.	Net indirect taxes on domestic production	Total taxes revenues (2) (as % of GNP)	Net (2) − (1)
West Bank	34,345 11.0	5,471 1.8	39,816 (12.8)	18,951	19,801	38,752 (12.4)	(1064)
Gaza Strip	15,073 10.4	3,125 2.2	18,198 (12.6)	12,945	2,583	15,528 (10.7)	−2,670
Total (occupied Palestinian territories)	49,418 10.8	8,596 1.9	58,014 (12.7)	31,896	22,384	54,280 (11.9)	−2,403

Source: Expenditure figures are from tables 25 to 28 and tax figures are obtained from Israel, Central Bureau of Statistics, _Judea, Samaria and Gaza Area Statistics_, (Jerusalem, CBS, 1985), vol. XV, No. 2, pp. 73 to 80.

250. It is, therefore, argued that the inhabitants of the territories in fact pay an "occupation tax" that can be conservatively estimated after 18 years at a total cumulative figure of $700 million for the West Bank alone. This refutes the Israeli claim that the low level of public expenditures and investment derives from budgetary limitations. If net fiscal transfers had been invested in the territories, rather than added to Israeli expenditures, it would have been possible to improve local services significantly and, in particular, to develop local economic infrastructures.[176]/

3. Revenues and expenditures of municipalities

251. In the absence of a national authority in the occupied territories, the municipalities of Palestinian cities and towns become the most important local institutions in respect of providing public services and collecting local taxes and fees. Were it not for the constraints of occupation, their role could have been instrumental in creating job opportunities and undertaking capital projects through community and rural development programmes.

252. Prior to 1967, municipalities played an important role in their localities, with the help of the central Government. Municipalities received a certain percentage of revenues from the tax on the sale of gasoline which constituted a significant portion of their budgets. The Jordanian Government exercised discretion in dividing revenues from this source among the municipalities. As for development projects, the Government placed a special fund at the disposal of the municipalities on easy terms. Loans were granted subject to the approval by the district commissioner. However, at the regional level the municipalities acted independently with regard to various social service projects. All these arrangements were abolished by Israel in 1967. A situation has since emerged whereby municipalities have been subjected to the legislative and executive authority of the military commander in the territories.[177]/ Although maintaining Jordan's budgetary provision for municipalities, the actual power, both legislative and executive, of municipalities has been severely curtailed. Municipalities are not allowed to embark on new projects (water, electricity, roads, school building, etc.) without the advance approval of the occupation authorities. In many cases, approval is either not granted or granted only after a long delay. This has led, at times, to a situation where some municipalities could not spend available revenues for badly needed projects and services.

253. In instances when municipalities resorted to the Jordanian-Palestinian Joint Committee for financial support, the Israeli military Government established a "Development Fund" and obliged all municipalities to transfer into this Fund whatever contributions they received from the Committee. When the implementation of this measure failed, Israeli authorities restricted the amount of funds to be brought into the territories for municipal and other purposes.

254. Municipalities cannot exercise legislative power, and they are therefore not allowed to introduce new taxes and fees or change their prevailing rates or their collection procedures without the prior approval of the Israeli

authorities. This is crucial, as many taxes and fees are not tied to levels of income and prices and are levied either at flat rates and/or imputed in an arbitrary manner.

255. It is, therefore, important that the revenues and expenditures of municipalities be viewed in the light of the above-mentioned constraints. Tables 28 and 29 give a consolidated picture of municipal budgets.[178/] Revenues, which are divided between "ordinary" and "extraordinary", amounted to as little as 4.6 per cent of GNP in 1984/85. Ordinary revenues have accounted for about 75 per cent of total revenues in the West Bank in the last five years and for 71.6 per cent in the Gaza Strip. Overall, they have represented more than 80 per cent in recent years, much of them coming from utilities such as water and electricity, followed by revenues from property taxes and fees. Extraordinary revenues comprise grants and loans from Arab and non-Arab sources, including the budget of the Israeli military Government in the occupied territories. In addition, they include income from municipalities' projects.

256. As noted, Jordan was a main source of income for the municipalities of the West Bank through loans and grants from the City and Village Development Bank and the Arab Bank. This source of funding was replaced, during the period 1979-1985, by the Jordanian-Palestinian Joint Committee. With the introduction of Jordan's Development Programme for the Occupied Territories (1986-1990), financing of municipal projects in the territories is envisaged through this Programme. Grants and loans from the Israeli administration in the territories underwent a steady decline over the period 1980-1984. The level of these loans and grants has often been adjusted in the light of revenues which the municipalities receive from Jordan and other Arab and non-Arab sources.

257. Owing to the unreliable nature of internal and external contributions to the budget of the municipalities in the territories, it has not been possible to depend on extraordinary revenues on a regular basis. Ordinary revenues seem to be more reliable, but they have not always been enough to meet the development requirements of municipalities, even within the limitations imposed by the Israeli occupation authorities on the new projects that are approved for implementation.

258. Current expenditures of the municipalities cover the administrative expenses of local services, engineering and technical expenditures and the cost of providing water and electricity. Construction of roads and buildings and other new infrastructural projects come under "capital" expenditures. Despite the relative increase in the level of both current and capital expenditures, the level of municipal services and development activities has followed a declining trend in real terms.

Table 28

Total municipal revenues, 1978/79 - 1984-85
(Thousands of current United States dollars and percentages)

Year	Ordinary revenues			Extraordinary revenues (Grants and loans from the Administration)	Total revenues	
	Total	Taxes, fees and others	Utilities		Amount	As % of GNP
1978/79	20,398.6	(8,532.6)	(11,865.9)	15,691.2	36,089.8	3.8
1979/80	25,092.7	(9,827.4)	(15,265.3)	22,533.0	47,625.7	4.1
1980/81	33,536.3	(8,170.3)	(23,414.3)	23,083.5	56,619.8	3.9
1981/82	32,564.3	(10,890.5)	(24,035.7)	17,176.1	49,740.4	3.5
1982/83	40,301.7	(13,258.4)	(27,043.2)	10,878.8	51,180.5	3.4
1983/84	56,707.0	(20,920.5)	(35,786.4)	12,563.5	69,270.5	4.1
1984/85	61,864.9	(22,078.5)	(36,341.6)	10,772.3	72,637.2	4.6

Source: Israel, Central Bureau of Statistics, Judea, Samaria and Gaza Area Statistics (Jerusalem, CBS, 1985), vol. XV, No. 2, table 1, pp.209 and 239.

Notes

- Decimal points are rounded for ease of computation.
- Conversion into United States dollars is based on period average market rates in IMF, International Financial Statistics, 1985 Annual Edition (Wash. D.C., IMF, 1985).

Table 29

Total municipal expenditures, 1978/79 - 1984/85
(Thousands of current United States dollars and percentages)

Years	Current*	Capital	Total	As % of GNP
1978/79	21,633.4	12,617.4	34,250.8	3.6
1979/80	22,920.2	17,667.4	47,270.0	4.0
1980/81	39,282.0	15,669.3	54,953.3	3.8
1981/82	38,148.8	11,042.1	49,190.9	3.5
1982/83	41,725.2	8,640.3	50,365.6	3.3
1983/84	49,741.7	14,361.0	64,102.7	3.8
1984/85	51,992.8	16,526.2	68,519.0	4.4

Source: Israel, CBS, Judea, Samaria and Gaza Area Statistics (Jerusalem, CBS, 1985), vol. XV, No. 2, table 2, pp. 210 and 240.

Notes

- Decimal points are rounded for ease of computation.
- Conversion into United States dollars is based on period average market rates in IMF, International Financial Statistics 1985 Annual Edition (Wash. D.C., IMF, 1985).

* Does not include loan repayments.

4.   The tax system

259. A detailed system of taxes, duties and fees was in force in the West Bank and Gaza Strip at the time of their occupation in 1967. As in most developing economies, the emphasis in the design and structure of the tax system reflected revenue considerations of the Government. Nevertheless, attempts were made as early as 1951, especially in the West Bank, to introduce also an element of equity in the tax burden based on the concept of "ability to pay". In view of the limited scope of the tax system as a whole, its potential role in the allocation, stabilization and distribution objectives of public policy was being promoted through a combination of monetary and fiscal instruments.

260. The different types of taxes prevailing in the territories by 1967 may be grouped under the two broad categories, namely direct and indirect taxes.

(a)   Direct taxes

261. These comprise taxes imposed on the income and wealth of individuals and juridical entities.

262. Income tax: This tax was in force in accordance with Law No. 25 of 1964 and covered the income of residents on a "global" basis from work, craft, business, profession or vocation and accruing as salaries and wages, profits, dividends, rent, interest and gains. It excluded agricultural income, interest on public loans, pensions, family and education allowances, non-profit organizations and juridical entities benefiting from the Investment Encouragement Law.[179]/ In addition, a number of disbursements and expenses were allowed as deductions for determining taxable income.[180]/

263. Salaries and wages, income of the self-employed and that of non-share-holding juridical entities were subject to progressive tax rates ranging from 5 to 50 per cent, with a marginal rate of 5 per cent between income brackets. Accordingly, taxable income was divided into 11 brackets, with steps of JD 400 moving to JD 2000, up to a total of JD 8000. The taxable income of share-holding companies was subject to a flat tax rate of 35 per cent.[181]/

264. It should be noted, however, that Income Tax Law No. 25 in Jordan was subsequently amended in 1975 and substantially revised in 1982 and in 1985 with a view to further meeting equity, resource-allocation and revenue considerations. These amendments entailed expanding income brackets, increasing exemptions and improving tax assessment and collection procedures. They did not apply to the occupied West Bank, where Israeli military orders have brought about the kind of changes deemed necessary by the occupation authorities. These changes have, inter alia, increased tax rates and reduced exemptions.

265. Property tax: In accordance with the provisions of Jordanian Tax Laws No. 11 of 1954 and No. 9 of 1967, a municipal tax on buildings and land located within the city limits was imposed at a rate of 17 per cent of the net annual rental value of buildings and 10 per cent of the net annual rental value of land. The taxes were collected by the Central Government (Ministry of Finance) on behalf of municipalities and, after deduction of collection charges, 42 per cent of the tax was transferred to municipal and village

councils as their share of total net collections. The balance of 58 per cent of the tax remained for the Government. In the assessment of the overall income tax liability of property owners, this percentage could apparently be deducted in order to avoid double taxation.

266. <u>Land tax</u>: While agricultural business was exempt from tax, the Land Tax Law of 1955 imposed a nominal fee of an average JD 1 per 1/4 of an acre of land planted with fruits and vegetables.

(b)   Indirect taxes

267. This category comprises various kinds of taxes and fees imposed at the central Government and municipal levels:

(a)   Customs duties and excises: Customs duties constituted the major source of Government revenues under this category, followed by excise duties on selected local products such as petroleum products, cement, cigarettes and alcoholic beverages, imposed in accordance with Law No. 13 of 1963;

(b)   Education tax: in accordance with Education By-law No. 1 of 1965, a tax at the rate of 3 per cent of the estimated annual rent of buildings was imposed on residents in municipal areas;

(c)   Fees and other charges: in accordance with Law No. 27 of 1952 and its subsequent amendments, fees and stamp duties were charged on various kinds of commercial and legal transactions.

(c)   Israeli policies and practices

(i)   Changes in tax laws

268. Following the Israeli occupation of the West Bank and Gaza Strip in June 1967, military proclamations were issued calling for the continued application of the prevailing laws in the territories, provided such application did not contradict the orders of the Commander of the occupation forces and the changes brought about by the establishment of Israeli military rule. Subsequently, many military orders were issued aimed at amending the prevailing tax system. Military Order No. 1106 authorized the civil administration to increase maximum income tax rates through by-laws in order to facilitate the amendment process. As noted earlier, a total of 177 military orders have effected significant changes in the tax system. In addition to changing the scope and rates of taxes, new taxes were imposed with a view to increasing Government revenues and aligning the tax system of the territories with that prevailing in Israel itself. These changes are briefly examined below.

(a)   The income tax law

269. Nowhere in the tax system of the territories are changes more pronounced and frequent than in the area of income tax. These changes pertain to rates, income brackets, methods of assessment, collection and appeal procedures,[182]/ and they are all aimed at maximizing the revenues of the occupation authorities.

270. From June 1967 to February 1985, 34 military orders were issued to amend income tax rates, income brackets and exemptions. The minimum level of taxable income was reduced from JD 400 to JD 40; tax rates were increased, ranging from 5.5 to 55 per cent with marginal rates of up to 5 per cent between income brackets; and the amounts of income under the 11 brackets were reduced to a maximum of JD 3,768, as against JD 8,000 applicable under income tax Law No. 25.

271. While the top rate has increased by 5 per cent, the amounts in taxable income brackets have been lowered in most cases by more than 50 per cent. It is obvious that, because of the lowering of taxable income brackets, a higher tax rate is now levied on amounts which generally represent less than half of the taxable bracket under the 1964 Law. Consequently, a taxable income of JD 1,600 which used to fall within the 15 per cent tax bracket under the 1964 Law has now moved up to the 33 per cent bracket, signifying an increase in tax payments of more than 100 per cent (see table 30). Workers and entrepreneurs are certainly discouraged when they see that a good portion of their marginal income is taken away, especially when the economy is increasingly moving into a recessionary state.

272. A comparison with income tax liability in Jordan puts the taxpayer in the territories at a great disadvantage. In Jordan, the tax threshold for a taxpayer with a spouse and four children was raised from JD 320 under the 1964 Income Tax Law to JD 1,400 under the 1982 Income Tax Law. Likewise, the deduction for each university student has been raised from JD 200 to JD 500. Taxpayers living in rented houses are eligible for a 50 per cent deduction on the amount of annual rent they pay. Medical expenses and insurance premiums are also deducted from taxable income.

273. Upon calculating the amount of income tax due on a sample of 10 income brackets ranging from JD 1,600 to JD 10,600 per annum, it is found that the overall rate has declined from 31.4 per cent under the 1964 Law to 13.8 per cent according to the 1982 Income Tax Law (see table 31).

274. The net impact of changes in the 1982 Income Tax Law of Jordan relative to a married couple with four children having an annual taxable income of JD 2,000 is that income tax due has dropped from JD 165 under the 1964 Law to JD 33 under the 1982 Law. However, as a result of the major amendments introduced by the Israeli authorities in the 1964 Law, the actual amount of tax due for a family of the same size in the territories is presently assessed at JD 299, which is nine times higher than in Jordan.

275. Israeli military orders have also lowered personal allowances for income tax purposes. In 1984, these allowances were lowered for all family sizes. While they were slightly increased later in 1985, they remain below the pre-1967 level (see table 32).[183/] The allowance ceiling in the West Bank stands at JD 314, which is only 22 per cent and 13 per cent of that prevailing in Jordan and Israel respectively. This is so despite the fact that per capita income in the West Bank is only 29 per cent and 72 per cent of per capita income in Israel and Jordan respectively.

Table 30

Comparison between income tax rates and brackets under 1964 law and after amendments through Israeli military orders, 1985

Income brackets and tax rates in March 1985		Income brackets and tax rates as in original Income Tax Law of 1964	
Taxable Income (JD)	Tax Rate %	Taxable Income (JD)	Tax Rate %
144 a/	5.5%	400	5%
396	7.7%	800	7%
648	11.0%	1,200	10%
900	16.5%	1,600	15%
1104	22.0%	2,000	20%
1284	27.5%	2,400	25%
1452	33.0%	2,800	30%
1632	38.5%	4,000	35%
2124	44.0%	6,000	40%
3024	49.5%	8,000	45%
3768	55.0%	more	50%

Source: Nidal R. Sabri, "The effects of taxes imposed on the population of the occupied Palestinian territories", a paper presented at the United Nations (HABITAT) Seminar on the living conditions of the Palestinian people in the occupied Palestinian territories, Vienna, March 1985, p.6.

a/   Converted into Jordanian dinars at the rate of IS 2,000 to one dinar.

Table 31

Tax due in accordance with the 1964 and 1982 Jordanian income tax laws

Annual taxable income (JD)	Tax due per 1982 (JD)	Tax due per 1964 Law (JD)
1,600	50	122
2,600	150	347
3,600	300	705
4,600	450	1,108
5,600	650	1,549
6,600	850	2,118
7,600	1,100	2,503
8,600	1,350	3,017
9,600	1,600	3,567
10,600	1,900	4,117
Total 61,600	8,400	19,153
Overall rate	13.8%	31.4%

Source: Based on Income Tax Law No. 25, 1964, and Income Tax Law No. 34, 1982.

Table 32

Personal allowances for income tax purposes
(Jordanian dinars)

Family status	West Bank 1964	present	Jordan	Israel
Single	150	150	400	737
Married	250	242	600	1,046
Married + 1 child	275	260	800	1,370
Married + 2 children	295	278	1,000	1,694
Married + 3 children	310	296	1,200	2,018
Married + 4 children	320	314	1,400	2,342

Source: (1) Article 14, Income Tax Law No. 25, 1964, Ministry of Finance, Amman, Jordan. (2) Income Tax Scale for Fiscal Year 1984-1985, issued by Officer-in-charge of Taxes at the Civil Administration. (3) Article 13, Income Tax Law No. 34, 1982, Ministry of Finance, Amman, Jordan. (4) Annual Income Tax Computation Scale, issued by the Department of Income Tax and Property, Ministry of Finance, Tel Aviv, March 1985.

276. With respect to business income tax, the Israeli authorities have also amended the Egyptian tax laws so that Gaza businesses, including the Bank of Palestine, have to pay 37.5 per cent tax on their income. Several industries in the Gaza Strip are claimed to be on the verge of closing.[184/]

277. The most striking change pertained to tax collection procedures embodied in chapter 14 of Law No. 25. This chapter was totally cancelled and replaced by Military Order No. 770 of November 1978 which obliged taxpayers to make advance payments on a monthly basis throughout the fiscal year and not after the end of the year, as had been the case. This pay-as-you-earn (PAYE) method of tax collection was enforced without giving due consideration to earnings. The monthly installment is based on an estimate which is equivalent to the total tax paid for the previous year. This method of assessment is based neither on the "Accrual" nor on the "Cash" method which is normally used in determining the income of taxpayers for a current fiscal year. It also bears no relation to the capital or the volume of business and/or profits of the taxpayer. The practice is particularly objectionable not only on legal grounds but also from an economic point of view, as it impinges on the limited resources available to businesses for investment and/or as working capital. The lack of an adequate banking system has forced businesses to either borrow at exhorbitant rates of interest to pay the tax in advance or face fines and even closure.

278. The advance payment of the tax is also practised in Israel itself, where the balance of the tax due is indexed to the cost of living. In the West Bank, however, the balance is indexed to the average exchange rate of the Israeli shekel to the Jordanian dinar. The final amount of tax collected in two similar cases has been higher in the West Bank than in Israel due to the fact that the exchange rate of the Israeli shekel has been depreciating faster than the increase in the cost of living. This practice is also followed in respect of all taxes which are assessed in Jordanian dinar but collected in Israeli shekels at the prevailing rate of exchange.

279. The advance payment of taxes was subsequently followed by Military Order No. 791 which imposed a fine of 1.5 per cent of the assessed tax on each 15 days' delay in payment, whereas this fine is set at 1 per cent in Israel itself. It should be noted, however, that most of the provisions of the two above-mentioned military orders are extracted from the Israeli Tax Law of 1961.

280. The advance payment of tax is also extended to include deductions at source of taxes on purchases, sales and services, a practice which results in double taxation and contradicts Jordanian law prevailing in the West Bank. Such an approach distorts the principle of income tax or other direct tax burden borne by taxpayers at the point of impact. Taxes so paid are likely to be added to the cost of business and largely passed on to the ultimate consumer, thus adding to the inflationary pressure.

281. In accordance with stipulations made in Law No. 25, a special court, known as the Court of Appeal for Income Tax Matters, was set up to consider appeals of taxpayers against the assessments and decisions of tax officers. The court, presided over by a judge with a rank not lower than "second level" and having two other judges with ranks not lower than "fourth level" operated under the jurisdiction of the Justice Ministry. In accordance with the law,[185]/ the verdict of the court could be further appealed against. Irrespective of the provisions of the law, Military Order No. 406 delegated the competence of the special Court of Appeal for Income Tax Matters to an "Objection Committee", which would present its recommendations for the consideration of the Military Commander, who would either accept or reject them (Military Order No. 172). The military orders have thus revoked judicial consideration of appeals at various levels and confined them to an administrative/military committee without judicial competence.[186]/ There is therefore no machinery within an established judicial system to deal with appeals. This has led to widespread discontent and attempts at evasion, as well as genuine reluctance to keep stringent records.[187]/ It has begun to act as a disincentive to work, particularly in the middle and upper-middle income groups who usually generate new wealth in an economy.

282. A similar practice is followed in respect of the appointment of "assessment officers". Despite the provisions of the Civil Service Code applicable in the West Bank until 1967, Military Order No. 120 of 1967 has authorized the Military Commander to appoint officials in the territories and confer upon them the competence he finds appropriate.[188]/

283. One of the most serious Israeli violations of the tax system of the territories involves the treatment of Israeli citizens (settlers) and juridical entities residing in the occupied territories. Under the generally accepted norms of tax law - the principle of the territorial application of taxes - the income of Israelis living in the territories ought to be taxed under Jordanian law, for such income is "derived, received or obtained" in these territories and not in Israel.[189]/ In practice, however, no Jordanian taxes are collected from Israeli citizens living in the territories. Companies and associations that were registered in Israel but operated in the territories paid their taxes directly in Israel while those registered in the territories paid no income tax at all.

284. In 1978, the Israeli Knesset changed the Israeli Income Tax Ordinance, stating that the income of an Israeli citizen which was earned, obtained or received in the territories will be regarded as income produced, obtained or received in Israel. The objective of this amendment was to prevent the territories from becoming tax havens for Israeli citizens through avoidance of the need to pay any taxes.[190]/ While this move has not ended the legal application of the Jordanian tax law, in practice it has prevented the territories from collecting the taxes due to them notwithstanding the illegality of the presence of Israeli citizens and juridical entities in the territories. The changes provided that if an Israeli citizen living in the territories paid taxes to the taxation authorities in the territories, he would be exempt from Israeli tax up to the amount that he had already paid in order to avoid double taxation.[191]/ This is a provision which is unilaterally applied by an increasing number of countries in view of the global treatment of income for tax purposes and the absence of double taxation agreements among countries. However, no separate tax is paid to the territories to begin with to justify such treatment under the Israeli tax system. The Israeli economy and Government therefore remain the sole beneficiaries of the economic activities of Israeli citizens in the territories and of their tax liabilities.

285. The same applies to income tax payments on the wages of, and to social security contributions made to the Israeli authorities by, more than 90,000 persons from the occupied territories working in Israel. In this case, however, there is no central authority to take this into consideration and extend a tax credit when assessing their overall income tax liability, as there is no double taxation arrangement between the territories and Israel.

286. As for Israeli juridical entities, those which are registered in Israel and which also operate in the occupied territories pay their taxes to the Israeli authorities in accordance with Israeli corporation tax rates. Here, too, the use of the territories benefits only the Israeli economy and Israeli Government budget. On the other hand, Israeli companies registered in the territories, with both management and ownership in the hands of Israelis, pay no local taxes and thus use the territories as a tax shelter. According to the Israeli Income Tax Commission and State Comptroller, there are some 267 to 300 Israeli firms registered in the West Bank.[192]/ A number of these companies are classified as "dummy" or "inactive" and thus have no tax liability. It is claimed, however, that those subjected to taxes paid less because Jordanian law has allowed them to give inflated figures for their expenses and thus reduce their taxable income. There are also doubts as to whether these companies have withheld income tax from the salaries of their employees. In fact, until new regulations were issued, Israeli firms in the territories had been able to avoid paying the value added tax.[193]/

(b) Property tax

287. In addition to the prevailing 17 per cent and 10 per cent tax on the net rental values of buildings and urban land respectively, the actual rent of such property was also made subject, as of 1 May 1985, to the 15 per cent value added tax (VAT). However, due to strong opposition among property owners, the application of VAT on such properties was suspended, though not altogether abolished.

(c) <u>Customs duties</u>

288. Imported machinery and other goods are indirectly charged customs duties as most local enterprises are not allowed to import their supplies directly from abroad. They can only do so via Israeli importers and Israeli agents for foreign firms. The Customs duties imposed are those applied to Israeli imports. They have an interventionist objective and are also aimed at increasing Government revenues. The actual range of tariffs is difficult to identify, as they are incorporated into the final prices of imported goods. Constant changes in these duties, due not only to the inflationary situation but also to economic policy, add to the difficulty of assessing the exact amount of duty imposed and to the uncertainty that confronts importers. An accepted approach for assessment purposes relies on the fact that in 1981 customs duties were levied at a rate of 100-150 per cent on consumer goods and around 40 per cent on non-consumer goods.[194]/ In addition, the purchaser has to pay the 15 per cent value added tax on transactions with importers.

289. The overall objective of this policy has been to safeguard Israeli products and influence the general level and pattern of the territories' imports from abroad. While there may be an economic justification for such duties to be applied on imports into Israel, the same cannot hold for the occupied territories. Israeli customs duties may be aimed at protecting domestic Israeli industries in which the occupied territories have no interest. As such, the payment of such duties by importers in the territories represents not only a participation in the protection of Israeli economic interests but also a contribution to Israeli Government revenues. In 1985, Israel supplied 89 per cent of the territories' imports from the rest of the world while Jordan provided 9 per cent, equivalent to a combined total of $659 million worth of goods. The contribution to the Israeli Government revenues from customs duties and from VAT on such a volume of trade cannot be underestimated.

290. The bonding system is also widely practised by the Israeli authorities, and the cost of this falls on the importers and end users. For example, vegetable oil imported through Jordan and over the bridges cannot be taken directly to Nablus for use in soap processing. The company concerned has to provide bonded warehousing close to a bridge to store the oil while it is being cleared. Afterwards, the company can transport the oil to its other warehouse in Nablus, thus incurring extra cost through apparently unnecessary duplication.[195]/

(d) <u>Excises</u>

291. Excises imposed on local industrial products (Law No. 16 of 1963) formerly covered a few articles such as cigarettes and matches. A wide range of major goods introduced locally are now subject to excise duties and fees, in accordance with the provisions of Military Orders Nos. 31, 643 and 740. By May 1985, the following rates were charged on some local products:

```
White soap ....... 20 per cent
Cosmetics......... 20-30 per cent
Detergents........ 20 per cent
Paints............ 15 per cent
Glass............. 10 per cent
Hides............. IS 1-2.5 per hide
```

(e)   Education tax

292. This tax was introduced at a rate of 3 per cent on the net rental value
of all property within municipal boundaries. The proceeds are credited to
education departments of municipal authorities and subsequently used in the
construction and maintenance of school buildings. The tax was raised to
5 per cent and later to 7 per cent (see Military Orders Nos. 501, 763 and 821).

(f)   Land tax

293. Following occupation, the rate of this tax was changed to
JD 0.6 per dunum and was subsequently raised three times. It now stands at
JD 2 per dunum, collected as a Government tax.

(g)   Social service tax

294. Prior to 1967, a tax at the rate of 10 per cent was collected on income
towards financing "social services". It was collected along with income tax.
Following the occupation, the tax has been incorporated into the income tax
itself and its proceeds are not used for welfare purposes.

(h)   Other taxes, fees and charges

295. A number of other fees and charges have also been substantially
increased. For example, fees for notaries and for power of attorney have been
increased, from 50 fils to 1.6 dinars and from 1 dinar to 10 dinars
respectively.[196]/ Similarly, special taxes on pharmacies and private medical
practitioners were introduced in 1981.[197]/ Apart from licences and fees,
there is another important source of Government revenues for the occupation
authorities, namely "fines" and "penalties" for security and other offences.
In 1984 alone, revenues from this source amounted to as much as a
quarter of a million Jordanian dinars.

296. Permits for crossing the bridges on the Jordan River out of or into the
territories have been used by the Israeli military authorities not only as a
security measure but also as a reliable source of Government revenues. These
permits were given almost free following the 1967 war. However, the
authorities began to impose fees for allowing people to travel. These fees
were periodically increased until, in 1986, they reached the equivalent of
JD 28 ($US 78) per permit for an adult and JD 3 ($US 8.4) for every child
visiting the territories. Visitors leaving the territories were charged
JD 5.5 ($15.40) per adult.[198]/ According to Israeli statistics, more than
400,000 persons (residents and visitors) crossed the bridges in 1985. This
provides an indication of the magnitude of the revenues collected by the
Israeli military authorities from this source alone. Table 33 gives a detailed
breakdown of the various types of fees charged on persons and vehicles
crossing the bridges. The heavy charges, accompanied by the worsening economic
conditions of the population in the territories, have adversely affected the
total number of crossings over the bridges in recent years. In 1986, the
Israeli authorities reduced the fee for visitors to JD 15 and for the
residents of the territories travelling abroad to 8 Jordanian dinars. Visitors
are also charged a departure tax of about 10 Jordanian dinars.

Table 33

Fees charged by Israeli occupation authorities on the bridges, 1986

	IS	$US
- Exit permit (for a resident of the territories, 14 years and above)	114.5	78
- Entry permit (for a visitor of 14 years and over)	114.5	78
- Fees on companions (residents or visitors)		
Below 12 years of age, each	12.6	8.6
Over 12 years of age, each	33.6	23
- Permit for a taxi driver to get to the bridge		
(per month)	225	154
plus parking fee (per month)	64	44
- Permit for a lorry driver (per month)	225	154
plus security inspection fee on return (per trip)	29	20
plus custom service fee (per trip)	21	14.5

Source : Al-Fajr, Vol. VII, No. 320, 27 June 1986, and field survey.

297. Pension contributions constitute another source of Government revenues. Pension schemes are available only to workers employed by the Government, who account for around 15 per cent of the employed labour force. Deduction and remuneration rates are fixed in accordance with Jordanian laws which were applicable in the territories before their occupation in 1967. The subsequent amendments which have resulted in substantially improved pension benefits in Jordan have been disregarded.

298. Pension benefits are paid to beneficiaries in shekels with ad hoc and partial adjustments aimed at reducing the adverse impact of depreciation in terms of the Jordanian dinar and/or the rising cost of living. As a result, the purchasing power of pension allowances is reduced below their original level. Deduction for pension purposes is carried at the rate of 7 per cent, and the proceeds are credited to an account which is operated by the Civil Administration. No investment of any form in the territories is financed from resources originating from pension contributions.

299. Contributions to social security schemes similarly provide the Government with another reliable source of revenues. No form of social security scheme is available to the two largest labour groups, namely workers in the private sector (whether owner-operators or employees) and workers employed in Israel. It is noted, however, that the wages of workers in the latter group are subject to social security deductions at rates on a par with those applicable to Israeli workers, but unlike the Israeli workers, workers from the territories are not accorded benefits in return.

(i) Imposition of a new tax (value added tax)

300. The Israeli authorities instituted, in August 1976, a tax on all goods
and services in Israel. The tax, referred to as value added tax (VAT), was
imposed at a flat rate of 8 per cent. The tax was simultaneously extended to
apply to Israelis living in the occupied territories. The legislative
technique was similar to that used in extending over the territories the
application of the Israeli Income Tax Ordinance. The provisions of the law
stated that the tax also applied to transactions carried out in the
territories by Israeli citizens.[199]/ The purpose was threefold, i.e. to
prevent the creation of a tax haven for Israelis in the territories, to raise
Israeli Government revenues and to further integrate the economic activities
of Israelis living in the territories.

301. The value added tax was also introduced at the same rate of 8 per cent in
the West Bank under By-law No. 31 of 1976 concerning fees and excise duties,
without any announcement of its imposition as a new tax. It was related to
Jordanian Law No. 16 of 1963. A new piece of legislation was thus superimposed
on the existing law. The rate of the tax was subsequently raised to
12 per cent in 1977. In 1982, a further increase of 3 per cent was effected,
raising the tax to 15 per cent payable by all businesses and entities except
crop-farming enterprises. As noted, the tax is also applied on imports
reaching the territories through Israel. The increase of the tax in 1982 in
both Israel and the territories was aimed at financing the Israeli invasion of
Lebanon,[200]/ which means that the inhabitants of the territories also had to
participate in financing that operation.

302. The introduction and subsequent increase of the tax triggered strong
opposition, especially among Palestinian businessmen and politicians, because
of its grave consequences on the economy and life of the inhabitants of the
territories and because of its violation of international law (the Geneva
Convention and the Hague Regulations) which forbids the imposition of new
taxes in occupied areas. However, when the issue was appealed to the Israeli
High Court of Justice in 1983, the Court ruled that the military Government
could levy value added tax on the residents of the territories. There was no
absolute prohibition on the imposition of new taxes in conquered
territories.[201]/

303. It should be noted, however, that VAT was introduced in Israel in order
to balance the loss of Government revenue due to other proposals which were
aimed at reducing some taxes. It was also in keeping with the introduction of
a similar tax (VAT) in most European countries. It was argued that the price
increases resulting from the imposition of VAT would be balanced by income-tax
reductions so that the total burden would remain unchanged. In addition, in
order to compensate low-income families which would not benefit from
reductions in direct taxes, it was envisaged to increase children's allowances
and old-age pensions, as well as social welfare services.[202]/ None of these
considerations apply to the occupied territories. As noted earlier, in
addition to this tax, the burden of a number of other taxes has been
simultaneously increased in the territories. The concessions made to Israelis,
in both Israel and the occupied territories, do not benefit the Palestinian
inhabitants of the territories. On the contrary, the tax burden of the average
Palestinian, in terms of both individuals and juridical entities, has been
continuously increased against a comparatively low and declining level of

income. Generally speaking VAT has evolved over the past few years to become one of the most serious fiscal constraints on the development of Palestinian industry and trade.

304. From the administrative point of view, VAT is also considered by the occupation authorities a useful instrument for controlling business activities at various stages, since it necessitates establishing and operating an elaborate system of book-keeping and all that that entails in terms of operational procedures. Most local Palestinian businesses are either unable to maintain such a system or unaware of the overall requirements. As a result, many small businesses have been confronted with penalties allegedly for lack of adequate records and non-payment of this and other taxes.[203]/

(ii) The tax system and economic activities

305. Since the 1950s, preoccupation with growth and development objectives has prompted policy-makers and planners in an increasing number of developing countries to accord special attention to ways and means of promoting savings and investment in the economy. In addition to the increasing involvement of the public sector in this process, particular emphasis has been placed on the crucial role of the private sector. Various measures have been resorted to in order to induce private savings and investments, thus contributing to the rapid growth and development of the economy. The tax system has increasingly been considered as a promising instrument for determining the pace and direction of efforts to achieve such a goal. In addition to its traditional role in serving as a major source of Government revenues, the tax system has also provided, through various incentives, the basis for influencing the magnitude and direction of resource allocations in the economy. Notwithstanding the conflicting nature of the two aims, many developing countries have offered tax incentives within the framework of investment encouragement schemes.[204]/

306. Jordan, along with other countries, introduced, in the mid-1950s, laws and regulations which provided incentives to the private sector for investment in industrial, tourist and transport projects. Income from agricultural activities was and still is tax-exempt. Many of the incentives and exemptions stipulated under the Investment Encouragement Laws Nos. 27 and 28 of 1955 were later replaced by Law No. 1 of 1967.

307. These laws provided exemptions from Customs duties on all machinery, equipment and other capital goods imported for approved investment projects or any approved expansion scheme. The profits of such enterprises were also exempt from income tax for up to six years after the production of goods or services. Buildings and land related to these investment projects were also exempt from property tax. The Government also provided, in some cases, the land for the location of these projects free of charge. Needless to say, these concessions were applied to all approved projects, whether located in Jordan itself or in the West Bank.

308. After 1967, new investment encouragment laws were enacted by Jordan, namely Laws No. 53 of 1972 and No. 6 of 1984, which provide more generous incentives for local, Arab and foreign investments in Jordan. In particular, the tax holiday period was increased, and projects in other sectors were added. The transfer of the foreign exchange equivalent of profits and the

original capital of non-Jordanians was equally guaranteed by law. The objective of all this was to promote savings and investment where propensities are high at the private sector level, even though it may be at the expense of some loss in Government revenues for the initial period. While the net effect of these incentives is difficult to determine here, it is widely believed that at a later stage the beneficiaries of the incentives may serve as new "tax handles" and lead to the creation of a broader tax base and, hence, more Government revenues, in addition to contributing to national income.

309. None of the old or new investment-related incentives are applied in the territories, although the relevant laws are theoretically still in force. On the contrary, as noted, a number of tax provisions have been amended and an administrative procedure created to the disadvantage of entrepreneurs. This is particularly the case as far as industry is concerned. Perhaps this approach stems from the overall declared policy of the Israeli authorities concerning economic development in the territories. As a result, new enterprises find it very difficult to survive the first few years of operation as they are beset by fiscal and monetary obligations.

310. The tax system in the territories is, therefore, used in its traditional role as the supplier of revenues to the Government. As such, its role in influencing entrepreneurial decisions on the allocation of resources leaves much to be desired. The treatment accorded, especially, to Israeli settlers in the territories provides a striking contrast. Giving a complete picture of the range of administrative, fiscal, monetary, commercial, legal and other concessions made to Israeli settlers falls beyond the scope of this study. Nevertheless, some of the financial incentives extended to Israeli businesses in some areas of the territories are indicative of the inequality in treatment. These businesses enjoy, inter alia, the following incentives: (a) an "investment grant" equal to 30 per cent of the enterprises' total investment in fixed assets; (b) a "concessionary loan" equal to 40 per cent of the total investment of fixed assets; (c) exemption from income tax on retained earnings for the first seven years; (d) a ceiling of 30 per cent on corporation taxes; (e) taxes on dividends to foreign investors limited to 10.5 per cent; (f) the waiving of the "employers' tax" for five years; (g) a number of import and export benefits once the business passes the start-up phase. In addition, aid for research-and-development may amount to as much as 54 per cent of the business's R and D outlays.[205]/

311. It may be inferred from this brief examination of some aspects of Government finance in the territories that public finance has not played its crucial role in contributing to the economic growth and development of these territories. The Government budget reflects a most restrained and passive outlook to growth and development needs in a dynamic setting. Ad hoc manipulations of taxes have made the tax system into a confused and fragmented set of fiscal measures which is characterized by deficiencies in concept and structures, inequitable in burden and prohibitive in terms of its actual and potential impact on economic activities. Given the rapidly deteriorating economic situation in the territories, there is an urgent need to restore the crucial role of the Government budget. The overall structure of the tax system, in particular, is in need of a thorough reform in line with the growing requirements of the Palestinian economy.

Chapter IV

EXTERNAL FINANCIAL RESOURCES AND THE DEVELOPMENT OF
THE OCCUPIED PALESTINIAN TERRITORIES

Introduction

312. It has been seen from the preceding discussion that the restricted local
financial resource base of the Palestinian economy has acted as a brake on the
territories' potential for mobilizing local resources for economic
development. Indigenous production capacity, measured by GDP, has become
increasingly incapable of covering outlays on the use of resources, as
demonstrated by private and public consumption expenditure, gross capital
formation and exports. Consequently, the overall process of financing
Palestinian economic development has become more dependent upon external
sources of finance. Given the particular nature of interaction of the
territories' economy with those of neighbouring countries (Israel and the Arab
countries), whereby the territories do not have the authority to regulate the
flows of trade and services, such dependency is neither surprising nor
necessarily undesirable.

313. In fact, it may be argued that only by maintaining these external
linkages have the territories been able to counter restrictions on the economy
at the local level and withstand the challenges posed within the context of
relations with the Israeli economy and the influences exerted by the Arab
economic environment over the past decade. However, the possible positive
aspects of such external links should be carefully examined in terms of the
ability of the local economy to generate over time the impetus for its own
development. With the growing gap between actual domestic production capacity
and total available resources to the economy, it has become necessary to
evaluate the effects of such trends upon economic development. Specifically,
it is of interest to discern the extent to which these patterns of external
linkages have sown the seeds of chronic structural shortcomings of
underdevelopment, an undesirable degree of dependence and the forfeiting of
economic independence to external forces.

A.   Factor income from abroad

314. Since the occupation of the West Bank and Gaza Strip in 1967,
far-reaching transformations have occurred in the ability of the territories'
economy to productively absorb the local labour force and lucratively deploy
local savings. This has led to the increasing significance of three distinct
but interrelated phenomona which are indicative of dependence on external
sources for employment and finance. These are labour in Israel, short or
long-term emigration for work in Jordan and elsewhere, and private and
official unrequited transfers from abroad. The first two of these are
discussed in the present section.

1.   Sources of factor income

315. Factor income from work in Israel, which became significant as of 1970,
results firstly from the daily movement of Palestinian labour into Israel for
employment. Whereas 12 per cent of the territories' labour force was employed
in Israel in 1970 (some 21,000 workers), the proportion had reached
37 per cent by 1984, representing a total of 90,300 workers.206/ Indeed, the

locally employed labour force of 151,000 in 1984 was still smaller than its 1970 level of 153,000.<u>207</u>/ Both the potential gains in terms of income from migration and the implicit cost of a decline in labour absorption at the local level after 20 years of occupation are visible. Regardless of its benefits or costs, this "labour export" feature of the territories' economy is not solely an outcome of occupation. There are indications that, prior to 1967, when the territories were under Jordanian and Egyptian administration, the migration rate had reached 25 per thousand (of population) in the mid-1950s.<u>208</u>/ However, the conditions of migration were certainly less inhibiting than at present, given the open borders with Arab countries and the absence of the present pattern of daily commuting to Israel. Moreover, the scale of the present "labour exports" by the territories is such as to indicate a relative and absolute contraction of local economic opportunities since the late 1960s.<u>209</u>/

316. The second relevant phenomenon is that which has gained momentum since the mid-1970s in response to the lack of local job opportunities and the attractions of lucrative employment in the oil-producing Arab States. These two factors pushed an increasing number of West Bank and Gaza Strip residents to emigrate and/or seek work abroad. This flow of labour involves three groups: (i) West Bank families who became refugees in 1967 in the East Bank - most of these lost their rights to reside in the territories, while some still maintain links with relatives and support them through remittances; (ii) residents of the territories who left the territories after 1967 and have since then taken up permanent residence abroad, usually with their immediate families, and who regularly transfer remittances to relatives in the territories; and, (iii) residents who work abroad for a certain period during each year, but regularly return to the territories to maintain their residency rights.<u>210</u>/

317. According to official Israeli statistics, the size of the latter group, i.e. those counted as residents but classified as "not in the labour force - working abroad", fluctuated from 16,000 to 19,000 between 1980 and 1984 (see chapter I, table 2 and also table 34 below). When added to the number of the territories' residents employed in Israel, the total number of persons working outside the territories stood at 91,300 in 1980 and rose to 106,300 in 1984. The proportion of the labour force employed abroad, other than in Israel, fell from 18-19 per cent during 1980-1983 to only 15 per cent in 1984, a concomitant of the economic downturn in the Arab countries in that year. The discussion below of "factor income" concerns this group and their counterparts working in Israel; remittances are grouped under "transfers" and are discussed in the following section.

318. Understandably, there are numerous problems in trying to estimate the size of each group and of the factor income or transfers (remittances) involved. Equally problematic sometimes are the contradictory definitions adopted by different sources in separating Palestinians' "factor income" from "transfers". This is partially due to restrictions under occupation as "migrants who used to leave the West Bank to return as they pleased could no longer do so without a 'reunion permit', which is accorded to them on condition that they stay outside the West Bank for certain periods that varied according to the emigrants' age. Moreover, a large number of Palestinians who were outside the West Bank when the war broke out could not obtain a 'reunion permit' and were forced to stay outside their homeland."<u>211</u>/ As for

migration since 1967, it did not only involve individuals, but also covered whole families, either as refugees in the immediate post-1967 period or over the subsequent years.212/ On the other hand, West Bank Palestinians in the Arab countries and elsewhere are statistically unidentifiable from East Bank Jordanians (as they hold Jordanian nationality).

319. The difference between permanent and temporary migrants is of special significance because of the different consumption, savings and remittance habits of the two groups, which are affected by the nature of the migration (duration of stay abroad), status in the labour-receiving country and the number of dependents that a migrant has in the host/home country.213/ Accordingly, not all of the migrant population can be assumed to be actively involved in the provision of financial resources to the occupied territories. There is evidence that of the total migrant population since 1967, up to 50 per cent has lost its right to return to the territories, as accorded by the "reunion permits" which are granted by the Israeli authorities to most migrants with families remaining in the territories.214/ Accordingly, it can be assumed that at most only a half of the migrant labour force, (i.e. some 76,000 persons from the migrant labour force, estimated in chapter I at about 152,000 in 1984) maintains regular links with the territories and transfers remittances to the territories.

2. Components of factor income

320. Factor income to and from the territories comprises three components: factor income from wages of Palestinians from the territories employed in Israel; factor income of Palestinians working in Jordan, other Arab States, and the rest of the world; and, other factor income from abroad (i.e. rent, profits, interest, and others). Payments for similar items to the rest of the world result in net factor payments to the territories. Although official data do not completely cover the three components, they are resorted to so as to depict the main trends in factor income flows. The figures should be treated with caution when analysing the role of external resources in the Palestinian economy.215/ The degree of discrepancy between official aggregate figures and estimates of certain components of factor income is such that it can alter findings with regard to the volume of gross national income and the analysis of the significance of different sources of factor income to the territories' economy.

321. Table 34 represents the official Israeli statistical series for the distribution of factor income payments to the territories according to two of its major components, namely wages from Israel (denoted by FII) and wages from the rest of the world (denoted by FIA). Accordingly, it can be seen that factor income from Israel (FII) grew steadily from $180 million in 1978 to almost $380 million in 1984, an increase of over 110 per cent, or an average of some 18 per cent per annum. In fact, FII peaked at $421 million in 1983, an especially prosperous year for the Israeli economy. Factor income from the rest of the world (FIA) also grew, but at a lower rate, from $61 million to $107 million during the period 1978-1984, a growth of 75 per cent, or some 12 per cent per annum. Thus, according to official Israeli statistics, the major component of factor income payments to the territories is that gained through employment in Israel. This component of factor income has accounted for almost 75 per cent of total factor income payments to the territories since 1978, except in 1984, when its share rose to 78 per cent.

322. An alternative calculation of net factor income, however, produces a very different result for FII, as depicted in table 34. This involves multiplying the net average daily wage (ADW) earned by Palestinians employed in Israel (i.e. net of taxes and other deductions at source) by the number of annual work days (WD), multiplied by the total number of Palestinians employed in Israel (TEI). The result (FII1) indicates a lower level of net factor income from Israel, growing from $122 million in 1978 to $189 million by 1984. Furthermore, the rate of growth of FII1 is less than that of FII, at some 55 per cent for the period 1978-1984, or about 9 per cent per annum. The figures for FII1 are between 50 per cent and 65 per cent smaller than those for FII over the period.

323. Certain shortcomings in the FII1 series can be discerned. The process of calculating according to average workdays, average wages and total number employed is bound to produce an estimate, rather than an accurate and definitive figure. Furthermore, the wage rate used is that for employees, who constitute, on average, some 97 per cent of all Palestinians employed in Israel. The 3,000 or so self-employed or employers from the territories working in Israel presumably have a somewhat higher income than that of employees.216/ The discrepancy between FII and FII1 could be explained by the fact that, whereas the former represents the gross wage bill paid to Palestinians employed in Israel, the latter is calculated according to net wages, i.e. after taxes have been deducted. However, the difference between FII and FII1 rose from 32 per cent of FII in 1979 to 50 per cent in 1984, as seen in the calculated series FII/FII1 in table 34. This differential between FII and FII1 could be due to taxation, pension and social security deductions, but this represents a large percentage deducted from gross wages.217/ A further problem with the official data is that FII plus FIA gives total factor income (TFI) which excludes other factor income payments (rents, interest and profits) which are also supposedly included in the total official calculations of factor income.218/

324. A final reason for treating the official series with caution arises from a comparison of the average per capita factor income of workers "in the rest of the world" and those in Israel. According to the official series, in 1980, for example, the 16,200 workers in the rest of the world earned a total of $94 million, or $5,800 per capita, while the 75,100 workers in Israel earned $275 million, or about $3,700 per capita. Accordingly, it could be said that in 1980, migration for work elsewere rewarded the migrant with some 57 per cent more than he could earn in Israel (assuming of course the availability of work). By 1984, the average per capita factor income from abroad had risen to $6,700, while that from Israel was some $4,200, with the percentage differential between the two levels still remaining almost the same, i.e. at 59 per cent. It is not certain, however, that such a (relatively) small differential could have the effect of making it worthwhile for Palestinians to leave the territories for work abroad, incurring the travel, residence and other costs and practical difficulties associated with migration. These problems, however, might be counterbalanced by the fact that income from the rest of the world, though gross, is not subject to taxes or deductions which are applied to gross wages from employment in Israel.

Table 34

Factor income to residents of the occupied Palestinian territories, 1978-1984

(ADW in current Israeli shekels; FII, FIA and FIIl in millions
of current Israeli Shekels;a/ TEI and ERW in thousands)

Year	FII	FIA	TFI	PCM WD	PA WD	ADW	TEI	FIIl	ERW	FII/ FIIl
1978	315 (180)	107 (61)	422 (241)		260	12	68.2	213 (122)		68%
1979	649 (255)	216 (85)	865 (340)	22	264	21	74.1	411 (162)		64%
1980	1409 (275)	483 (94)	1892 (369)	21.6	259	40	75.1	788 (154)	16.2	56%
1981	3595 (314)	1047 (91)	4642 (405)	22	264	108	75.8	2165 (189)	16.4	60%
1982	8510 (351)	2802 (115)	11312 (466)	21.9	263	247	79.1	5138 (212)	18.7	60%
1983	23689 (421)	7934 (141)	31623 (562)	21.6	259	603	87.8	13712 (244)	18.7	58%
1984	110684 (377)	31259 (107)	141943 (484)	21.7	260	2360	90.3	55408 (189)	16	50%

Explanatory note:

FII: Gross factor income from Israel (CBS figures)
FIA: Factor income from abroad (CBS figures)
TFI: Total factor income payments to the territories (FII + FIA)
PCM WD: Per calender month work days
PA WD: Annual work days (PCM WD x 12)
ADW: Average daily wage of employees in Israel (net)
TEI: Total territories' residents employed in Israel
FIIl: Net factor income from Israel (PA WD x ADW x TEI)
ERW: Total territories' residents employed abroad (CBS figures for
         "not in the labour force - working abroad")

a/ Figures in parentheses are in current millions of United States dollars.

Sources:

- Dollar figures calculated according to annual average $US/JD and IS/$US
exchange rates, from IMF, International Financial Statistics (Wash. D.C., IMF,
1985), pp. 384-85 and 364-7.
- For FII and FIA figures:
    - 1978-1980 figures from R. Meron, Economic Development in Judea, Samaria
    and the Gaza District, 1970-80 (Jerusalem, Bank of Israel, 1983), p. 8;
    - 1981, 1982 figures from D. Zakai, Economic Development in Judea, Samaria
    and the Gaza District, 1981-82 (Jerusalem, Bank of Israel, 1985), p. 59;
    - 1983, 1984 figures from D. Zakai, Economic Development in Judea, Samaria
    and the Gaza District, 1983-84 (Jerusalem, Bank of Israel, 1986), p. 65.

Table 34 (continued)

- For PCM WD, PA WD, ADW, TEI, and FIIl:

  - PA WD and ADW for 1978 estimated according to 1977 and 1978 data; TEI for 1978 from Israel, Central Bureau of Statistics, Quarterly Statistics of the Administered Territories 1982, vol. XII;
  - All figures for 1979 from Royal Scientific Society, Financial and Banking Conditions in the Occupied West Bank and Gaza Strip (Amman, RSS, 1985), p. 117;
  - All figures for 1980 calculated from Israel, Central Bureau of Statistics, Judea, Samaria and Gaza Area Statistics (Jerusalem, CBS, vol. XV, No. 1, 1985), p. 114;
  - All figures for 1981-1984 calculated from Israel, Central Bureau of Statistics, Judea, Samaria and Gaza Area Statistics (Jerusalem, CBS, vol. XV, No. 2, 1985), p. 174;
  - ERW figures 1980-1984 calculated from Israel, CBS, Statistical Abstract of Israel 1985 (Jerusalem, CBS, 1985), p. 721.

325. It would appear, therefore, that the official Israeli data (FII and FIA) underestimate factor income from the rest of the world and overestimate the factor income accruing from labour in Israel. Indeed, since figures for factor income from the rest of the world (FIA) are net (no tax or social security payments are subsequently transferred against these), the analysis of the role and significance of factor income from employment in Israel will differ depending on which series (FII or FIIl) is being used. Israeli series also exclude other factor income payments (rent, interest and profits) which should be accounted for in arriving at a total figure for factor income payments to the territories (see the following paragraphs). On the other hand, the aggregated statistics (FIIl) might underestimate net earnings from employment in Israel. Finally, it is likely that actual factor income from abroad is greater than that officially reported, possibly as a result of the undeclared entry of such income into the territories made possible by the absence of formal financial channels through which such flows normally pass.

326. There is an additional component in factor income flows which, when added to the two already discussed, allows for the calculation of total factor income accruing to the territories. This component includes rent, profits, dividends and interest paid to the territories' residents from investments in the rest of the world. The main element in these flows is probably that of interest on deposits held by local residents with banks in Jordan and elsewhere. Other items, such as rent from property owned abroad, or dividends and profits made on investments inside Israel (stock market speculation, investments in Israeli company shares or other holdings), are also likely sources for non-wage factor payments. There is no primary statistical data for this item, and therefore a series cannot be estimated. However, the sum of earnings of workers in Israel and the rest of the world and the factor income from property and investments provides total factor income payments to the territories (TFII) (see table 35). Net factor income is then calculated by subtracting from TFII the total paid out by the territories to factors of production of other economies (Israeli, Arab or other), denoted as FIO.

Table 35

Factor income payments of the occupied Palestinian territories,
GDP & GNP (market prices), 1978-1984
(Millions of current Israeli shekels and percentages)a/

Year	TFII b/	FIO	NFI	GDP	GNP	NFI/ GDP	NFI/ GNP
1978	430	13	417	1252	1669	33%	25%
	(246)	(7)	(239)	(717)	(956)		
1979	881	25	856	2124	2980	40%	29%
	(346)	(10)	(336)	(835)	(1171)		
1980	1981	61	1920	5489	7409	35%	26%
	(387)	(12)	(375)	(1071)	(1446)		
1981	4856	138	4718	11195	15913	42%	30%
	(425)	(12)	(413)	(979)	(1392)		
1982	11312	80	11232	25339	36571	44%	31%
	(476)	(13)	(463)	(1044)	(1507)		
1983	31623	821	30802	62631	93469	49%	33%
	(562)	(14)	(548)	(1115)	(1663)		
1984	141913	4207	137706	318099	455805	43%	30%
	(484)	(14)	(470)	(1085)	(1555)		

Explanatory note

    TFII: Total factor income payments to the West Bank and Gaza Strip
          (aggregate official figures)
    FIO: Factor income paid out (wages, rent, interest, profits)
    NFI: Net factor income (i.e. TFII - FIO)
    GDP: Gross domestic product
    GNP: Gross national product (i.e. GDP + NFI)

    a/ Figures in parentheses are in millions of current United States
dollars.

    b/ The TFII figure, taken from official Israeli series, is slightly
larger than the sum of the two components of TFI in table 34 for the years
1978-1982. For 1983 and 1984, TFI is equal to TFII. This results from
different calculating methods used by the two sources (CBS for the aggregate
TFII and Bank of Israel for the components FII and FIA). Both series exclude
any calculations of other factor payments.

Table 35 (continued)

Sources:

   - Dollar figures calculated according to annual average $US/IS exchange
   rate, from IMF, International Financial Statistics (Wash. D.C., IMF,
   1985), pp. 364-7.

   - TFII, FIO and NFI figures: 1978-1983 figures calculated from Israel,
   Central Bureau of Statistics, Judea, Samaria and Gaza Area Statistics
   (Jerusalem, CBS), vol. XV, No. 1, April 1985, pp. 164, 167, 171, 174.
   Figures for 1984 calculated from Israel, Central Bureau of Statistics,
   Judea, Samaria and Gaza Area Statistics (Jerusalem, CBS), vol. XV, No. 2,
   December 1985, pp. 71, 73, 78 and 80.

   - GDP: 1978-1983 figures calculated from Israel, Central Bureau of
   Statistics, Judea, Samaria and Gaza Area Statistics (Jerusalem, CBS),
   vol. XV, No. 1, April 1985, pp. 164, 167, 171, 174. Figures for 1984
   calculated from Israel, Central Bureau of Statistics, Judea, Samaria and
   Gaza Area Statistics (Jerusalem, CBS), vol. XV, No. 2, December 1985,
   pp. 71, 73, 78 and 80.

327. The level of net factor income (NFI) payments to the territories rose
from $240 million in 1978 to $470 million by 1984. In 1983, the significant
expansion still being experienced in the Israeli economy helped to generate
$550 million from factor income in Israel and elsewhere. It is probable that
most of the factor income payments by the territories is in the form of
interest paid on loans from Israel, Jordan or elsewhere, returns on
investments made by Israeli or Arab sources in the territories, and rent for
property in Jordan and the rest of the world. Whatever wages are paid to
non-residents working in the territories are most likely minimal.[219/] The
FIO series in table 35 exhibits a relative stability, growing only slowly and
maintaining a generally low level of under $15 million until 1984. This
underscores the fact that, despite dependence on external financial sources,
the territories provide less attraction to external financial interests or
labour for productive or profitable deployment.

3.   Role of factor income

328. The inclusion of net factor income in gross national product (GNP) allows
for an examination of the extent of resources generated outside the economy.
Table 35 shows the growing degree of dependence of the territories' economy
upon the employment of its labour force abroad. In 1968, when a relationship
had not yet been clearly defined between the Palestinian economy and the
Israeli and Arab environment, factor income from abroad represented less than
3 per cent of GNP.[220/] Factor income accounted for 25 per cent of GNP in
1978, reaching 30 per cent by 1984. It had already peaked at 33 per cent or
$550 million in 1983, illustrating the interplay of weak domestic economic
growth and external financial dependence. By comparing factor income with
gross domestic product (GDP), it can be seen that, even for the highest level
of GDP ($1,115 million) recorded in 1983, factor income equalled 49 per cent

of domestic output. It appears that, while the economy has been unable to
develop its own sources of finance, the size of external resources in the form
of factor income has grown, thus acquiring an increasingly significant role in
the overall financing of economic growth and development. Domestic economic
growth has witnessed annual fluctuations (positive and negative), while factor
income has grown steadily. In 1980, when GDP stood at $1,071 million, factor
income was $375 million, representing 35 per cent of GDP and 26 per cent of
GNP. By 1984, though GDP had hardly grown from its 1980 level and stood at
$1,085 million, factor income had continued to increase, reaching
$470 million, or 43 per cent of GDP and 30 per cent of GNP.

329. There is no information available about the pattern of allocation of
factor income within the territories' economy, either sectorally or according
to its deployment between consumption, savings and investment. As already
noted, up to 40 per cent of gross factor income from Israel is transferred to
the Government before it enters the territories in the form of income tax,
social security and other deductions by Israeli employers. There is no basis
for assuming that net factor income has any specific role, except to
compensate for the lack of indigenous sources of income needed for private
consumption and investment. Notwithstanding this role, factor income flows
cannot be distinguished from other (local or foreign) sources of income unless
earmarked for certain purposes. There is, therefore, little analysis that can
be undertaken of its developmental role, except in terms of its comparative
position vis-à-vis GDP, as discussed above. In this respect, it is evident
that factor income from abroad has an important role in supplementing the low
level of domestic output by guaranteeing a source of income for over 100,000
(in 1984) of the employed labour force. Together, these services performed by
factor income flows are vital and increasingly prominent in the territories'
economic development.

330. In other economies which have developed a high degree of dependency on
migrants' remittances, a wide range of schemes has been used to attract
foreign exchange, but such schemes have been totally absent in the case of the
occupied territories. Many labour-exporting countries have attempted to
increase total remittances through official channels and encourage workers to
put their savings into "productive investments" rather than spend them on
luxury consumer goods.[221]/   There is differing evidence on the success of
such efforts, which include foreign exchange deposit schemes, premium exchange
rates for remittances, and the channeling of workers' earnings into productive
investment through official programmes.[222]/   However, the possibility of
recourse to such options in the process of managing and benefiting from the
"migratory chain" in all its stages, and especially those options concerned
with optimal use of the resources generated, has been non-existent in the
experience of the Palestinian economy, primarily because of the absence of an
indigenous authority to evaluate and regulate such issues.

331. One area in which a special position and role for factor income might be
perceived relates to the differential status of the beneficiaries of these
flows. The main recipients of factor income are the 90,000 Palestinian migrant
workers in Israel (1984 figures), for whom this income is the major, if not
sole, source of subsistence. It is difficult to estimate the proportion of
income from work in Israel which is deployed in savings or investment,

although much is expected to be devoted to immediate consumption needs, while
some might be used for home, farm or workshop improvement. Moreover, as noted,
the lack of a banking system has made it almost impossible to mobilize the
small savings of individuals. The second major group of beneficiaries are the
families of those 16,000 residents of the territories who work elsewhere but
not in Israel. Factor income from the rest of the world in this case might
have a more prominent role to play after providing for household consumption
requirements, namely financing home-building or serving as a sort of
"start-up" capital for small commercial or industrial businesses in the
territories. Only with the third component of factor income, that which
accrues through interest on savings or investment abroad and rent on property
abroad, might there exist a definite local investment role for factor income
payments. However, in view of uncertainties in the local situation, recipients
of this category of income might consider factor income as a secure source of
income for immediate consumption expenditure. Nevertheless, it is possible
that factor income payments of this type find their way into limited direct
investment in the territories.223/

332. On the whole, whatever local uses are made of factor income, it should be
noted that a portion of it never enters the territories, either being
appropriated by government as taxes and other deductions (see section B.2
below), spent outside the territories, or kept abroad, including in banks in
Amman, because of lack of attractive opportunities and channels for its
deployment in the territories. Nevertheless, much of factor income accruing to
Palestinians working in Israel is spent in the territories, "... since these
workers live in the region and many of them return home daily. Residents of
the areas who work in Jordan and other countries spend a smaller proportion of
their income in the areas. The decline in emigration to Jordan and the Gulf
States for purposes of employment, and the subsequent increase in employment
in Israel and the areas themselves are likely to increase domestic demand, and
consequently the gross domestic product."224/

B.   Financial transfers

1.   Gross and net transfers to the occupied territories

333. In addition to factor income, another type of external financial
resources is available to the occupied territories, namely that represented by
unrequited transfers (remittances, official aid), which have become
increasingly prominent in recent years, especially with the growth of
Palestinian, Arab and international interest in providing financial support to
the territories and their inhabitants. The increase in official and private
aid to the territories has supplemented private transfer flows originating
from the "permanent" migrants abroad (i.e. those who have lost their residency
rights but maintain family links in the territories). When combined with the
factor income accruing to the territories, the scale of external financial
flows in the economy acquires an even greater significance.

334. It is possible to view the flow of transfers to the territories in terms
of its three major forms. The first involves flows from Israeli and Jordanian
government institutions to individuals or institutions in the territories.
These include Israeli military government transfers to local authorities,

other institutions or individuals. The second major source of transfers to the
territories consists of Palestinians who emigrated from the territories after
1967, but who still support family members in the territories. Although this
latter component is comparable to factor income from work abroad, it differs
in one important respect, namely, it originates from "non-residents" and is
thus considered as an extra, non-domestic source of finance accruing to the
territories. The third component of transfers to the territories, namely
official aid, can be broken down according to its two main sources, Arab and
non-Arab international aid. The first involves transfers from official
Jordanian, Palestinian and other Arab sources to institutions in the
territories, mainly municipalities and local charitable societies, and to
individuals and various businesses and commercial enterprises in different
sectors. This form of aid has grown noticeably in recent years. The other
constituent of official aid which has also become increasingly prominent
recently is transfers from non-Arab international agencies to local
institutions or individuals, for use for relief or development purposes. Until
the late 1970s, this item was almost solely composed of transfers from the
United Nations Relief and Works Agency for Palestine Refugees in the Near East
(UNRWA). Since then, other United Nations and private voluntary organizations
have also become involved in the process. Consequently, the territories'
economy has also grown increasingly dependent on this source of finance in
recent years.

335. Like factor income, these payments to the territories should be balanced
against transfers to the rest of the world. Whereas residents do transfer
funds for safekeeping and deposit in Jordanian banks, the bulk of these
transfers from the territories appears to be destined to Israel in the form of
taxes (income, value added tax and others) and transfers to government (social
security or insurance payments). Transfers to Israel have grown noticeably in
the past few years, thus indirectly lessening the potential economic impact of
private and official transfers to the territories.

336. The volume of net transfers (specified in official data as the difference
between all transfers to the territories and transfers out of the territories,
and designated as NT in table 36) increased until 1981, when it reached a peak
of $120 million. By that year, the increase in Arab and international aid had
begun to show, while economic conditions in the Arab oil-producing States were
still prosperous enough to allow the generation of sizeable remittances by
migrants. As of 1982, however, NT began a decline which continued until 1984,
when it fell below its 1979 level of $88 million. It can be seen from table 36
that one component of NT, namely transfers to private persons in the
territories (PT), 225/ grew gradually from $61 million in 1978 to a peak of
$95 million in 1982, only to decline in following years, reaching $84 million
in 1984. This is not surprising in the light of the decrease in remittances
from non-resident migrant workers. However, transfers to private persons have
accounted for over half of all transfer payments (TPC) credited to the
territories since 1979. This share reached 58 per cent in 1980, and has
fluctuated between 51 and 55 per cent since. It remains the largest component
of transfer payments to the territories.

Table 36

Transfer payment aggregates of the occupied Palestinian territories - gross national product, 1978-1984
(Millions of current Israeli shekels)ᵃ/

Year	PT	TPC	PT/TPC	TPD	TPN	NT	GNP
1978	106	221	48%	62	159	159	1669
	(61)	(127)		(36)	(91)	(91)	(956)
1979	180	351	51%	126	225	225	2980
	(71)	(138)		(50)	(88)	(88)	(1171)
1980	427	741	58%	263	478	584	7409
	(83)	(145)		(51)	(94)	(114)	(1446)
1981	1057	2089	51%	725	1364	1364	15913
	(92)	(183)		(63)	(120)	(120)	(1392)
1982	2310	4169	55%	1598	2571	2598	36571
	(95)	(172)		(66)	(106)	(107)	(1507)
1983	5192	9497	55%	4347	5150	4819	93469
	(92)	(169)		(77)	(92)	(86)	(1663)
1984	24689	...	51%	...	...	25529	455805
	(84)	(165)		(72)	(93)	(87)	(1555)

Explanatory note

PT   =   Private transfers from abroad not entailing a quid pro quo

NT   =   Net transfers from abroad (including private and public)

TPC =   Transfer payments credit (i.e. current transfers to the territories)*

TPD =   Transfer payments debit (i.e. current transfers from the territories)*

TPN =   Transfer payments net (TPC-TPD, or NT)

GNP =   Gross national product

* Official series for transfer payments (TPC/TPD) for 1981-1983 are published as of 1985 in United States dollars. These data differ in some cases from the calculations made above from shekels to dollars. This is due to the fact that in periods of accelerating inflation, it is preferable if calculations can be made on a more frequent basis than according to annual exchange rates, e.g. in quarterly periods. It appears that the official series in dollars does this, producing dollar figures for transfer payments which are higher than those calculated above. This does not affect major trends discussed. However, it is necessary to use the NT series for calculating GNP, while examination of the TPC/TPD figures allows for a more detailed look at the components of transfers.

ᵃ/ Figures in parentheses are in millions of current United States dollars.

Table 36 (continued)

Sources:

- Dollar figures for PT, NT, GNP, and for 1978-1983 TPC, TPD and TPN calculated according to annual average $US/IS exchange rate in IMF, International Financial Statistics (Wash. D.C., IMF, 1985), pp. 364-7.

- PT, NT, GNP figures for 1978-1983 calculated from Israel, Central Bureau of Statistics, Judea, Samaria and Gaza Area Statistics (Jerusalem, CBS), vol. XV, No. 1, April 1985), pp. 164, 167, 171, 174; figures for 1984 calculated from Israel, Central Bureau of Statistics, Judea, Samaria and Gaza Area Statistics (Jerusalem, CBS), vol. XV, No. 2, December 1985, pp. 68, 73, 75, and 80.

- TPC, TPD, TPN: 1984 United States Dollar figures from Israel, Central Bureau of Statistics, Statistical Abstract of Israel 1985 (Jerusalem, CBS, 1985), p. 712; 1981-1983 Israeli shekels figures from Statistical Abstract of Israel 1984, (Jerusalem, CBS, 1984); 1978-1980 Israeli shekel figures from Statistical Abstract of Israel 1981, (Jerusalem, CBS, 1981), p. 720.

2. Components of transfers

(a) Transfers between occupied territories and government

337. While the benefits accruing to the territories through their relation with the Israeli economy might be apparent in terms of job and income opportunities (as well as any other possible benefits from trading links), the costs are not so easily perceived. One way to measure costs, other than estimating the indirect effects of competition and domination in various productive and marketing spheres, 226/ is to look at the scale of financial resources transferred by the territories to government in the form of indirect production, value added and income taxes and other such transfers. This will shed further light on the overall discussion of movement of financial resources in and out of the territories. Official data series are available for transfers from government and local authorities to the territories' inhabitants; these are presented in table 37 and denoted as G. Similarly, there are official data series for two of the major components of transfers out of the territories, namely indirect production taxes and income taxes, presented in table 37 as Tp and Ti respectively. The sum of these two flows to government is denoted by the series in table 37 calculated as Tt, while the net transfers to government (G - Tt) are denoted as NTG. It can be seen that transfers and subsidies from government almost doubled between 1978 and 1984, from $9 million to $17 million. Concurrently, the share of G in total transfer payments to the territories (TPC) also increased, from 7 per cent in 1978 to some 11 per cent in 1984. The growth in this share is especially noticeable as of 1982, the year in which the total level of transfers to the territories began to decline. The overall increase in the share of transfers from government should be seen in the light of the gradual decline in total transfer payments to the territories. The balance of transfers to the territories is accounted for by remittances and aid.

Table 37

Selected components of transfer payments of the
occupied Palestinian territories, 1978-1984
(Millions of current Israeli shekels and percentages)a/

Year	G	G/TPC	Tp	Ti	Tt	Tt/GNP	NTG
1978	15	7%	38	68	106	6%	-91
	(9)		(22)	(39)	(61)		-(52)
1979	26	7%	50	135	185	6%	-159
	(10)		(20)	(53)	(73)		-(62)
1980	61	8%	140	305	445	6%	-384
	(12)		(27)	(75)	(87)		-(75)
1981	164	8%	396	765	1161	7%	-997
	(14)		(35)	(67)	(102)		-(87)
1982	438	10%	1030	1835	2865	8%	-2427
	(18)		(42)	(76)	(118)		-(100)
1983	1073	10%	3768	5787	9555	10%	-8482
	(19)		(67)	(103)	(170)		-(151)
1984	4914	11%	22384	31896	54280	12%	-49366
	(17)		(76)	(109)	(185)		-(168)

Explanatory note:

G: Government and local authority transfers/subsidies
TPC: Transfer payments credit (i.e. = current transfers to the territories)
Tp: Indirect domestic production taxes
Ti: Income tax and other transfers to government and local authorities
Tt: Tp + Ti
GNP: Gross national product
NTG: G - Tt (i.e. net transfer flows to government and local authorities)

a/ Figures in parentheses are in millions of current United States dollars.

Sources:

-Dollar figures calculated according to annual average $US/IS exchange rate, from IMF, International Financial Statistics (Wash. D.C., IMF, 1985), pp. 364-7.

-TPC and GNP figures used in above calculations are taken from table 36.

-All other figures: for 1978-1983 calculated from Israel, Central Bureau of Statistics, Judea, Samaria and Gaza Area Statistics (Jerusalem, CBS), vol. XV, No. 1, April 1985, pp. 164, 167, 171, 174; figures for 1984 calculated from Israel, Central Bureau of Statistics, Judea, Samaria and Gaza Area Statistics (Jerusalem, CBS), vol. XV, No. 2, December 1985, pp. 68, 73, 75, and 80.

338. It can also be seen in table 37 that the volume of transfers out of the territories in the form of taxes trebled between 1978 and 1984. Whereas some $60 million was transferred in 1978 by the territories to Israeli and local government authorities in the form of income, production and value added taxes and other transfers (duties, fees, fines, etc.), this amount reached $185 million in 1984. It appears that the bulk of these transfers were actually made to Israeli authorities - either to the income tax departments in Israel itself or to the tax departments of the Israeli administration in the territories. Of the total tax bill of 1983 and 1984, for example, some $11 million and $12.5 million respectively was paid to Palestinian local authorities as property and fuel taxes, rates and various fees.227/ This local government revenue constituted under 7 per cent of the total tax transfers (Tt) by the territories' inhabitants in those two years, both directly to the local authorities and through the civil administration. This means that the balance of taxes and other transfers to "government and local authorities" is most likely destined for the Israeli Government and its civil administration in the territories.228/

339. The scale and significance of the transfer of Palestinian financial resources to Israeli authorities can be seen in relation to a number of indicators, including GNP. As shown in table 37, the proportion of GNP transferred to Israeli and local authorities through taxation alone has doubled, from 6 per cent in 1978 to 12 per cent in 1984, with the increase most noticeable since 1982. The amount of tax thus transferred to Israeli authorities in 1984 ($170 million) was equivalent to 46 per cent of the gross factor income from employment in Israel, 16 per cent of GDP and 11 per cent of GNP, more than double all private transfers received from abroad, and some $7 million more than the $165 million total of transfer payments credited to the territories.229/ In fact, the transfer flows to government in both 1983 and 1984 were some $6 million more than total government expenditure (including its transfers to the territories) in that year.230/ This means that a significant proportion of tax revenue does not appear to be spent by the government in the territories, and that the government can subsidize all its expenditure in the territories through tax revenue alone (i.e. not including other revenue sources). Many of the potential benefits resulting from these newly emergent patterns of dependency on external finance can be lost through this high rate of transfer to Israeli authorities of domestically and externally generated resources.

(b) Migrants' remittances

340. In one study of the role of remittances in the Jordanian economy, it is argued that approximately one third of the Jordanian labour force abroad consists of migrants of West Bank origin and that the same proportion of remittances transferred to Jordan through official channels are due to these West Bank migrants.231/ However, because of the lack of financial security and incentives for investment in the territories, only a portion of remittances which are transferred to Jordan are subsequently transferred to the West Bank. This amount, assumed to be enough to cover cost-of-living increases, is estimated at a level equivalent to the total remittances to Jordan in 1975, plus an increase of 20 per cent per annum. The balance of remittances reaching Jordan remains in the East Bank (for consumption, savings or construction purposes).

341. It is possible to construct two series of figures based on official Jordanian data for transfer payments, as is done in table 38, one of which shows the portion of remittances transferred to the West Bank (REM in table 38) while the other details the amount assumed to be kept outside the territories (REM1). According to these figures, the amount of transfers to the territories from this one source alone grew from $110 million in 1978 to $257 million in 1984. These figures are well above the total for transfer payments to the territories from all sources provided by Israeli statistics (TPC in table 36). Though such alternative estimates shed doubt upon official Israeli statistics, there are sound reasons for believing that the REM series exaggerates the actual level of transfers.[232]/

Table 38

Remittances of migrants from the occupied Palestinian territories working abroad, 1978-1984 a/
(Millions of Jordanian dinars)b/

Year	REM	REM1	REMT
1978	33	27	60
	(110)	(88)	(198)
1979	40	25	65
	(132)	(83)	(215)
1980	48	37	85
	(159)	(124)	(283)
1981	57	66	123
	(173)	(200)	(373)
1982	69	70	139
	(194)	(196)	(390)
1983	82	63	145
	(226)	(174)	(400)
1984	99	72	171
	(257)	(187)	(444)

Explanatory note

REM: Remittances of West-Bank-origin labour force abroad transferred to the territories

REM1: Remittances of West-Bank-origin labour force abroad kept in Jordan.

REMT: REM + REM1 (total remittances due to West Bank origin migrants abroad and transferred to Jordan through official channels).

a/ According to the method used to calculate these series, 36 per cent of the total remittances actually transferred to Jordan from abroad are due to migrants of West Bank origin (see chapter I, section A). However, since 1975, it is assumed that : (a) not all remittances which are transferred to Jordan are subsequently transferred to the territories ; and, (b) a base amount equivalent to total remittances transferred in 1975, plus an estimated 20 per cent of that amount per annum to account for cost of living increases, was actually transferred to the territories (REM). The remainder, REM1, is either saved in Jordan and elsewhere, or used for home-building or consumption expenditure abroad.

b/ Figures in parentheses are in millions of United States dollars.

Table 38 (continued)

Sources:

Figures are calculated according to the method in I. Zaghloul, Transfers of Jordanians and Their Effect on the Jordanian Economy (Amman, Central Bank of Jordan, 1984), p. 11. REMT is equal to 36 per cent of total annual remittances to Jordan recorded in official Jordanian balance-of-payments statistics.
Dollar figures calculated according to annual average $US/JD exchange rate, in IMF, International Financial Statistics (Wash. D.C., IMF, 1985), pp. 384-85 and 364-7.

342. Ultimately, the significance of this series is not to be found in the degree to which the figures for remittances are precise. Rather, the presentation of such alternative data series shows how official Israeli estimations of transfer flows from abroad underestimate the weight of migrants' remittances in terms of supporting the territories' inhabitants. Also, to the extent that such alternative data series are accurate, official national account figures, such as those used in this study, can be seen to seriously distort the actual picture. Consequently, the scale and potential of financial resources in the occupied territories remains an issue of the utmost importance to researchers and policy-makers alike.

(c) External aid

343. A third type of transfers was also noted, namely that of official aid from a variety of Palestinian, Arab and other sources of a private, governmental and intergovernmental nature. These transfers, which have become increasingly substantial in recent years, are generally easier to trace than others. They also have perhaps the most important role, both present and potential, in the provision of financial resources for development in the occupied territories. Since these transfers represent an expression of humanitarian and political will and commitment to assisting the Palestinian people, they are less subject to changes in local or regional economic fortunes than are other sources of external finance (i.e. factor income, including remittances).[233]/ However, this component of transfers is under the direct control of Governments or funding agencies. Such aid is the only source of external finance available to the territories whose deployment and size can be actively influenced by a wide range of factors, from changes in funding agencies' priorities and outlook, to the declared (and/or perceived) aspirations of the inhabitants of the territories, not to mention the policies and priorities of the occupation authorities. In the light of this and the relatively large size of external aid, its constitution and role deserve special scrutiny.

344. The following paragraphs examine external aid to the territories according to several criteria: source (Arab and the rest of the world), deployment (sectorally, by major donor agency) and type (grants and loans). Though exact data for all years under review (i.e. 1978-1984) are not available, estimates are possible for the main items under consideration. An initial analysis of the data presented below sheds further doubt on the precision and reliability of official statistics related to external financial

flows to the territories. It reveals a much greater pool of untapped financial resources actually and potentially available to the territories than official data series indicate. In turn, this implies higher levels of gross and per capita national income as well as consumption expenditure and, probably, uninvested and unutilized savings.

(i) Arab and Islamic aid

345. The scale and composition of aid from Arab sources to the territories is detailed in table 39. There are five major Arab sources of aid to the territories.234/ The longest existing form of aid is that received by the West Bank from the Jordanian Government since 1967 to cover the wages and pensions of civil servants, rent paid on government premises, subsidies to municipalities, guarantees on bank loans to public institutions, direct grants, education and health services. Complementing government transfers is the semi-official charitable aid provided to West Bank welfare and charitable societies by their Jordanian East Bank counterparts. Further sources comprise Arab and Islamic States which undertake projects through the "Jerusalem Fund" to preserve the Arab and Islamic heritage in Jerusalem, and regional development funds and banks which have become involved in funding specific projects in the territories (e.g. a large-scale irrigation works in the Fara'a area of the Ghor Valley in the West Bank is funded by the Arab Fund for Economic and Social Development). The major source of aid to the occupied territories since 1979 (and the major channel for Arab aid) has been the Jordanian-Palestinian Joint Committee for the Support of the Steadfastness of the Palestinian People in the Occupied Homeland (referred to henceforth as the Joint Committee) which was established at the Arab States' summit meeting of November 1978, held in Baghdad, Iraq.

346. The Joint Committee was intended as a common Jordanian-Palestinian body for the receipt of official Arab funds and their subsequent disbursement to Palestinians in the territories for purposes of what is termed "steadfastness".235/ The Joint Committee was meant to receive from the major Arab oil-producing States236/ an annual budget of $150 million for a 10-year period commencing in 1979. Between 1979 and 1985, however, the total receipts of the Committee from these sources amounted to just under $400 million (when they should have been over $1 billion).237/ The Committee became fully operational early in 1979 and was active until early 1986, when its activities were temporarily suspended. It had official representation at the ministerial level of both the PLO and the Jordanian Government and worked with the support of a "Technical Bureau" based in Amman, Jordan. This Bureau had the task of receiving and/or formulating project proposals, evaluating them and making recommendations on appropriate action to the Committee. Funding, when approved, was done either directly or, more often, through various Jordanian financial institutions or specialized banks which were entrusted with the task of managing the Committee's funding activities (grants or loans) within their particular field of competence.

347. Despite a variety of operational and political problems affecting its activities, it was able to channel significant amounts of Arab funds into the territories. In addition to serving as a major source of external finance to the territories, the operations of the Joint Committee have been significant in that they represented a common Palestinian-Arab effort on behalf of the Palestinian people to develop appropriate indigenous capacity for maintaining

Table 39

Estimates of private and official Arab unrequited transfers to the occupied Palestinian territories, 1978-1984, by source
(Millions of current Jordanian dinars)[a]

Year	JGT	JNGO	ARIS	JJPC	TAIA
1978	8.2	.6		NA	
	(26.9)	(2.0)	(4.25)		(33)
1979	6.2	.7		12.83	
	(20.6)	(2.3)	(4.25)	(42.7)	(70)
1980	6.4	.8		24.48	
	(21.4)	(2.7)	(3.6)	(82.1)	(110)
1981	6.65	.9		25.15	
	(20.1)	(2.7)	(3.6)	(76.2)	(103)
1982	6.9	1		33.04	
	(19.6)	(2.8)	(2)	(93.8)	(118)
1983	7.15	1		13.75	
	(19.6)	(2.7)	(2)	(37.9)	(62)
1984	7.35	1		12.66	
	(19.2)	(2.6)	(10)	(33)	(65)

Explanatory note

JGT: Jordanian Government salaries and pensions to West Bank residents; Jordanian Government rent paid for premises in West Bank; Other Jordanian Government transfers: aid to municipalities, guarantees on loans by commercial banks, direct grants, education and health.
JNGO: Aid from Jordanian non-governmental organizations - religious endowments and charitable associations;
ARIS: Arab and Islamic States' aid (including Jerusalem Fund);
JPJC: Jordanian-Palestinian Joint Committee grants and loans;
TAIA: Total transfers from Arab and Islamic sources: total Arab and Islamic aid.

a/ Figures in parentheses and those for ARIS and TAIA are in millions of current dollars.

Sources:

- Dollar figures calculated according to annual average $US/JD exchange rate, from IMF, _International Financial Statistics_ (Wash. D.C., IMF, 1985), pp. 384-85.
-JGT, JNGO, ARIS figures calculated from data in Royal Scientific Society, _Financial and Banking Conditions in the Occupied West Bank and Gaza Strip_ (Amman, RSS, 1985), pp. 91 -112.
- JPJC figures provided by Jordanian-Palestinian Joint Committee, Technical Bureau, Amman, 1986.

the local economic base. Through its experience, it stimulated discussion, criticism and evaluation of what could and should be done to support the territories and contribute to their development. The Joint Committee can thus be understood as a sort of testing ground for the Palestinian people's capacity to guide its own development, despite the limitation of its role and the constraints under which it operated. In the light of the limited scope of Palestinian experience in development funding and project management activities and the fact that international organisations have been most prominently identified with such activities in the territories, the unique nature of the Committee's experience cannot be overemphasized.

348. The work of the Committee suffered from a number of handicaps, too detailed and complex to evaluate fully here. These included the constraints imposed by the Israeli authorities upon entry of funds into the territories, especially those identified as originating in the Committee, the occasionally unclear project support criteria, management and staffing difficulties, operational limitations on attempting to enact a global development-relief effort from outside the territories, limited participation by aid recipients in policy and project formulation and implementation, the practical problems of ensuring field supervision and follow-up, maintaining the Committee's resource base and isolating its work from the interference of political factors.[238]/

349. The major component of official Jordanian transfers to the territories is in the form of salaries and pensions to government employees in the West Bank. Total Jordanian government transfers to the occupied territories (JGT) stood at some $27 million in 1978, but fell to $21 million in 1979. This reduction was concurrent with the commencement of operations by the Joint Committee in 1979 and its assumption of certain financial responsibilities of the Jordanian Government, mainly those connected with municipal assistance. In subsequent years, while the dinar value of JGT slightly increased, their equivalent value in terms of the United States dollar declined to around $19 million, owing to a fall in the value of the Jordanian dinar. Meanwhile, direct Arab and Islamic States' aid to the territories (denoted as ARIS) increased from some $4 million in 1978 to $10 million in 1984 with the commencement of the funding of the Ghor Valley irrigation project. However, after 1979, the bulk of Arab transfers to the territories was allocated by the Joint Committee. From a level of some $43 million in 1979, the Joint Committee's disbursements rose to a peak of $94 million in 1982 and fell to their lowest level ever of $38 million in 1983 and $33 million in 1984. In 1985, however, the last year in which Joint Committee funds were disbursed on a significant scale, the level of funding rose to JD 15.6 million, or some $40 million.[239]/ Thus, in the 1979-1985 period, though the Joint Committee allocated a total of JD 156 million, (approximately $462 million) for projects in the occupied territories, only some JD 137 million was actually disbursed, equivalent to something over $405 million. The difference between allocations and disburments to projects is due to the unfulfilled commitments of donor States, which accounted for 12 per cent of allocations. Between 1979 and 1983, the share of Joint Committee funding in total official Arab transfers to the territories was over 60 per cent, reaching 80 per cent in 1982; by 1984, its share had fallen to just over 50 per cent.

(ii) Other external aid

350. Other external aid to the territories comes from a wide range of sources. The situation reflects the extent to which different elements of the international community perceive needs for funding in the territories and accordingly have mobilized resources to address them. There are two major categories of (non-Arab) external financial sources operating in the territories: international agencies (United Nations) and private voluntary organizations (PVOs). The United Nations has been involved in providing relief and welfare services to Palestinian refugees since 1949. The United Nations Relief and Works Agency for Palestine Refugees in the Near East (UNRWA) has had substantial programmes in the West Bank and Gaza Strip involving expenditures on education, health and limited social and welfare services. More recently, the United Nations Development Programme (UNDP) has been channelling resources to productive, social welfare and infrastructural development projects in the territories, though on a smaller scale than UNRWA. Various PVOs have also become increasingly active in project funding in the territories in recent years. United States-based PVOs receive private contributions as well as official United States Government contributions (from the United States Agency for International Development (USAID)) to finance their growing programmes in such fields as education, health and community and economic development. Meanwhile, PVOs based in a number of European States (especially the Federal Republic of Germany, the United Kingdom, the Netherlands, Sweden, Norway and Switzerland) have been active in similar fields, disbursing both official aid and private contributions in the territories. A third, and more recent, actor in international financing of development efforts in the territories is the European Economic Community (EEC), which has worked directly or through European PVOs to fund projects in the territories.

351. Whereas aid from Arab sources is primarily motivated by considerations of Arab solidarity and support for what is seen as Palestinian "resistance" to Israeli encroachments on the territories' economy and resources, other international aid is motivated by different factors. On the one hand, aid from UNRWA and some PVOs is rooted in humanitarian concerns regarding certain basic needs of Palestinians (primary education, health care, material support for hardship cases) that are catered for insufficiently by government or local institutions. However, much of PVO and UNDP funding is aimed at addressing immediate "developmental" requirements, in the same way as commercial or State finance acts in other countries. The emphasis is on agricultural and small industrial projects, community development and various self-help schemes, job-creation projects and women's advancement programmes, as well as certain larger infrastructural requirements.

352. This range of interests is by no means solely the domain of international agencies. Usually, it is local Palestinian PVOs which have already initiated such activities and seek international funding for them. Also, some of the Arab aid reaching the territories, including that from the Joint Committee, has been directed towards development projects, even though much is allocated to more "traditional" needs (social welfare, education and health, municipal services and infrastructure). Yet it should be emphasized that, while most international PVOs consider their role as "developmental" and UNRWA provides "humanitarian relief", the Joint Committee is explicitly oriented to support "steadfastness". These differences are important because they largely

determine the areas in which different agencies will deploy funds and the sort of local institutions with which they will work. They have also acquired increasing relevance recently as agencies' priorities have become the focus of a vivid debate between those who hold that "steadfastness", or keeping people on the land, is the only feasible goal for aid donors as long as the Israeli occupation continues, and others who are of the opinion that aid should and can aim at promoting 'development' or "improving the quality of life".[240/]

353. As can be seen from tables 40 and 41, the bulk of non-Arab transfers to the territories are UNRWA expenditures serving refugees in the West Bank and Gaza Strip. In almost every year under examination, UNRWA transfers have accounted for more than 80 per cent of all international aid to the territories. This is not surprising considering that UNRWA provides primary education, health care, shelter, sanitation and other basic services to some 785,000 registered refugees in the territories. Indeed, the average annual expenditures from other sources, including UNDP, EEC and PVOs, appear small or insignificant compared to transfers from UNRWA. This is not, in fact, strictly the case, since it is only in the late 1970s that many other agencies commenced their programmes, and they have since developed them. Thus, whereas UNDP implemented a programme including 23 projects between 1980 and 1986 and totalling some $9.5 million in resources (i.e. an average annual expenditure figure of under $1.4 million), an indicative planning figure of $17 million was set for total programme expenditure for the five-year period 1987-1991 (i.e. an average annual figure of almost $3.5 million).[241/]

354. Other international sources, such as USAID-supported PVOs, have also increased their funding levels, while new agencies have recently commenced activities or are increasing their commitments (e.g. EEC and some European based PVOs). Some of the PVOs involved are dedicated solely to Middle East or Palestinian activities, such as American Near East Refugee Aid (ANERA), the Near East Foundation (NEF), the Middle East Council of Churches (MECC), Holyland Christian Mission (HCM), the United Palestine Appeal (UPA), the American Middle East Educational and Training Service (AMIDEAST) and the Welfare Association. Others are internationally active agencies with varying degrees of Palestinian commitment, such as the Community Development Foundation (CDF), affiliated to the United States-based organization Save the Children, Catholic Relief Services (CRS), OXFAM, Terre des Hommes (TDH), Co-operation for Development (CD), the Mennonite Central Committee (MCC) and the Protestant Association for Co-operation in Development (EZE). The interests of these agencies, as attested to by lists of some of their programmes, cover the range of humanitarian, welfare and development concerns: vocational training courses, university scholarships, land reclamation projects, building loan funds, higher education institutional support, small business start-up schemes, hospital expansion and equipment, community water projects, day-care centres, mother and child health programmes, agricultural marketing and production techniques support, small industry support and numerous other projects in such fields. In sum, therefore, it is seen that there are a large number of agencies active in providing financial resources in varying forms and degrees to the territories, from a range of political, developmental and operational viewpoints, and assisting most sectors of the territories.

Table 40

Estimated international (non-Arab) unrequited transfers to
the occupied Palestinian territories, 1978-1984, by source[a]/
(Millions of current United States dollars)

Year	UNRWA	UNDP	EEC	USPVO	EURPVO	INTRA
1978	37.4			7.0	2.0	46.4
1979	39.0	1.0		7.0	3.0	49.0
1980	51.9	1.0		7.0	3.0	62.9
1981	59.5	1.0	1.0	7.0	3.5	72.0
1982	61.9	1.0	1.0	7.0	3.5	74.4
1983	60.5	1.0	1.0	7.0	4.0	73.5
1984	65.1	1.0	1.0	7.0	4.0	78.1

Explanatory notes:

UNRWA: Expenditures by UNRWA in the West Bank and Gaza Strip
UNDP: Average annual expenditure by UNDP in the West Bank and Gaza
Strip;
EEC: Average annual expenditure by EEC in the West Bank and Gaza Strip;
USPVO: Average annual expenditures by United-States-based PVOs in the
West Bank and Gaza Strip (CDF, ANERA, CRS, MCC, NEF, AMIDEAST,
HCM);
EURPVO: Average annual expenditures by European based PVOs in the
West Bank and Gaza Strip (EZE, TDH, MECC, OXFAM, CD, CA);
INTRA: Total transfers (expenditures) by international agencies to the
territories.

[a]/All figures (except UNRWA) are approximations of annual expenditures
and do not necessarily represent actual transfers in those specific years.

Sources:

UNRWA: Data supplied by UNRWA;
UNDP: In the 1985 Report of the Administrator to the UNDP Governing
Council (DP/1985/18), total spent and committed funding figures are
provided for the 1980-1984 period ($5.1 million); on the basis of these,
it is possible to arrive at an annual average figure - the level of
actual expenditure in each year is not available;
EEC: Field interviews with EEC representative office in Amman, in 1986,
on total expenditure from 1981 to 1984 (over $4 million); on the basis of
these, it is possible to arrive at an annual average figure - the level
of actual expenditure in each year is not available.
USPVO: In M. Benvenisti, U.S. Government Funded Projects in the West Bank
and Gaza Strip, 1977-1983 (Palestinian sector) (Jerusalem, West Bank Data
Base Project, 1984), the annual USAID contribution to United States PVOs
between 1979 and 1983 was quoted as $6.9 - $6.5 million. This provides
the basis for the average annual figures above; annual reports of the
main agencies (AMIDEAST, ANERA, CDF, CRS and NEF) allow for cross
checking and confirmation of these figures for recent budgetary years;
EURPVO: From data in annual reports and as communicated by agencies
(EZE, TDH, CD, MECC).

Table 41

Estimated transfers to the occupied Palestinian territories by selected international agencies in 1984
(Millions of current United States dollars)

Agency	Amounts
Private Voluntary Organizations - Total	11.0
ANERA	1.0
CDF	2.3
CRS	2.0
AMIDEAST	1.8
MECC	1.8
Other PVOs	2.1
Non-Arab International Agencies - Total	67.1
UNRWA	65.1
UNDP	1.0
EEC	1.0
Arab Agencies and other Governments - Total	65.0
JPJC	33.0
Jordanian Government and others	32.0
Grand total	143.0

Source: Estimates are based on Benvenisti, M., U.S. Government Funded Projects in the West Bank and Gaza Strip, 1977-1983 (Palestinian sector) (Jerusalem, West Bank Data Base Project, 1984); Data provided by PVOs and from their annual reports; and tables 39 and 40.

Note: All figures (except UNRWA) are approximations of annual expenditures and do not necessarily represent actual transfers.

(iii) Deployment of external aid

355. It can be seen from table 42 that the pattern of allocation of external transfers to the territories from the major funding sources discussed was heavily biased in favour of social development and welfare services. This is to be expected in the case of UNRWA, for example, which disbursed 55 per cent and 19 per cent of its expenditures during the period 1979-1985 on education and health respectively. Another 14 per cent of UNRWA's expenditures went to social welfare (food distribution and emergency relief) services. However, the pattern of expenditure of the Joint Committee was naturally more diversified, given its wider range of commitments and aims. The Committee's expenditures in the period also strongly favoured social and infrastructural projects. Educational institutions (universities, post secondary colleges and vocational training, primary and pre-school education) received the largest share of Joint Committee funding, namely some 25 per cent of the total disbursements, or almost JD 35 million (approximately equivalent to $100 million). Health

Table 42

Sectoral distribution of aid to the occupied Palestinian
territories from selected agencies (various years)

Sector	UNRWA 1979-1985 $m	UNRWA 1979-1985 Percent	JPJC 1979-1985 JDm	JPJC 1979-1985 Percent	USPVO 1977-1983 $m	USPVO 1977-1983 Percent	UNDP 1980-1986 $m	UNDP 1980-1986 Percent
Agriculture	–	–	10.74	8.0	10.1	28.1	1.5	17.0
Water/sewage	–	–	1.91	1.0	12.3	34.3	2.2	25.0
Social/community services	–	–	–	–	1.2	3.3	0.7	8.0
Health	79.4	19.5	2.59	2.0	0.7	1.9	2.8	31.8
Education	225.3	55.3	34.57	25.0	3.1	8.6	1.5	17.0
Roads/transport/ municipalities	–	–	21.94	16.0	1.7	4.7	–	–
Electricity	–	–	9.09	6.6	1.8	5.0	–	–
Industry	–	–	6.05	4.4	.5	1.4	0.1	1.1
Social welfare/ culture/religion	56.7	13.9	21.86	16.0	4.5	12.5	–	–
Housing	2.3	.6	21.97	16.0	–	–	–	–
Other	43.4	10.6	6.76	5.0	–	–	–	–
Total	407.2	100.0	137.48	100.00	35.9	100.0	8.8	100.0

Explanatory note:

UNRWA: Total expenditures by UNRWA in West Bank and Gaza Strip;
JPJC: Total expenditures by Jordanian-Palestinian Joint Committee in West Bank and Gaza Strip;
USPVO: Project funding proposals for the West Bank and Gaza Strip of three major United-States-based PVOs (Catholic Relief Services, Community Development Foundation and American Near East Refugee Aid) approved by Israeli authorities;
UNDP: UNDP-sponsored projects completed or under implementation (i.e. committed funding) in the West Bank and Gaza Strip

Sources:

UNRWA: Data supplied by UNRWA, 1986;
JPJC: Data supplied by JPJC, Technical Bureau, Amman, 1986;
USPVO: From M. Benvenisti, U.S. Government Funded Projects in the West Bank and Gaza (1977 - 1983) (Jerusalem, West Bank Data Base Project, 1984), table 8;
UNDP: Calculated from "Programme implementation - special programmes of assistance - assistance to the Palestinian people, report of the Administrator" (DP/1986/22), 13 March 1986, annex I.

services (hospitals and related large-scale projects) received the second
largest share of the Committee's funding (18.9 per cent, or some
JD 26 million). The third largest sectoral allocations were in three different
areas, each receiving around JD 22 million, or 16 per cent of the Committee's
disbursements. These three areas comprised: (i) support for municipalities'
services, roads and transport (especially bus co-operatives): (ii) social
welfare needs (unemployed graduates' stipends, hardship cases) and religious
institutions (repair and upkeep of Muslim waqf, i.e. endowment properties and
religious places in Jerusalem); and (iii), aid to housing co-operatives and
home building. The remainder went to agricultural projects and co-operatives
(7.8 per cent of expenditure), provision of electricity for villages and
support of the Nablus and Jerusalem electricity companies (6.6 per cent), aid
to small industries and workshops (4.4 per cent), public health
(2.0 per cent), land purchase and other activities (5 per cent).

356. United States-based PVO funding went mainly to drinking water and sewage
projects (34 per cent; over $12 million) and a variety of agricultural
development projects, including irrigation ($10 million or 28 per cent of
approved expenditures). Social welfare (community services and food provision)
and education (scholarships, support to universities and pre-school education)
received some 16 per cent and 9 per cent respectively of PVOs' approved
expenditures. Industry did not benefit greatly from either PVO or UNDP
funding, receiving under $1 million from the two sources. The concern for
health and educational services is also apparent in the allocation of UNDP
expenditures until 1986, with 32 per cent and 17 per cent of committed
resources going to health and education respectively. Infrastructural needs
received the second largest share of UNDP's funding (25 per cent) in the
period under review. The unique position of UNDP and its favourable relations
with the parties concerned has allowed it to take the initiative in this
sector. UNDP funding has also been directed to agricultural projects for both
training and productivity enhancement (17 per cent of expenditure), while
various general vocational training and educational projects have received a
similar share of UNDP funds.

357. It is likely that the increasingly active posture adopted by
international development funding and relief agencies will continue to be
evident in coming years. The only possible exception to this is the disruption
of significant Arab aid through the Joint Committee which continued throughout
1986, with temporary alternative arrangements being set in place as of late
1986.242/ The pattern of allocation of aid, however, might alter with
changes in the priorities of both the funding agencies and the recipients.
Indeed, the pattern to date, which has strongly favoured health, education and
social welfare at the expense of industry, related infrastructure, agriculture
and other productive and related sectors (tourism, construction, transport,
trade), is the outcome of a variety of factors, including donors' and
recipients' outlook.

358. However, an important factor which colours the eventual pattern of
disbursement is the policy guidelines laid down by the Israeli authorities.
It has been argued forcefully that the procedure whereby some PVOs, including
United States-based ones, and UNDP submit proposals to the authorities results
in some proposals oriented towards production or economic development being
turned down, while infrastructual and social service projects are
approved.243/ However, there are indications that such factors are becoming
less influential, perhaps as the authorities develop more flexible guidelines

in this regard.244/ In addition, a number of PVOs and international agencies, as well as the Joint Committee, decline to submit proposals to the authorities, either in order to avoid delays and refusals or out of an unwillingness to recognize the legitimacy of Israeli occupation authority in such areas. If approval is required for legal or other reasons, it is left to the local institution or PVO to enter into whatever contacts are necessary to secure project initiation and funding. On the whole, therefore, while locally perceived and expressed priorities have an initial effect in determining the pattern of deployment of international transfers to the territories, the final outcome can be altered by various other factors, including donors' preferences, operational and technical considerations, and the policies of the Israeli authorities towards such projects.

(iv) <u>Terms of aid: grants, loans and financing arrangements</u>

359. In order to obtain a clearer idea of the conditions affecting aid disbursement to the occupied territories, it is instructive to examine the terms on which external agencies make such unilateral transfers available. Specifically, an attempt has been made here to investigate the loan component of Arab and other aid, as opposed to its concessionary element, and the degree of local participation compared to external financing. Consequently, it is revealed that the bulk of agencies operating in this sphere have not, at least until very recently, included loan programmes (either through direct or revolving fund arrangements) as a suitable or feasible tool for delivery of aid. Instead, direct grants have been the favoured form of aid in most cases, while local participation in finance has been encouraged by tying external grants to local counterpart funds.

360. Accordingly, it is seen that the aid extended by the three major United States-based PVOs active in the territories (ANERA, CDF, CRS) to development projects between 1977 and 1983 equalled, on average, 44 per cent of total project budgets, with the balance of the project budgets provided by the local beneficiaries or from Jordanian and other sources of aid.245/ All of the aid provided by these PVOs was in grant form, as was the case with aid from United Nations agencies, including UNRWA and UNDP. In another example, it is seen that the grants made to projects in the West Bank and Gaza Strip by the Middle East Council of Churches (MECC) in 1984, mostly in community and rural self-help programmes, were equivalent to some 57 per cent of the total project costs.246/ In addition to the local participation in finance, the projects aided by MECC also included a number of loan-based programmes in housing and for small businesses, though these were equivalent to only 9 per cent of externally provided aid and 5 per cent of total project expenses. Such non-concessionary terms of finance appear to have become increasingly favoured by PVOs in recent years, with more of them initiating revolving fund or other loan arrangements.247/ One of the agencies that has been active in the territories, namely CDF (the local branch of the United States-based Save the Children), has recently initiated a revolving small-scale enterprise credit fund of $1 million in the West Bank.248/ With the growth and increased stability of local credit or banking institutions, such as the recently re-opened Cairo-Amman Bank, it is possible that an institutional climate favouring a greater degree of locally secured and managed loan programmes will take effect in external aid activities.

361. Though the loan element has become apparent only recently in PVOs' programmes, it was an essential element of the aid programme supervised from 1979 onwards by the Joint Committee. From its inception, the Committee was

able to offer a significant proportion of its total aid to the territories in the form of loans. This was largely possible because of the involvement of Jordanian banking institutions in the aid and loan procedures established and followed by the Committee. Thus, the Housing Bank in Amman managed individual or group housing projects in the territories, the Jordanian Co-operative Organization supervised co-operative loans in agriculture, industry, water, electricity, housing and craft projects, and the Industrial Development Bank in Amman was responsible for disbursing loans for industrial, tourist and transportation projects. When loans to individuals, firms or local authorities could not be channelled through the existing Jordanian financial institutions, the Committee itself became a source of direct loans to projects such as aid for village electrification, loans to agricultural firms, and Gaza Strip municipality housing projects. The Committee adopted certain guidelines for the processing and approval of loan applications which differed from one sector to another. These guidelines included certification establishing the loan applicants' need and creditworthiness, a personal guarantee for each loan from a person residing in Jordan (East Bank), a repayment schedule whose periods ranged from 15 to 20 years, and a management fee of 1 per cent; all loans disbursed directly by the Committee were interest free. As can be seen in table 43, of JD 58 million of Committee aid disbursed between 1979 and 1985 (not including certain important sectors also aided by the Committee such as municipalities, education and social welfare), JD 49 million, or some 84 per cent, was in the form of loans. Of this total, JD 15 million, or 31 per cent, was disbursed directly by the Committee, and the balance went through Jordanian financial institutions. The sectors where loan arrangements were most prevalent were in housing and electricity (98 per cent each of total aid), agriculture (84 per cent), industry (79 per cent), and transportation (77 per cent). Those fields where the Committee was most active as a direct source of loans were electricity, agriculture, public health and religious affairs (though the total disbursement in the latter two sectors was relatively small).

Table 43

Jordanian Palestinian Joint Committee loan disbursements, 1979-1985
(Millions of current Jordanian dinars and percentages)

Sector	Total aid disbursed	Loans disbursed	Loans as % of disbursement	Direct loans	Direct loans as % of loans
Agriculture	10.74	9.06	84.4%	4.88	53.9%
Industry	6.05	4.79	79.2%	-	-
Transportation	4.32	3.32	76.7%	-	-
Water	1.91	0.05	2.6%	0.01	22.0%
Electricity	9.09	8.98	98.8%	8.88	98.9%
Housing	27.98	22.62	98.4%	1.22	5.3%
Public health	2.59	0.05	1.9%	0.05	100.0%
Religious affairs	0.83	0.10	12.0%	0.10	100.0%
Total:	58.51	48.97	59.8%	15.14	30.9%

Source: Data supplied by Jordanian-Palestinian Joint Committee, Technical Bureau, Amman, 1986.

C.   **External financial sources and the occupied territories' development**

1.   **The relative importance of different components of transfers**

362. The importance of unilateral transfers to the occupied territories has
been highlighted in terms of their different components, including migrants'
remittances and aid from Arab sources and from international agencies. It is
possible to obtain a rough idea of the relative importance of each of these
sources from table 44. Whereas remittances (REM in table 44) accounted for the
bulk of transfers in 1978, Arab aid (TAIA) became the prominent element in
external aid as of 1979, with the commencement of the Joint Committee's
operations. This remained the case, with international aid (INTRA) having the
third largest share of total transfers (TOTRA), until 1983, when Arab aid
began to fall off, though remittances continued to grow. Consequently, the
role of international financing in the territories became more prominent.
Indeed, it might since have become the leading element of transfers from
abroad to the territories, with the expected fall in migrants' remittances
commencing in 1984. The significance of the figures in table 44 rests not only
in what they indicate about the relative weight of different external
financial sources. Of similar importance, as was the case with other
statistical series proposed above (e.g. factor income payments), is that the
figures for total transfers to the territories (TOTRA), based on the sum of
the three components mentioned, surpasses the official Israeli data for total
transfer payments to the territories (TPC). Here again, there are valid
grounds for doubting the reliability of official series and thus calling into
question the range of national income statistics presently available for the
territories. Further, it implies that the role of external resources in the
development of the territories is even more substantial than assumed and thus
deserves even greater consideration in any analysis of, or active involvement
in, the economy of the occupied Palestinian territories.

Table 44

**(Minimum) estimates of total private and official transfers to
the occupied Palestinian territories from abroad, 1978-1984[a]/**
(Millions of current United States dollars)

Year	REM	TAIA	INTRA	TOTRA	TPC
1978	55	33	46	134	127
1979	66	70	49	185	138
1980	79	110	63	252	145
1981	86	103	72	261	183
1982	97	118	74	289	172
1983	113	62	73	248	169
1984	128	65	78	271	165

Explanatory notes:

REM: Remittances of emigrant labour force abroad transferred to the
       territories (minimum estimate);

TAIA: Total transfers from Arab sources;

INTRA: Total transfers (expenditures) by international sources;

Table 44 (continued)

TOTRA: Gross transfer payments from abroad (not including Israeli
        government expenditure - see table 37).

TPC: Total transfer payments credited to the territories from abroad,
        according to official Israeli statistics

a/   (All figures have been rounded, in light of their approximate
nature).

Sources:

REM: The figures here are equal to half the supposed transfers
        recorded as REM in table 38, to provide a reasonable minimum
        approximation of workers' remittances (this series is used
        bearing in mind the limitations upon it, as discussed in section
        B.2 above);

TAIA: From table 39;

INTRA: From table 40;

TPC :   From table 36.

2.   Factor income and transfers within overall sources of Palestinian
        national income

363. A final angle from which it is instructive to view the role of external
finance in the territories' development involves comparing the performance of
factor income and transfers. By examining data for net national disposable
income (NNDI), it is possible to discern the shares of both net factor income
(NFI) and net transfers (NT) in overall national resources. NNDI grew steadily
from $1,047 million in 1978 to $1,749 million in 1983, an average annual
increase of some 13 per cent (see table 45). In the same period, NT at first
grew, but subsequently fell below their 1979 level, such that NT accounted for
8.7 per cent of NNDI in 1978 but only 4.9 per cent in 1983. In 1984, though
the level of NT remained almost constant, the general slowdown in the economy
due to other factors (stagnation in domestic product and factor income) meant
that NT's share of NNDI rose slightly to 5.3 per cent. It would appear,
therefore, that the significance of transfers from abroad in overall financial
resources of the territories has diminished in the past few years, with a
stagnation in their absolute level and a fall in their share of NNDI.

364. As might be expected, the combination of NFI and NT to the territories
highlights even more sharply the extent of the dependence of the territories
upon a pattern of economic relations which is totally removed from its
control. Following 1978, between 31 per cent and 36 per cent of income at the
disposal of the territories was generated through labour in Israel and the
rest of the world and through transfers received from a variety of private and
public sources, mainly Arab, Palestinian and international. In 1983, when GDP
had reached its highest point, 36 per cent of the territories' net disposable
income originated in factor income and transfers, also equivalent to
57 per cent of GDP. In 1984, this share declined slightly to 51 per cent of
GDP. The situation in both expansionary and recessionary years since 1980
depict a chronic dependence and continued weakness of domestic productive
capacity.

Table 45

Net current transfers, factor income, net national disposable income
and gross domestic product in the occupied Palestinian territories,
1978-1984
(Millions of Israeli shekels and percentages)a/

Year	NT + NFI	NNDI	NT/NNDI	(NT + NFI) /NNDI	/GDP
1978	576 (330)	1828 (1047)	8.7%	32%	46%
1979	1081 (424)	3205 (1259)	7.0%	34%	51%
1980	2504 (489)	7993 (1560)	7.3%	31%	46%
1981	6082 (533)	17276 (1512)	7.9%	35%	54%
1982	13830 (570)	39169 (1614)	6.6%	35%	51%
1983	35621 (634)	98288 (1749)	4.9%	36%	57%
1984	163235 (557)	481344 (1642)	5.3%	34%	51%

Explanatory note

NT: Net current transfers from abroad (private and public)
NNDI: Net national disposable income (GNP + NT)
GDP: Gross domestic product
NFI: Net factor income from abroad

a/   Figures in parentheses in millions of United States dollars.

Sources:

NT + NFI calculated from NFI series in table 35 and NT series in table 36;
NNDI figures for 1978-1983 calculated from Israel, Central Bureau of
Statistics, Judea, Samaria and Gaza Area Statistics (Jerusalem, CBS),
vol. XV, No. 1, April 1985, pp. 164 and 171; figures for 1984 calculated
from Israel, Central Bureau of Statistics, Judea, Samaria and Gaza Area
Statistics (Jerusalem, CBS), vol. XV, No. 2, December 1985, pp. 68 and 75.
Percentages calculated from NNDI figures above and GDP figures in
table 35.
Dollar figures for NNDI calculated according to annual average $US/IS
exchange rate, in IMF, International Financial Statistics (Wash. D.C.,
I.M.F., 1985), pp. 364-7.

365. As noted, the bulk of these external resources is in the form of factor income. Transfers accounted for 27 per cent of all external resources in 1978, and steadily declined thereafter, to reach 16 per cent in 1984. As employment of Palestinians in Israel continued to increase over the period, and with the recent decrease in Palestinian and Arab aid and migrants' remittances, the share of resources generated in Israel rose from some 55 per cent of total transfers and factor income in 1978 to 67 per cent in 1984. This allows for further precision in identifying the nature of the territories' reliance on external finance. It can be seen that not only is the economy increasingly dependent on external sources of finance, but that this trend appears to be largely in the direction of finance originating in Israel. Were it not for the continued flow of transfers to the territories from Arab and international sources, the degree of dependency on this source of income would be even greater, thus deepening and further complicating an already disturbing subordination of the Palestinian economy to Israeli financial and economic interests. [249]/

Chapter V

CONCLUSIONS AND RECOMMENDATIONS

366. The present chapter draws on the findings and conclusions reached in the study and examines the possibilities for feasible solutions to the problems encountered by the economy of the occupied territories, with emphasis on the specific role of the financial sector. It is hoped that the proposals would contribute to the formulation of guidelines for policy action at various levels in the territories, both by the parties directly concerned and by the international community. As such, attention is focused on some of the main issues that are of vital importance to the future of the Palestinian economy.

A.   General economic situation

367. The period immediately following the 1967 occupation of the territories by Israel was characterized by high rates of economic growth in the territories. However, that momentum could not be sustained because of radical structural changes brought about in the economy of the territories through measures embodied in a series of military orders. As a result, the level of domestic output and its contribution to gross national product have been steadily falling in recent years.

368. While the relative share of the traditional sector in domestic output has rapidly declined, the share of industry has virtually stagnated while labour has become increasingly dependent on employment opportunities in Israel and the rest of the world. The closure of banks and other financial institutions, since the occupation of the territories, has deprived these and other sectors of the economy from short-term and long-term sources of finance. That lack of financing has acted as a serious bottle-neck in efforts to expand output in these sectors. In the area of trade, the territories have been gradually transformed into the largest single importer of Israeli (non-military) products with a growing balance of trade deficit that can only be met from workers' remittances and transfers from abroad.

369. The inability of domestic output to meet rising demand and the growing import of goods from Israel, coupled with the use of a depreciating Israeli currency as legal tender in the territories, have manifested themselves in high level of prices. This has, in turn, affected the level of savings and investment in the economy of the territories with the existing financial institutions unable to absorb some of the liquidity that is injected from abroad.

370. Domestic contribution to savings has been negative. The rising trend in total private disposable income from all sources has not been adequately reflected in the level of personal savings. Gross capital formation has also followed a declining trend in recent years. Although the private sector accounts for the bulk of total capital formation, much of the investment has been in buildings and construction works, which have been largely aimed, inter alia, at meeting the acute shortage in housing and as a hedge against high rates of inflation. The continued political and economic instability, lack of investment opportunities in commodity-producing sectors, and land confiscation practices of the occupation authorities have further pushed private savings into speculative activities.

371. In general, the economy of the territories is at present characterized by a high degree of fragmentation reflecting an increasing distortion in the structure of output and income, a widening gap between domestic and national output, and a high degree of openness that renders it vulnerable to outside economic and political forces. The lack of appropriate institutions to safeguard the interest of the local economy through various policy instruments has further compounded the problems of indigenous economic management in the territories and has led to the increasing subservience of the local economy to the economy of the occupying authorities.

372. Bold measures are needed to reverse this state of affairs, including the following: (a) initiating a policy aimed at developing the economy of the territories; (b) accelerating capital accumulation designed to increase productive capacity in agriculture and industry; (c) providing incentives to encourage local and foreign investors in productive sectors of the economy; (d) easing restrictions and licensing procedures on production and marketing in agriculture and industry; (e) promotion of equitable trade relations between Israel and the territories, especially with regard to existing limitation on Palestinian agricultural exports to Israel; (f) allowing the re-emergence of local financial institutions and promoting their financial intermediation; (g) increasing employment opportunities in other sectors; and, (h) promoting the entrepreneurial spirit that has served as the basis for economic endeavour and achievements in the territories. Only through such a conscious policy and commitment, coupled with concrete measures at various levels, can the economy of the territories be expected to move out of stagnation and set itself on a course of sustained growth and development. Indeed, the success of such an approach equally necessitates the creation and development of indigenous bodies capable of managing the economy on a day-to-day basis and charting its future course.

373. It should be noted, however, that the policy orientation of measures aimed at reviving the economy of the territories should reflect the aspirations of the Palestinian people in the territories, articulated in terms of overall development objectives and strategies. Given the resource endowments of the economy, its present distorted structure and future prospects, the following basic objectives may be considered, among others, to serve as a frame of reference for designing appropriate policy measures required in each area of economic and social endeavour:

(a) Accelerate the growth of the domestic economy at a rate sufficient to sustain natural increases in population and to bring about improvements in the level of per capita income;

(b) Increase productivity in the neglected areas of agriculture and industry and expand the output of essential goods by promoting import substitution industries based on local raw materials, and by diversifying exports, thus reducing the overall foreign exchange gap and deficit in the balance of trade;

(c) Stabilize the general price level and reduce the prices of essential commodities;

(d) Create productive employment opportunities throughout the territories to absorb both natural increases in the labour force and migrant Palestinian workers employed in Israel and the rest of the world;

(e) Accelerate the rate of development expenditures with the view to creating the basic infrastructural facilities that provide external benefits to the economy, and increasing the absorptive capacity of the territories for further productive investment;

(f) Establish and strengthen appropriate financial institutions aimed at mobilizing, allocating, and managing domestic resources in line with the needs of the economy; and,

(g) Establish the requisite institutional capabilities within the public administration of the territories for the effective formulation and implementation of economic and social policy measures.

374. Undoubtedly, the realization of such objectives, which are in line with the expressed needs of the territories, would be dependent upon institutions capable of handling the crucial interplay of various economic and social policy instruments. Obviously, such institutions are lacking in the territories and the issues involved are dealt with by facilities operated by or under the direction of the occupation authorities.

375. This study has examined one of the important auxiliary areas, namely, finance, which contributes towards the realization of certain economic and social needs whether or not expressed in terms of societal goals. The institutional and policy shortcomings in this area are striking not so much because of their lack of development but because of the deterioration that the financial sector has experienced since the occupation of the territories.

B. Money and banking

376. Following the occupation of the West Bank and Gaza Strip in 1967, the Israeli authorities immediately issued military orders closing all banks and credit institutions operating in these territories and declaring the Israeli currency as legal tender. Subsequently, however, the Jordanian dinar was also allowed to circulate in the West Bank while the Egyptian pound was declared illegal in the Gaza Strip. There is, thus, no specific currency belonging to the territories. The rapid depreciation of the Israeli currency, coupled with significant trade with Israel, has closely tied the territories to Israeli economic realities, which are characterized, _inter alia_, by high rates of inflation. Branches of Israeli banks were opened in the territories with the majority located in major Israeli settlements serving the Israeli settlers. With these developments, the role played up to 1967 by the Central Banks of Jordan and Egypt was taken over by the Bank of Israel.

377. Consequently, the inhabitants of the territories lost a system that managed monetary activities through regulating the money supply, directing credit and supervising the operations of banking and other financial institutions with a view to promoting production, employment, income and investment in the territories. There has been inadequate disclosure regarding monetary statistics in the territories to allow a thorough evaluation of the operation of the system that has emerged under occupation, especially where analysis of the behaviour of monetary aggregates and their interaction with economic activities would reflect on the policy instruments at work.

378. Branches of Israeli banks that have been opened in the territories have not succeeded in restoring the pre-1967 level of banking operations. In particular, they have not been able to play the conventional and fundamental role of intermediating between Arab depositors and borrowers for the mobilization and allocation of resources into the economy of the territories. A great portion of the resources raised by these banks from the territories is transferred to and used in Israel under balances held with banking headquarters. Moreover, apart from providing some common banking operations, the role of those banks in providing medium-term and long-term finance for the growth and development of the Palestinian economy has been minimal, if any.

379. Consequently, and following 20 years of occupation, the territories do not enjoy the services of banks and other specialized financial institutions designed to promote the growth and development of vital sectors of the economy. Businesses operating in these areas have been obliged to meet their short-term and long-term financial needs by falling back on their meagre savings and/or by resorting to the prohibitive practices of the informal financial market which is characterized by high rates of interest and difficult guarantee requirements. Even then, the amounts have remained very limited and the conditions rather exacting. External efforts made, for instance, through the Jordanian-Palestinian Joint Committee, to rectify this continued anomaly by providing medium-term and long-term finance were confronted with restrictions. As such, development finance needs of the Palestinian economy have not been met during the past 20 years of occupation.

380. The situation has been particularly serious in rural areas where the cost and conditions of finance, even for seasonal credit, are far beyond the ability of an average inhabitant. Such credit has been largely supplied by money-lenders, suppliers of agricultural inputs, marketing middlemen, and other similar sources. Rural co-operative institutions, which usually provide credit on acceptable terms, are themselves plagued by a shortage of capital and of technical and managerial cadres. This situation is ironic when compared with that of rural areas in the developing economies in general where the credit needs of the inhabitants have not only attracted the attention of local authorities on a priority basis but have also attracted the involvement of an array of organizations from the international community.

381. The role of insurance companies in finance is equally negligible, if not non-existent. The operations of local companies are generally confined to car insurance. The revenues so accumulated are largely kept as bank deposits in view of restrictions on new investment projects. Branches of Israeli insurance companies transmit premium dues to the accounts of their headquarters in Israel. As such, the potential role of the insurance business is not reflected in the economic scene.

382. Efforts to redress the situation have not met with success. The absence of an indigenous banking system, coupled with the dual, if not triple, currency standard, and the growing credit needs of the economy have prompted local informal facilities to emerge and fill the gap. The role of money-changers has been significant in this respect. The major part of their business has been exchanging Israeli and Jordanian currencies that accrue to the inhabitants of the territories. They have not been able to fill the crucial gap in financial intermediation. The recent relative stability of the Israeli currency, coupled with high real rates of interest, the continuing

decline in the international value of the United States dollar and, most importantly, the fall in the volume of remittances and transfers to the territories do not augur well for the business of money-changers. The recent move by the Israeli authorities to regulate and tax the activities of money-changers is likely to add to the problems confronting them. Renewed efforts are needed to replace the very fragile, vulnerable and ad hoc arrangements by appropriate financial institutions reflecting the dire needs of the economy in the areas outlined above.

383. Attempts to reopen local banks in the Gaza Strip resulted only in the reopening of the Bank of Palestine in 1981 which operates under the direct supervision of the Bank of Israel. The reopening coincided with the worsening of the economic situation in the Strip. However, due to numerous restrictions imposed on its operations, the bank has had only a marginal impact on the financial and credit conditions in the Strip. Unlike the branches of Israeli banks operating in the Strip, the Bank of Palestine is not allowed to deal in foreign exchange, or to open new branches covering a wider geographic area, or have a say in the approval of investment projects. These restrictions have inhibited the bank from financing foreign trade and attracting deposits in foreign currencies, from serving localities that lack banking and credit facilities, and, above all, from carrying the crucial function of financial intermediation. Coupled with the limited capital and the continued devaluation of the Israeli currency, these constraints have forced the bank to follow a conservative approach in its lending operations. A re-examination of these and other issues that have stifled the operation and role of this bank is urgently called for. This is particularly needed at this crucial juncture as the Gazan economy is experiencing the most severe recession in 20 years of occupation.

384. In the West Bank, efforts to reopen banks since their closure in 1967 were met with various conditions not in line with the laws and regulations prevailing at the time of its occupation. After numerous attempts, the branch of the Cairo-Amman Bank was finally allowed to open late in 1986, in Nablus, under certain conditions. While the reopening of the branch signals the beginning of a move in the right direction, much of the success expected from it will depend on the manner in which the branch is treated in terms of its resource base and on the nature and scope of its operations. This is important in order to prevent the repetition of the experience of the Bank of Palestine.

385. First of all, the resources of the newly opened branch need to be augmented through external contributions until it has succeeded in mobilizing adequate domestic savings. The Central Bank of Jordan may be able to serve not only as a repository of reserves but also as a promoter and the lender of last resort in order to help the branch take calculated risks. The bank could also be allowed to open its other branches elsewhere in the territories with a view to mobilizing the savings of inhabitants over a wider area and thus to carry out financial intermediation and provide credit to the urgent priority areas of the economy, especially agriculture, industry and housing. The interrelationship of its branches should increase the overall capacity of the bank for credit creation throughout the territory. It is also vital for the newly opened branch to establish links with existing formal and informal entities such as co-operatives, insurance companies, money-lenders and the large number of professional institutions in order to mobilize greater

savings. It is important for the branch to avoid developing an urban bias in its operations whether directed to financing trade or industry. The branch may be allowed to deal in foreign currencies so as to enlarge the scope of its operations and enable it to compete with the branches of Israeli banks operating in the territories.

386. The branch may also be allowed to operate with a flexible range of interest rates in order to raise real rates of interest above the level of inflation thereby influencing the choice between alternative uses of private savings. If need be, this could be accompanied, according to the laws prevailing in the territories, by other incentives, such as tax exemption on income from bank deposits or income from newly established businesses. The branch can play a pioneering role in this process. In order to further influence the possible insensitivity of the market to a single rate of interest, a system of differential rates of interest for different types of credit could be instituted to help direct resources to desired areas. A complementary tax policy could further strengthen the effectiveness of such measures. In view of the loose nature of the market, it is possible that such measures may not produce high results in the immediate future. However, this should not be construed as a sign of their ineffectiveness. In an effort to develop an entrepreneurial outlook for autonomous investments, it may be necessary to accept a longer gestation period for the effectiveness of these measures.

387. It should be noted, however, that parallel to these efforts attention may also be given to promoting financial discipline among the users of bank services. An adequate scheme could be developed for evaluating credit applications and monitoring loans in order to ensure their effectiveness and provide for the prompt repayment of principal and interest.

388. Bearing the complexity of the measures outlined above, the success of the newly opened branch would be largely dependent upon its ability to develop an adequately qualified technical and managerial cadre. Such a cadre is needed to evaluate the economic and financial viability of proposals.

389. Finally, an appropriate legal frame of reference is needed to support the efforts of the branch by providing the necessary basis for its mutual contractual obligations and these of its clients in accordance with laws and regulations of the territories. Similarly, the role of the Central Bank of Jordan with respect to the operations of the branch, including its dealings in Jordanian dinars as well as Israeli shekels and other currencies, needs to be specified.

390. Despite recent developments, the institutional arrangements to meet the medium-term and long-term financing needs of agriculture, industry, tourism and housing are still lacking. The position of small farmers, industrialists and businessmen remains precarious. Specialized financial institutions are needed to provide support to private initiative in these areas. The effort to establish an Arab finance house deserves full support as it promises the creation of the nucleus of an arrangement for long-term financing including the possibilities of attracting external bilateral and multilateral resources on concessional terms.

C. Public Finance

391. General government budgets, both of Israel and of local Palestinian authorities, serve as the fiscal determinant affecting the level of income and demand, providing basic services, influencing economic activities and promoting growth and development. It should be noted, however, that the limited size of the government budget, coupled with the lack of a growth and development-oriented policy, has rendered the role of the budget marginal with respect to these tasks.

392. Despite a breakdown of government outlays for current and development purposes, the overall level of government revenues and expenditures reflects a neutral budget approach in the territories. As such, it moves from a certain given level of revenues to determine outlays. Total expenditures in general and those for developmental purposes constituted a negligible portion of national income. The continuing inflationary pressure has further reduced the impact of these limited outlays. As a result, the territories seem to suffer from a low level of basic government services at various levels in such areas as education, health, welfare, public works, postal services and telecommunications. With respect to development outlays, the low level of contribution by the public sector to gross domestic capital formation has left various physical and human infrastructural facilities, which provide external benefits to the economy, virtually unattended. The lack of a policy favouring and encouraging private investment in productive sectors has prompted the contribution by the private sector to gross capital formation to be concentrated in housing and construction works. It is, therefore, the level of autonomous external resources that has had some impact on income and demand as well as economic activities in the territories during much of the two decades of occupation.

393. The only area where an interventionist government budgetary policy has been pursued is in taxation. Numerous military orders and proclamations, issued since 1967, have effected significant changes in the tax system. In addition to changing the structure and rates of existing taxes, the new taxes imposed have been intended not so much to stimulate economic activity as to increase government revenues and align the tax system of the territories to Israeli economic interests. In fact, it has been solely these objectives that have prevailed behind the changes rather than the resource allocation, equity, and/or stabilization objectives of public policy. Those latter objectives generally provide the overriding considerations for any changes to be effected in a tax system. These may have been considered irrelevant in the context of the territories' economy under occupation.

394. In the area of income tax, the threshold for taxable income was reduced through a reduction in the minimum level of taxable income, personal and family allowances as well as exemptions. In addition, both marginal and overall effective rates were increased throughout the schedule. As a result, a higher tax rate is now levied on amounts that generally represent less than half of taxable income under the laws that prevailed in the territories at the time of their occupation. This has put the inhabitants of the territories at a disadvantage when compared to the more liberal attitude reflected in Jordan and Israel itself despite a higher level of per capita income indicating increased ability to pay taxes. Under the present recessionary situation, there is hardly any merit in either retaining, or adding to, the distortions that affect the incentives to work, save and invest.

395. The most striking change in the income tax law pertains to the collection procedures embodied in chapter 14 of the law that prevailed in the territories at the time of occupation. Those procedures have been altogether replaced by military orders introducing measures that have affected the assessment and collection of taxes. More importantly, the court of appeal for income tax matters and the right of taxpayers to subsequent recourse to higher judicial bodies have been delegated to an "Objection Committee" with the Military Command having the final say in the matter. As such, appeals at various levels have been revoked and confined to an administrative/military committee.

396. It may be stated that the haphazard changes introduced in the income tax law, such as the abolition of its administrative procedures that have left assessment and interpretations to tax inspectors, recourse to coercive measures in tax collection, and, above all, the arbitrary way of treating tax appeals, seem to have eroded public confidence in the purpose and objectivity of the income tax system. No direct or indirect participation of the taxpayers was solicited before the introduction of changes into the income tax system. The legality of the measures aside, it was of paramount importance that those changes, if introduced within the frame of law, could have also been accompanied by detailed manual of operation for the benefit of both taxpayers and tax officers. The actual involvement of the public, through their legitimate institutions and interest groups, in all these aspects, is considered a major factor in the effectiveness of any tax system. The application of this important measure leaves much to be desired in the territories.

397. One area deserving further elaboration relates to tax assessment of artisans and traders who either are unable or unwilling to keep books. An objective and realistic approach could rely on such factors as capital, volume of business, type of trade, the normal level of profit, location and other pertinent issues. These factors can be determined in consultation with local authorities, chambers of commerce, taxpayers' professional associations and tax experts and can serve as an alternative to the direct analytical assessment based on inadequate records. Such an approach is bound to eliminate the climate of mistrust and disagreement which has strained relations between taxpayers and tax authorities.

398. It is equally necessary to consider establishing standardized systems of accounts that have adequate and clear instructions coupled with appropriate training on the methods and techniques involved. The local authorities could play an important role in organizing training programmes on various aspects of the tax system including assessment procedures, accounting techniques and methods and other aspects of tax administration. It is only through such a realistic and systematic approach that acceptable solutions may be found to the problems confronting both taxpayers and the authorities.

399. The success of all such efforts would obviously depend on a number of factors. In the first place, taxpayers need to be convinced that the tax laws applicable are those that prevailed in the territories prior to occupation and that amendments to those laws are only introduced in line with changes effected in these laws. Secondly, procedure for tax assessment and collection should be made more realistic, as noted above. Thirdly, revenues from all taxes should be clearly and adequately reported and spent on the most pressing needs of the territories. In all these matters, the taxpayer needs to be given a feeling of fairness and participation in the efforts made to improve

his living conditions, thus instilling in him the pride of contributing to that end in order to ensure the creation of a dynamic atmosphere encompassing all aspects of life in the territories, irrespecive of their present political status.

400. An important development which has affected the scope of the income tax law of the territories relates to the manner in which the income of Israeli citizens (settlers) and juridical entities, residing in the territories, is treated by the Israeli authorities for tax purposes. Under the principle of "territorial application of taxes", the income of Israelis residing in the territories should normally be subjected to the laws of the territories where such income is "derived, received or obtained".

401. According to an amendment introduced in the Israeli income tax ordinance, the income of an Israeli produced in the territories is considered as income produced, obtained or received in Israel and, thus, is subject to Israeli income tax. Meanwhile, the amendment provided the taxpayer with a credit equivalent to the amount of tax that may have already been paid to the territories which was intended to avoid double taxation - a common feature of many national tax systems. However, in practice, no taxes were paid to the territories. The share of the territories in the taxes and whatever amount was due to the Israeli authorities have both ended up in the Israeli treasury. The objective behind the amendment was to prevent the territories from becoming a tax haven for Israeli citizens and juridical entities. In fact, Israelis residing in the territories were paying virtually no taxes until the amendment was enacted in the Israeli law. No statistics are issued to ascertain the magnitude of the revenues due to the territories from this source.

402. Another area where the Israeli Government has followed an interventionist policy concerns the imports of the territories. The customs duties imposed on these imports are those applied to imports of Israel. This is supplemented by the payment of the value added tax on Israeli importers. The overall objective has been to safeguard Israeli products and to raise government revenues. Here also, no detailed statistics are made available to ascertain the relevance of these duties to the territories' economy and/or to assess the amount of revenues accruing to the Israeli budget.

403. In addition to the changes introduced in the tax system of the territories, a tax introduced in Israel in 1976, referred to as the Value Added Tax (VAT), was subsequently extended to the territories under the category of "fees and excises" covering almost all transactions. Here also, the purpose was to avoid creating a tax haven for Israelis in the territories and to raise government revenues. When the issue was appealed by the inhabitants of the territories, based on international conventions, the decision to extend the tax to the territories was upheld by the Israeli High Court of Justice.

404. The legal aspect of the tax aside, its imposition carries elements of inequity in the territories. The introduction of the tax in Israel was defended on the grounds that the price increases resulting from it would be balanced by income tax reductions so that the total tax burden would remain unchanged. In addition, in order to compensate low income families that would not benefit from reductions in direct taxes, it was envisaged to increase children's allowances, old-age pensions and social welfare services. None of

these compensatory considerations has applied to the inhabitants of the territories. On the contrary, as noted earlier, the burden of a number of taxes has increased against a relatively low and declining level of domestic income. On the whole, the VAT has evolved over the past few years to become one of the most serious fiscal constraints to the development of Palestinian industry and trade. Indeed, maintaining the tax, if legally justified, necessitates a thorough re-examination of the tax system in general and the income tax in particular.

405. Given the prevailing atmosphere surrounding the attitude of the Government towards the Palestinian economy, the tax system has been largely confined to its traditional role of providing revenues for the Government. As such, its role in resource allocation through influencing entrepreneurial decisions has been nil. None of the existing old and/or new investment-related incentives are at work in the territories, although the relevant laws are theoretically still in force. On the contrary, the amendments of existing taxes and the imposition of new taxes have served to discourage entrepreneurs. This appears in stark contrast to the range of incentives extended to Israeli settlers and their businesses in the occupied territories.

406. The Palestinian economy in its present state is in dire need of assistance and support. As in the area of monetary policy, fiscal incentives can go a long way towards providing such support for the realization of a number of the objectives outlined in the early part of this chapter. In fact, a combination of monetary and fiscal incentives based on the prevailing laws of the territories could encourage productive investments. The tax system by itself can play a significant role in this process. The benefits accruing from tax incentives would not only induce investments even in marginal areas by increasing the rate of return but would also serve to diversify businesses geographically throughout the territories despite difficulties of shortages in basic services. In view of high tax rates and limited allowances, the benefit of any tax incentive offered to both individuals and juridical Palestinian entities would be high. It may be argued that such incentives could represent a loss of the already low-level government revenues. While this may be true in the short-run, in the long-run they are believed capable of creating an atmosphere favourable to investment that would provide more "tax handles", thus broadening the tax base in the economy as a whole.

407. Efforts could concentrate on promoting the corporate business enterprises. The corporate tax rate could be lowered and applied also on the profits of limited liability companies as well as other forms of economic enterprises and/or organizations. Undistributed profits of these entitites could be taxed at a flat rate lower than the present one. Any distribution of profits could be subjected to the individual income tax at the prevailing rates. In cases where profits are distributed, an additional flat rate, which would be equal to or less than the marginal rate of income tax at its initial bracket, could be withheld and subsequently taken into account when assessing overall tax liability of the recipients of such profits. In the absence of an adequate banking system, and capital market, such a move could, at least, promote self-financing to a certain extent.

408. The shortcomings of the tax system briefly outlined could be individually examined in detail along with their possible solutions to prevailing problems. However, an ad hoc treatment of these shortcomings is not likely to

contribute to the improvement of the tax system as a whole. In fact, the
fragmented structure of the tax system is the product of such ad hoc
treatments that have been aimed primarily at raising revenues for the
Government. While the tasks of the tax system in regard to equity,
stabilization and, above all, allocation have continued to be neglected, as in
the case of the instruments of monetary policy, the lack of an overall
economic outlook is considered to have been behind the piecemeal approach in
amending the tax system.

409. It is, therefore, necessary to envision an overall reform of the tax
system as an integrated and co-ordinated set of policy measures guided by
short-term and long-term economic and social objectives in the territories.
Such an approach is more likely to bring the conceptual and structural aspects
of taxation into line with the requirements of a dynamic fiscal system aimed
at assisting the process of economic and social change and development in the
territories.

410. The assistance of the international community in the improvement of all
the areas outlined in this chapter could appropriately be solicited. In
addition to finding solutions to the anomalies mentioned, such assistance is
crucial for establishing and developing indigenous institutions with
appropriate technical and managerial capabilities. The accumulated experience
of the United Nations in these and other related areas could be called upon.

D.   External resources

411. The pressing inadequacy of the domestic sources of finance, both public
and private, has forced the inhabitants of the territories to rely
increasingly on external financial support for their subsistence and
accumulation of capital. As with the increasing remittances of workers in
Israel, the interaction which has developed between the territories and the
Arab countries has enabled the territories to counter the range of
restrictions imposed on the local economy and to meet the challenges posed by
the increasing links with the Israeli economy. However, any possible positive
aspect of such external flows into the territories must be seriously examined
in terms of the capacity that those flows create within the local economy to
generate, over time, the impetus for sustained growth and development. The
absence of a regulatory body has rendered this issue more critical as the
volume and orientation of these flows remain beyond the control of the
territories.

412. Two distinct but interrelated sources of external finance have emerged
for the territories, namely factor income and unrequited transfers from
abroad. Factor income largely comprises the earnings of Palestinian residents
of the territories working in Israel and Arab countries because of the lack of
local employment opportunities. By the early 1980s, the size of the
Palestinian migrant labour force in Israel alone had reached almost two fifths
of total Palestinian labour force in the territories. According to Israeli
statistics, factor income from labour in Israel has amounted to almost
four fifths of total factor income payments to the territories. The
contribution of total factor income to GNP has steadily increased since
occupation as more Palestinian labour has been displaced and consequently
absorbed outside the territories. At one point, this contribution amounted to
almost half of gross domestic output - a very high ratio indeed. In absolute
terms, it has lately followed a declining trend.

413. The lack of appropriate policies and measures has caused much of the income from this significant source to be absorbed in high-level consumption, which has led to an increasing deficit in the balance of trade of the territories. The contribution of factor income to investment has been in housing and construction works, with agriculture and industry continuing to suffer from shortage of financial resources for short-term as well as long-term purposes. The increasing reliance on factor income from one source (that is, labour in Israel) has further added to the vulnerability of the territories' fragile economy. Its contribution to the creation of a sound basis for the sustained growth and development of the Palestinian economy has been virtually nil.

414. The lack of indigenous financial institutions has been a further limiting factor in the amount of factor income deployed through formal channels and into productive investments. The various incentive schemes (such as, higher interest rates on foreign exchange deposits, premium exchange rates and/or productive investments) that labour-exporting countries have devised in order to attract more remittances from their labourers abroad, have been absent in the territories. While for the majority of Palestinian workers abroad, factor income may just be sufficient to sustain their subsistence, for many other families it has been a supplementary source of income. However, in view of limitations, a portion of such income never enters the territories. Not only have incentives for productive investments been lacking for this category of income earners, but restrictions have been imposed on the actual size of funds permitted entry to the territories. These restrictions have only recently been relaxed - at a time when the level of economic activity, especially in the labour-importing Arab oil-producing countries, is at its lowest.

415. The entire issue of exporting labour and its resultant income is in need of serious consideration in view of the deteriorating economic situation in the territories. Some of the incentive schemes designed along the guidelines indicated above for the revival of the Palestinian economy can serve as a useful frame of reference for efforts aimed at enhancing the contribution of this source of income to economic growth and development.

416. The second major external source of finance, that is, private and official transfers, has also become increasingly important in recent years. It has, in fact, reduced the total reliance on the factor income of Palestinian workers in Israel. Combined with factor income it gives the overall scale of external financial flows an even greater significance. Such transfers include flows from Israeli Government institutions, Palestinians who emigrated from the territories since 1967 and official aid from Arab and non-Arab sources.

417. While the level of transfers from Israel has increased, that of the territories to Israel has increased at a faster rate, thus indicating a negative net transfer from the territories vis-à-vis Israel. This situation supports the claim that the territories are in effect paying an "occupation tax". The occupation authorities thus obtain more resources from the territories in the form of taxes and other payments than they transfer to it. The present deteriorating state of the territories' economy can hardly support such a development.

418. As with factor income to residents of the territories working in Israel and elsewhere, the remittances of Palestinian migrants who maintain family ties with the territories constitute another significant element in the total of external resources. According to non-Israeli statistics, this source of income has provided the territories with a sizeable amount annually since 1980. This indicates an even greater degree of involvement of migrants' remittances in the local economy than reported by Israeli statistics and consequently a greater degree of reliance on non-domestic sources of finance.

419. Other Arab and non-Arab international support has increasingly served as a substantial source of finance to the territories, reflecting a continued expression of humanitarian assistance and of political will and commitment of the international community. However, given the present status of the territories, the magnitude of and areas for deployment of such resources are likely to be influenced by a wide range of factors that lie beyond the control of the territories.

420. As for Arab sources of finance, the assistance of the Jordanian Government has continued to flow to the territories since 1967 in the form of wages and salaries of Palestinian civil servants, rent paid on government premises, subsidies to municipalities, guarantees on bank loans to local Palestinian institutions, direct grants, and provision of education, health and other services. This is complemented by assistance from Jordanian semi-official charitable institutions. Other Arab and Islamic sources include transfers from the Jerusalem Fund, Arab Fund for Economic and Social Development, and the Jordanian-Palestinian Joint Committee. The Committee, which was created in 1978, serves as an institutional arrangement to channel Arab aid for the "steadfastness" of the Palestinians in the territories.

421. The Joint Committee was able to channel significant amounts of Arab funds into various socio-economic sectors of the territories and to manage those funds. The share of the Committee in total Arab funding in the territories had reached four fifths. However, aid from this source began to decline in recent years owing primarily to unfulfilled commitments of donors. Nevertheless, the magnitude and breadth of its operations, coupled with the active role played by local Palestinian institutions in development projects, illustrate the capacity of the Palestinian people to direct and manage resources in different social and economic activities. Much of the resources channelled have gone into education followed by health services, municipalities, welfare, housing, agriculture, small industries and artisans. Through its vast experience and relations with a large number of institutions, both in and outside the territories, the Committee has, in effect, served as a development agency and has increasingly provided a forum for stimulating an integrated approach to dealing with economic and social issues confronting the territories.

422. Despite these successes, however, the work of the Committee has suffered from a number of difficulties. These include the constraints imposed by the occupation authorities on the entry of funds into the territories, staffing and managerial inadequacies, problems related to project formulation, a total freeze in Arab contributions, implementation and evaluation of loans including field supervision, and others. These shortcomings deserve serious examination at this critical time and especially as resources have again begun to be made available to it for investment in the territories. Both within the framework

of the Joint Committee and local Palestinian institutions, there exists a great potential for further development of the indigenous capacity to formulate, evaluate, programme and co-ordinate present and future international aid efforts to the territories.

423. Non-Arab international sources of finance comprise mainly those of the United Nations system and international private voluntary organizations that also disburse much of the official aid from the United States of America and European countries to the territories; recently the European Economic Community has also emerged as a separate source, however small. The bulk of assistance under these sources has continued to be provided by the United Nations Relief and Work Agency for Palestinian Refugees in the Near East (UNRWA) in such social welfare and development areas as education, health, shelter, sanitation and other basic welfare services to refugees throughout the territories. The contribution of UNRWA is increasingly being supplemented by contributions from other United Nations organizations, including the special programme of the United Nations Development Programme (UNDP), which has been concentrated on education and infrastructural activities, and those of other agencies in various areas within the context of a United Nations programme of economic and social assistance to the Palestinian people as called for by the General Assembly. Private voluntary organizations have also stepped up their assistance in various areas through a large number of projects ranging from humanitarian to welfare and some developmental activities benefiting agriculture.

424. It should be noted, however, that irrespective of the source, the approval of the number and nature of proposals for funding has often reflected considerations not in line with the apparent ranking of priority needs of the territories. Therefore, while locally perceived and expressed priorities have an initial effect in determining the pattern of deployment of external aid in the territories, the final outcome has been altered by various other factors. These include donors' preferences, operational and technical considerations, and the policies of the occupation authorities towards the nature and direction of external aid.

425. On the whole, external aid has largely consisted of grants, primarily because of the lack of institutional finance facilities to assist in making local counterpart funds available whether at the public or private sector level. The loan component of projects was originally witnessed in the territories in funding by the Joint Committee. Only recently have direct or revolving fund arrangements also been considered a suitable tool for the delivery of external aid through private voluntary organizations. However, the amount of resources that could be allocated for the revolving fund arrangements has been rather limited.

426. An increase in the use of external aid is dependent not only on the relaxation of procedures for the approval of projects but also on the creation and development of local financial institutions capable of providing local counterpart funds. Along with greater involvement of local financial institutions in the channelling and management of factor income and remittance flows and a strengthening of the local Palestinian capacity to influence the deployment of aid to the territories, increased local participation in financing development efforts can assist in providing a more effective utilization of external financial resources.

Notes

1/ 1 dunum = 1,000 m^2 = 0.25 acre approx.

2/ "Living conditions of the Palestinian people in the occupied Arab territories - Report of the Secretary-General" (A/35/533), 1980, para 29. Other sources put the total land area of the occupied territories at around 6,124,000 dunums, with 5,755,000 dunums in the West Bank and 369,000 dunums in the Gaza Strip. See P.G. Sadler and B. Abu Kishk, "Palestine: options for development" (TD/B/960), p. 15.

3/ "Living conditions of the Palestinian people in the occupied territories - Report of the Secretary-General" (A/39/233), 1984, appendix II, p. 63.

4/ "Living conditions of the Palestinian people in the occupied territories" (A/40/373), 1985, p. 3. See also Meron Benvenisti, West Bank Data Base Project, A Survey of Israeli Policies, (Washington and London, American Enterprise Institute for Public Policy Research, 1984), p. 19.

5/ Over 90 per cent of the land seized is privately-owned. Land classified as 'State Domain' had not been finally approved by the Jordanian authorities at the time of the outbreak of the 1967 war. According to the usual legal procedures in Jordan, individual land owners are given a period of time, after preliminary registration, to prove entitlements. This procedure was interrupted by the 1967 war and Israel ignored its application. See "Continued exploitation in spite of the world (Israeli colonization in the West Bank)", (Amman, mimeograph, 1980), p. 6. Also see Joan Mandell, "Gaza: Israel's Soweto", in Middle East Research and Information Project, No. 136/137, October-December 1985, p. 11.

6/ Dudley Madawela, "Living conditions of the Palestinian people in the occupied Palestinian territories", a background paper for a United Nations seminar of the same title, Vienna, 25-29 March 1985, p. 10.

7/ For details, see Meron Benvenisti, 1986 Report: Demographic, economic, legal, social and cultural developments in The West Bank, (Jerusalem, West Bank Data Base Project, 1986), pp. 6 and 31-32.

8/ Some sources put the proportion of refugees at 80 per cent of the total population of the Strip. See F. Bseiso, "Basis for planning the support policy of national steadfastness in the occupied territories", Shoun Arabiya, (in Arabic), No. 48, December 1986, p. 124.

9/ Calculated from Israel, Central Bureau of Statistics, Statistical Abstract of Israel 1986 (Jerusalem, CBS, 1986), p. 45.

10/ See Kosseifi's figures.

11/ Israeli data for migration since September 1967 is presented in table 2. The discrepancy between the two sets of figures arises from the fact that, unlike the calculated figures, official data does not include the population growth of migrants once they have left the territories. Also see S. Gabriel and E. Sabatello, "Palestinian migration from the West Bank and Gaza: economic and demographic analysis", in Economic Development and Cultural Change, vol. 34, No. 2, January 1986, p. 249-252.

12/   Based on an assumed 20 per cent rate for labour force participation, which is conservative in so far as that is the rate characterizing the labour force of the territories and it is well below that of other Palestinian communities (see ECWA, "Final report on the economic and social situation and potential of the Palestinian Arab people in the region of Western Asia" (E/ECWA/166/Add.1), 3 May 1983, p. 79). Also see I. Zaghloul, Transfers of Jordanians and Their Effect on the Jordanian Economy (Amman, Central Bank of Jordan, 1984), p. 11, (in Arabic).

13/   United Nations, Social, economic and political institutions in the West Bank and the Gaza Strip (New York, United Nations, 1982), p. 17.

14/   United Nations, The Legal Status of the West Bank and Gaza (New York, United Nations, 1982), pp.25-38.

15/   See Israel Defence Forces, Proclamations, Orders and Notices, vol. 1, Proclamation No. 2, (Jerusalem, IDF, 1968).

16/   Israel, Ministry of Defense, Co-ordinator of Government Operations, Judea, Samaria, Gaza District, Sinai and Golan Heights - A Twelve Year Survey, 1967-1979, October 1979, p.2.

17/   Also see Meron Benvenisti with Ziad Abu-Zayed and Danny Rubinstein, The West Bank Handbook: A political lexicon (Jerusalem, Jerusalem Post, 1986), p. 77.

18/   "Living conditions..." (A/39/233), p. 47.

19/   Royal Scientific Society, Financial and Banking Conditions in Occupied West Bank and Gaza Strip (in Arabic) (Amman, RSS, 1985), pp. 5-6.

20/   United Nations, The Legal Status ..., p. 32.

21/   M. Benvenisti et al, The West Bank Handbook ..., pp.23-25.

22/   M. Benvenisti, 1986 Report ..., pp. 39-40; and M. Benvenisti et al, The West Bank Handbook ..., pp. 23-25.

23/   For a concise coverage of Israeli measures aimed at altering the judicial system of the occupied territories, see United Nations, The Legal Status ..., pp. 38-47. Also see P.G. Sadler, N. Kazi and H. Jabre, Survey of the Manufacturing Industry in the West Bank and Gaza Strip (Vienna, UNIDO, 1984), pp. 48-61 and Raja Shehadeh, The West Bank and the Rule of Law, (Geneva, International Commission of Jurists, 1980), pp. 13-45.

24/   Albert Waterson, Development Planning: Lessons of Experience (Baltimore, Maryland, John Hopkins Press, 1965), pp. 249-292.

25/   For a further examination of the objective and impact of these decisions on the economy of the occupied territories, see Economic and Social Commission for Western Asia, The Economic and Social Situation and Potential of the Palestinian Arab People in the Region of Western Asia (summary), (New York, United Nations, 1985), pp. 31-34.

26/   Ibid. p. 34.

27/   Susan Hattis Rolf, "The territories: an economic question", Jerusalem Post, 27 February 1986, p. 10.

28/   See chapter IV below, and UNCTAD, "Selected statistical tables on the economy of the occupied Palestinian territories" (UNCTAD/ST/SEU/1), 10 July 1986, tables 2 and 3.

29/   For further details, see UNCTAD, "Recent economic developments in the occupied Palestinian territories" (TD/B/1102), pp. 5-6.

30/   See World Bank, World Development Report 1985 (New York, Oxford University Press, 1985), p. 151.

31/   For more information on this point, reference is made to Savings for Development. Report of the international Symposium on the Mobilization of Personal Savings in Developing Countries, Kingston, Jamaica, 4-9 February 1980, (United Nations publication, Sales No. E.81.II.A.6).

32/   World Bank, World Development Report 1985.

33/   Shlomo Frankel, "Israel's Economic Crisis", Merip Reports, October-December 1985, p. 21. See also George Abed, "Israel in the orbit of America: The political economy of a dependency relationship", in Journal of Palestine Studies, No. 61, Autumn 1986, p. 49.

34/   "Living conditions of the Palestinian people in the occupied territories - Report of the Secretary-General" (A/40/373), 1985, p. 7.

35/   Benvenisti et al., The West Bank Handbook..., p. 3.

36/   Sara Roy (West Bank Data Base Project), The Gaza Strip Survey (Cambridge, Harvard University Press, 1986), p. 139.

37/   For more details on the contribution of the Israeli authorities to the industrial sector of the occupied territories, reference is made to Hillel Frisch, Stagnation and Frontier Arab and Jewish Industry in the West Bank (Jerusalem, West Bank Data Base Project, 1983).

38/   It was stated by Mr. Y. Rabin, Israeli Minister of Defence, that "there will be no development (in the Occupied Territories) initiated by the Israeli government, and no permits will be given for expanding agriculture or industry (there), which may compete with the State of Israel", in The Economist, "A light unto (some) nations", Development Report, January 1986, p.3.

39/   See Abdel Razek Hassan, The Position of Palestinian Industry in the Occupied regions since 1967; The West Bank and Gaza Strip, 1985, pp. 7-8, and Ziad Abu-Amr, "The Gaza economy since 1948", in G. Abed (ed.) Economic Development Under Prolonged Occupation (forthcoming).

40/   See World Bank, World Development Report, 1985, pp. 178-179. See also ESCWA, National Accounts Studies, Bulletin No. 7, 1985.

41/   World Bank, <u>Industrial Strategy for Late Starters: The experience of Kenya, Tanzania and Zambia</u>, IBRD, Staff Working Papers, No. 457, p.3.

42/   See P.G. Sadler <u>et al</u>, <u>Survey of the Manufacturing Industry ...</u>, pp. 22-23.

43/   By comparison, the total number of establishments in 1965 had reached 3,716 units employing a total of 17,101 persons. See ECWA, "The industrial and economic trends in the West Bank and Gaza Strip" (E/ECWA/UNIDO/WP.1), 1981, p. 8.

44/   See M. Benvenisti, <u>A Survey of Israeli Policies</u>, pp. 15-18.

45/   "Living conditions ..." (A/39/233), p. 27.

46/   <u>Ibid</u>, pp. 17-18.

47/   Al-Fajr, 9 January 1987. Also see M. Benvenisti, <u>A Survey of Israeli Policies</u>.

48/   M. Benvenisti, <u>1986 Report</u>.

49/   For more information on this issue reference may be made to Abdul-Ilah Abu Ayyash, "Israel regional planning policy in the occupied territories", in <u>Journal of Palestine Studies</u>, 1976, vol. V, Nos. 3 and 4, pp. 83-106. See also Antoine Mansour, <u>Palestine: une économie de résistance en Cisjordanie et à Gaza</u> (Paris, L'Harmattan, 1983), pp. 90-96, and Sara Roy, <u>The Gaza Strip Survey</u>, pp. 58-59.

50/   <u>Jerusalem Post</u>, 6 May 1986.

51/   For example, two Gaza Strip exporters had their export licenses revoked and were to be fined for having 'illegally' diverted 150,000 crates of citrus fruit from an intended East European market to West European markets (<u>Haaretz</u>, 15 January 1986).

52/   See <u>Jerusalem Post</u>, 6 May 1986.

53/   M. Benvenisti, <u>1986 Report</u>, p. 7.

54/   This figure fluctuated between 60 per cent and 74 per cent from 1978 to 1985.

55/   However, it should be noted that industry is not a major contributor to GDP and that most industrial exports are part of a production process directly linked to the Israeli industrial sector. See UNCTAD, "Recent economic developments...", para. 22.

56/   Since the mid-1970s, the territories have served as a market second only to the United States for Israeli goods. Excluding Israeli exports of diamonds to the United States, the territories are the largest single market for Israeli exports. See F. Gharaibeh, <u>The Economies of the West Bank and Gaza Strip</u> (Boulder Co., Westview Press, 1985), p. 110.

57/   Strictly speaking, Palestinians working in Israel are not 'migrants' in that they reside in the territories and work in Israel - labour mobility is a more accurate description of the process.

58/   See discussion above on population.

59/   Palestinian sources quote higher levels of unemployment than those officially reported; see International Labour Conference, Report of the Director General on the Situation of Workers in the Occupied Arab Territories, 72nd Session (Geneva, ILO, 1986), pp. 20-21.

60/   See, for example, Jerusalem Post, 19 January 1986. Along with other foreign workers in Arab oil-producing countries, Palestinians have been among the first victims of expenditure and employment cutbacks. This is also indicated in official Israeli data, which report a fall in the territories' residents working abroad from almost 19,000 in 1984 to 16,000 in 1985.

61/   There has been a growing proportion of higher educated graduates among the territories' unemployed labour force. See, for example, Arab Graduates' Club, Unemployed Graduates in the West Bank and Gaza Strip, a Statistical Bulletin (Jerusalem, 1985) (in Arabic).

62/   This fall reflected the operation of a number of factors: attempts at competing in the local market with Israeli agriculture and freeing surplus labour; the attraction of higher wages from employment in Israel; pressure on cultivated area posed by Israeli settlement policy.

63/   For an analysis of recent data related to the characteristics of Palestinian migrant labour, see UNCTAD, "Recent economic developments ...", paras. 28-29.

64/   Israel CBS, Statistical Abstract of Israel 1986, p. 696.

65/   Jordanian-Palestinian Joint Committee, "Report on the housing project in support of national steadfastness in the occupied territories", (in Arabic), 1986, p. 4.

66/   Bakir Abu Kishk, "The contribution of the housing sector to the economy of the occupied territories", paper presented to the United Nations (HABITAT) Seminar on the living conditions of the Palestinian people in the occupied territories, March 1985, p. 10. Also, see: (i) Edward Balassanian, "Policy recommendations to alleviate the housing problem in the occupied Palestinian territories", paper presented to same Seminar, pp. 14-15; and (ii) "Living conditions..." (A/40/373), p. 19.

67/   "Living conditions..." (A/39/233) p. 20.

68/   F. Gharaibeh, The Economies..., p. 97.

69/   A. Rabinovich, "Arab villages engage in pre-emptive activity", Jerusalem Post, 12 December 1986.

70/   "Living conditions..." (A/39/233), p. 21.

71/   Jordanian-Palestinian Joint Committee, "Report on the housing project ...", p. 13. See chapters II and IV for further details on the operations of the Joint Committee.

72/   Balassanian, p. 2.

73/   See: (i) P.G. Sadler and B. Abu Kishk, Palestine: options..., pp. 41-42; and (ii) Bakir Abu Kishk, "The contribution of the housing sector...", p. 16.

74/   See Allan Gerson, Israel, the West Bank and International Law (London, Frank Cass, 1978), p. 116; and United Nations, The legal status..., pp. 17-20.

75/   M. Benvenisti et al, The West Bank Handbook..., pp. 113-121.

76/   United States, Department of State, Country Reports on Human Rights Practices for 1985 (Wash. D.C., GPO, 1986), p. 1276; see also M. Benvenisti, A survey of Israeli Policies, p. 61.

77/   The Chairman of the Israeli Settlements' Council in the West Bank puts the total number of Israeli settlers in the West Bank alone at 60,000. See News From Within, No. 8, 15 November 1985.

78/   Sara Roy, The Gaza Strip Survey, pp. 134-135.

79/   M. Benvenisti, 1986 Report..., pp. 29 and 34.

80/   B. Ashhab, Al-Fajr, 24 October 1986. See also Jerusalem Post, 1 March 1986.

81/   M. Benvenisti, 1986 Report..., p. 49.

82/   Al-Fajr, 27 June 1986.

83/   For more information on Israeli settlement policy, see M. Benvenisti, A survey of Israel's policies, pp. 49-69.

84/   Ha'aretz, 16 January 1986, and, Jerusalem Post, 3 December 1986.

85/   M. Benvenisti, 1986 Report..., p. 51.

86/   For further information, see Ibid. pp. 52-62, and Sara Roy, The Gaza Strip Survey, pp. 135-150.

87/   New Outlook, January/February 1986, pp. 35-37.

88/   M. Benvenisti, 1986 Report..., pp. 16, 51.

89/   See R.D. Ottensooser "The Palestine pound and Israel pound - transition from a colonial to an independent currency" (Thèse No. 101, Université de Genève, 1955, pp. 13-17).

90/   Ibid., p. 31.

91/   Ibid., p. 41.

92/   Ibid., p. 58. Also see: S.B. Himadeh, Economic Organization of Palestine (Beirut, American University of Beirut, 1938), chapter IX; and R. Nathan et al., Palestine: problem and promise (N.Y., Public Affairs Press, 1946), chapter 19.

93/   Comprising Transjordan and those parts of Palestine which it held under the terms of the Armistice Agreement with Israel of 3 April 1949; ibid., p. 114.

94/   In actual fact, only notes ceased to be legal tender in Jordan after 1950, whereas the legal tender of Palestine coins was extended due to a shortage of the new Jordanian coins.

95/   See Financial Structure of Jordan, (Amman, The Central Bank of Jordan, 1986), p. 5.

96/   For more information, see Central Bank of Jordan, The Law of the Central Bank of Jordan, Amman, Law No. 23, 1971 and provisional Law No. 4, 1975.

97/   Appointed by the Governor of the Bank of Israel. See Bank of Israel, Israel's Banking Legislation, (Jerusalem, Bank of Israel, 1982) p. 53.

98/   See Israel Defence Forces, Notices, Orders and Appointments, Judea and Samaria and Gaza District Areas, Military Orders Nos. 194, 471 and 705, and subsequent regulations further elaborating on the scope and implementation of these orders.

99/   Harris, Lawrence, "Money and finance in the West Bank and Gaza", (mimeographed report, Open University, November 1985, pp. 8-12.

100/   F. Gharaibeh, The Economies..., pp. 124-125.

101/   Israel Defence Forces, Notices, Orders..., Orders Nos. 7, 18, 26 and 30 (1967), and No. 705 (1981). Military Order No. 7 excluded the Ottoman Bank. Military Order No. 706 (1981) subsequently removed the Bank of Palestine from the list of closed banks. See section 3(b) below for more details.

102/   Ibid., Military Orders Nos. 26, 33, 45 and 74 (1967) and 445 (1971).

103/   Ibid., Military Orders Nos. 9 and 21 (1967), 445 (1971), 487 (1972), 640 (1980), 671 (1980), 719 (1981), 767 and 1024 (1982).

104/   F. Gharaibeh, The Economies..., p. 125.

105/   Brian Van Arkadie, Benefits and Burdens: A report on the West Bank and Gaza Strip Economies since 1967, (New York, Carnegie Endowment for International Peace, 1977).

106/   Ibid., p. 104.

107/   Israel Defence Forces, <u>Notices, Orders...</u>, Military Orders Nos. 13, 34, 41, 76, 83 and 89 (1967), 155 and 179 (1968), 721 (1977), and 823 (1980).

108/   See instructions of 4 August 1981 relating to Military Order No. 258 (1969).

109/   F. Gharaibeh, <u>The Economies...</u>, p. 123.

110/   Israel Defence Forces, <u>Notices, Orders...</u>, Military Order No. 258 (1967) and its subsequent amendment, 163 (1968), 719 (1981) and 1070 (1983). See also Bank of Israel, <u>Foreign Exchange Control, Explanatory Guide</u>, (Jerusalem, Bank of Israel, 1981), chapter III, pp. 19-21 and chapter IV, section (b).

111/   Israel Defence Forces, <u>Notices, Orders...</u>, Military Order Nos. 299 (1969), 750 (1982) and 805 (1983).

112/   <u>Ibid.</u>, see also, Civil Administration, Judea and Samaria, <u>Annual Report, 19th year of Administration, 1985</u> (Jerusalem, Civil Administration, 1986), p. 2.

113/   L. Harris, "Money and finance...", chapter 3, p. 4. The text of the relevant military orders can be found in Israel Defence Forces, <u>Notices, Orders...</u>, Military Orders 751 (1982) for the Gaza Strip and 974 (1982) for the West Bank.

114/   Israel Defence Forces, <u>Notices, Orders...</u>, Military Order Nos. 543 and 680 (1976).

115/   For further details on foreign exchange dealings in the Gaza Strip, see amendments of 4 November 1981 to Military Order No. 719 (1981).

116/   Bank of Israel, <u>Israel's Banking Legislation</u>, chapter IV, section 2 (a), p, 23.

117/   Dan Zakai, <u>Economic Development in Judea, Samaria and the Gaza District, 1983-1984</u>, (Jerusalem, Bank of Israel, 1986), p. 72.

118/   Antoine Mansour "Monetary situation: constraints and proposals for possible remedies", a paper submitted to the Habitat Seminar on the Living Conditions of the Palestinian People in the Occupied Palestinian Territories, Vienna, 25-29 March 1985.

119/   L. Harris, "Money and finance...", p. 16.

120/   Yusef A. Sayigh, "The Palestinian Economy under Occupation", <u>Journal of Palestine Studies</u>, vol. XV, No. 4, Summer 1986, pp. 50-51.

121/   Arie Bregman, <u>Economic Growth in the Administered Areas, 1968-1973</u> (Jerusalem, Bank of Israel, 1974), p. 95.

122/   Antoine Mansour, "Monetary dualism in the West Bank", Journal of
Palestine Studies, vol. XI, No. 3, Spring 1982, p. 105. For details on
maintaining savings in stable currencies see C.L. Ramirez-Rojas, "Monetary
substitution in developing countries", Finance and development, June 1986,
vol. 23, No. 2, pp. 35-38.

123/   F. Gharaibeh, The Economies..., p. 124.

124/   A. Mansour, "Monetary situation...", p. 6.

125/   "Living conditions... (A/39/233), p. 37.

126/   B. Van Arkadie, Benefits and Burdens..., p. 104.

127/   Jerusalem Post, 5, 14, and 19 May 1981.

128/   L. Harris, "Money and finance...", p. 16.

129/   Ibid., pp. 16-17.

130/   Ibid., p. 16.

131/   F. Gharaibeh, The Economies..., p. 126

132/   Royal Scientific Society, Financial and banking conditions...,
pp. 96-99. It should be noted that as of 1979, the Jordanian-Palestinian Joint
Committee took over much of the task of assisting the municipalities. See
chapter IV for further details on the operations of the Joint Committee.

133/   Ibid., pp. 97 and 99.

134/   L. Harris, "Money and finance...", pp. 27-29.

135/   Ibid.

136/   Z. Abu-Amr, "The Gaza economy...", p. 37.

137/   Jalal Dawoud, "The Bank of Palestine in Gaza Strip", in Samed,
No. 18, 1981, pp. 3-20 (in Arabic).

138/   Israel Defence Forces, Notices, Orders..., Military Order No. 706
of 1981.

139/   Jerusalem Post, 5 June 1986.

140/   Al-Fajr, 6 June 1986, p. 3.

141/   Al-Fajr, 6 June 1986.

142/   L. Harris, "Money and finance...", pp. 22-23.

143/   Musa Arafeh et al., The Cooperative Movement in Jordan (Amman,
Jordan Co-operative Organization, 1977), p. 5.

144/   Information obtained from senior ACC staff.

145/   M. Arafeh et al., The Cooperative..., p. 5.

146/   L. Harris, "Money and finance...", p. 24.

147/   Ibid., chapter 3, pp. 2-13.

148/   The Economist, Quarterly Economic Review, Syria, Jordan,
4th Quarter 1980, p. 20.

149/   The Economist, Quartely Economic Review, Jordan, No. 1, 1986, p. 14.

150/   Jerusalem Post, 16 May 1986.

151/   L. Harris, "Money and finance...", chapter 3, p. 13.

152/   Jerusalem Post, 19 September 1986. In fact, the Value Added Tax
(VAT) Department of the Military Authorities recently issued regulations
requiring Palestinian money changers to submit to the Department daily
accounts of their transactions, with the names and ID card numbers of their
customers. The purpose is to make money changers keep accurate accounts in
order to make Arab businessmen pay their VAT in full, a tax imposed in the
territories in the mid-1970s at a rate of 17 per cent (Al Fajr,
14 November 1986, p. 14).

153/   Jerusalem Post, 19 September 1986.

154/   Jerusalem Post International Edition, 27 September 1986, p. 5.

155/   Al-Fajr, 10 October 1986, p. 9.

156/   Jerusalem Post (Supplement), 10 November 1986, p. 4.

157/   V.V. Bhatt, "Improving the financial structure in developing
countries", in Finance and Development, June 1986, pp. 20-22.

158/   The Economist, "A light unto some...", pp. 1-4.

159/   This is in line with the provisions of the Basle Concordat of 1983
as an international agreement on the supervision of international banks'
foreign establishments. For further information, see L. Harris, "Money and
finance...", chapter 5, pp. 11-124.

160/   S.B. Himadeh, Economic Organisation..., p. 507.

161/   Ibid, pp. 509-510.

162/   Ibid, p. 511.

163/   France, Ministry of Economic Affairs, National Institute of Economic
Statistics and Studies, Memento Economique, La Palestine, Série M2 (Paris,
Presses Universitaires de France, 1948), p. 146.

164/   S.B. Himadeh, Economic Organization ..., p. 552.

165/   Ibid, p. 544.

166/   R.D. Ottensooser, The Palestine Pound ..., p. 70.

167/   Namely the revenues raised privately by the Jewish Agency and other Zionist bodies for activities in the Jewish Sector of Palestine, France, Ministry of Economic Affairs, National Institute of Economic Statistics, op.cit., pp. 146-150.

168/   World Bank, World Development Report 1985, pp. 224-225.

169/   For further details on the conceptual aspect of this issue, see Richard Musgrave, Fiscal Systems (New Haven and London, Yale University Press, 1969), pp. 69-87 and 207-216.

170/   International Labour Conference, Report of the Director-General, Annexes, Report on the Situation of Workers in the Occupied Arab Territories, (Geneva, ILO, 1984), paragraph 27.

171/   Al-Fajr, 11 April 1986, pp. 1 and 13. For further details on the health situation and related services in the West Bank, see "West Bank health researched", in TANMIYA (Development), (Welfare Association), vol. 2, Issue 1, March 1987, p. 7.

172/   For further details, see South, October 1986, p. 127.

173/   See also "Population, employment and public funding on the West Bank, 1985", New Outlook, January/February 1986, pp. 35-37.

174/   Henry Selz, "Poverty is not the issue", Merip Reports, October-December 1985, p. 24.

175/   See World Bank, World Development Report 1985, pp. 226-227.

176/   M. Benvenisti, 1986 Report ..., p. 19. See also S. Roy, The Gaza Strip Survey, p. 76.

177/   Daniel Elazar, Judea, Samaria and Gaza : views on the present and future (Washington, D.C., American Enterprise Institute, 1982), pp. 107-109.

178/   For a more detailed discussion of municipal receipts and outlays, reference is made to, Royal Scientific Society, Financial and Banking Conditions..., pp. 5-52.

179/   The Hashemite Kingdom of Jordan, Income Tax Law, No. 25, 1964, articles 5 and 87.

180/   Ibid, articles 9-15.

181/   Ibid, article 24.

182/   Nidal R. Sabri, "The effects of taxes imposed on the population of the occupied Palestinian territories", a paper presented at the United Nations (HABITAT) Seminar on the living conditions of the Palestinian people in the occupied Palestinian territories, Vienna, March 1985, p. 4.

183/   Exemption under Palestinian individual income tax for a married couple in 1943 was 300 Palestine pounds, see R. Nathan et al, Palestine..., p. 612.

184/   Al-Fajr, 6 June 1986.

185/   The Hashemite Kingdom of Jordan, Ministry of Occupied Territories Affairs, Occupied Territories Affairs, May 1986 (Arabic), pp. 48-54.

186/   Ibid, p. 51.

187/   P.G. Sadler et al., Survey of the manufacturing industry..., pp. 38-40.

188/   Hashemite Kingdom of Jordan, Occupied Territories Affairs, p. 52.

189/   D. Elazar, Judea, Samaria and Gaza..., pp. 75-76.

190/   Ibid. p. 76.

191/   Ibid.

192/   Jerusalem Post, 12 May and 20 November 1986.

193/   Jerusalem Post, 20 November 1986.

194/   P.G. Sadler et al., Survey of the manufacturing industry..., p. 39.

195/   Ibid, p. 40.

196/   United Nations, The legal status..., p. 42.

197/   R. Locke and A. Stewart, Bantustan Gaza (London, Zed press, 1985), pp. 10-17.

198/   Al-Fajr, 27 June 1986.

199/   D. Elazar, Judea, Samaria and Gaza..., pp. 76-77.

200/   Bank of Israel, Economic Review, 56, April 1985, p. 77. See also Economist, Quarterly Economic Review, 1982, 2nd Quarter, p. 17.

201/   N. Sabri, "The effects of taxes...", pp. 9-10.

202/   David Horowitz et al., Economy of Israel (New York, Keter Publishing House, 1973), pp. 129-131.

203/ For a detailed coverage of tax penalties imposed on the inhabitants of the territories, see (i) "Report of the Special Committee to Investigate Israeli Practices Affecting the Human Rights of the Population of the Occupied Territories - note by the Secretary-General" (A/40/702), 1986, pp. 60-62; (ii) "Selected chronology of economic issues and related activities in the occupied Palestinian territories (West Bank and Gaza Strip) 1985-1986" (UNCTAD/ST/SEU/2), 1 July 1986, p. 76.

204/ Recent approaches also advocate that the Government should run a budgetary surplus, which would allow the Government to alleviate some of the shortcomings of the capital market by making resources available to the private sector for investment in desirable areas and at the same time embark on infrastructural projects aimed at increasing the perceived rate of return on private investment. See Maris I. Blejer and Adrienne Cheasty, "Using fiscal measures to stimulate savings in developing countries", Finance and Development, June 1986, vol. 23, No. 2, pp. 16-19.

205/ Jerusalem Post, 1 November 1986.

206/ Calculated from Israel, Central Bureau of Statistics, Statistical Abstract of Israel 1985 (Jerusalem, CBS, 1985), p. 725.

207/ Ibid.

208/ See for example, S. Gabriel and E. Sabatello, "Palestinian migration...", p. 249.

209/ For a thorough treatment of the scale, conditions and trends of employment of Palestinians from the territories in Israel, see International Labour Conference, Report of the Director General, Appendices, Report on the Situation of Workers of the Occupied Arab Territories, (Geneva, International Labour Office, 1986).

210/ It should be noted that there are different methods of classifying financial flows of migrant labour, according to the different status of migrant groups in the host countries. Thus, "the International Monetary Fund identifies three categories of financial flows associated with migrants, only one of which is called workers' remittances. Labour income is the factor income accruing to temporary labourers (staying less than 12 months) working abroad. Workers' remittances is the value of the private transfers from workers residing abroad for more than a year. Migrants' transfers are a set of counter entries to the flows of goods and changes in financial assets that arise from migration (change of residence) and are thus equal to the net worth of migrants ..." in G. Swamy, International Migrant Workers' Remittances: Issues and Prospects (Wash. D.C., World Bank, 1981), p. 6. The definition used by the World Bank aggregates the three categories in defining remittances (primarily for data manageability reasons). In the present study, the IMF approach is adopted, though the third category mentioned, i.e. migrants' transfers, is not calculated: discussion here of factor income covers the IMF's labour income, while remittances and transfers refer to the IMF's definition of workers' remittances.

211/   G. Kosseifi, "Forced migration of Palestinians from the West Bank and Gaza Strip", Population Bulletin of ESCWA, No.27, December 1985, p. 75.

212/   Ibid., pp. 79-81.

213/   G. Swamy, International Migrant ..., p. 5.

214/   In G. Kosseifi, op. cit., p. 82.

215/   This is also noted by the Israel, Central Bureau of Statistics, which states that, among other data, the reliability of those items in national accounts which include transactions between residents of the territories and Israel, including receipts by workers employed in Israel, is "especially poor". Israel, Central Bureau of Statistics, Judea, Samaria and Gaza Area Statistics (Jerusalem, CBS, vol. XV, No. 2, 1985), p. 82.

216/   Calculated from Israel, Central Bureau of Statistics, Judea, Samaria, ..., vol. XV., No. 2, p. 174.

217/   In addition to income tax payments, it has been reported, that "... Arab workers have to pay the Israeli defense tax, insurance fees, social security fees and Histadrut membership dues (which may come to as much as 40 per cent of their wages) but they receive no benefits in return". See J. Hiltermann, "The emerging trade union movement in the West Bank", Merip Reports, October-December 1985, p. 28. Official Israeli statistical publications confirm that "direct taxes which were deducted from the employees' wages (recorded in the item 'transfer payments to Israel') are to be deducted from income from work in Israel". Israel, Central Bureau of Statistics, Judea, Samaria, ..., vol. XV, No. 2, p. 83.

218/   In the Bank of Israel Research Department series of publications, from which the FII and FIA series are taken (see the sources for table 36), the sum of these two components leave no room for any other component, contrary to the explanations offered for the official series. Israel, Central Bureau of Statistics, Judea, Samaria, ..., vol. XV, No. 2, p. 86.

219/   This does not cover the illegal activities of around 55,000 Israeli settlers in agricultural and industrial sectors of Israeli settlements in the territories.

220/   Calculated from Israel, Central Bureau of Statistics, Statistical Abstract of Israel 1985 (Jerusalem, CBS, 1985), p. 708.

221/   G. Swamy, International Migrant ..., p. 39.

222/   See, Ibid, and A. G. Chandavarkar, "Use of migrants' remittances in labour exporting countries", Finance and Development, June 1980, for interesting discussions of these and related issues.

223/   Most studies on experience in other countries "have pointed out that the single largest investment favoured by emigrants is in urban real estate, agricultural land and housing... In the presence of such strong preferences for real assets that will appreciate with inflation and that are relatively risk free, investment schemes may not be particularly popular", G. Swamy, International Migrant ..., p. 41. However, as has been noted in a study of the use of remittances in labour-exporting countries, "when evaluating the effect of remittances on the local savings and investments of labour-export countries, care should be taken against considering that all 'consumption' is necessarily unproductive. Even if the maintenance of the family (including housing and education) is part of consumption, it does not follow that in low income countries, these expenditures are less desirable than 'investment'... The act of using remittances for consumption of basic needs goods eminently conforms to the actual prerequisites for development founded on 'basic needs'... If the available data on the use of remittances in the labour-export countries is worrying, this is not because consumption absorbs the bulk of remittances, but because they reflect the absence of a coherent policy which aims to mobilize savings made from these remittances for the benefit of productive investment"; A. G. Chandavarkar, "Use of migrants' remittances ...", p. 39.

224/ D. Zakai, Economic Development in Judea, Samaria and the Gaza District, 1981-82 (Jerusalem, Bank of Israel Research Department, 1985), p. 60.

225/ This should not be confused with remittances. Official series do not provide data for remittances per se, but rather cover all transfers to private persons, indicated by the PT series.

226/ The volume of agricultural and industrial imports from Israel and the degree of dependence upon Israel as a "convenient" and close market for the territories' exports are relevant in this respect.

227/ Calculated from Israel, Central Bureau of Statistics, Statistical Abstract of Israel 1985 (Jerusalem, CBS, 1985), pp. 745-746.

228/ There is one discrepancy that arises between this series of data on tax and other transfers, and the series in table 36 for transfer payments from the territories (TPD). It might be expected that the TPD figure would include, as its major component, the sum of tax transfers designated by Tt. However, in all years since 1978, Tt is larger than TPD by between 50 per cent to 150 per cent. This means that despite the fact that Tt represents taxes to government, a large percentage of these are not considered as part of the territories' "debited transfer payments" in balance-of-payments calculations (i.e. the source of the TPD series). This implies, therefore, that either the tax deducted by employers of Palestinian migrant workers in Israel is not considered to be part of the transfer flow from the territories, and/or that a proportion of the tax revenue represented by Tt is actually paid to the locally based Israeli civil administration (in addition to the part of Tt which goes to Palestinian local authorities) and consequently is not considered as a transfer payment by the territories. Accordingly, the series TPD might be the best indicator of indigenous Palestinian resources taxed and transferred by the Israeli authorities, over and above those income taxes and other deductions collected by employers in Israel itself and by the civil administration for its activities in the territories.

229/ Calculated from figures for factor income (FII) in table 34, GDP and GNP in table 35, and transfer payments to the territories (TPC) in table 36.

230/ Figures for the Tt series are from table 37. Government expenditure figures for 1983 are calculated from Israel, Central Bureau of Statistics, <u>Judea, Samaria and Gaza Area Statistics</u> (Jerusalem, CBS), vol. XV, No. 1, April 1985, pp. 163 and 170 and for 1984 from Israel, Central Bureau of Statistics, <u>Judea, Samaria ...</u>, vol. XV, No. 2, pp. 67 and 74.

231/ I. Zaghloul, <u>Transfers of Jordanians ...</u> .

232/ The REM series depends on figures for West Bank migrants outside Jordan which are substantially higher than alternate estimates for the total West Bank migrant population inside and outside Jordan. As seen in chapter I, the size of the West Bank-origin labour force assumed by the REM series to be working outside of Jordan (110,000 in 1980) is significantly larger than that arrived at through alternate calculations for all West Bank migrants residing permanently outside the territories, in Jordan and elsewhere (96,000 in 1984). The 96,000 figure includes West Bankers living in Jordan, while the 110,000 figure excludes this group. Another problem with the series is the probability that at most only half of Palestinian migrants still have family ties with the territories and can be assumed to be involved in the transfer of remittances. Accordingly, much less (up to half) of the remittances reaching Jordan can be assumed to end up inside the occupied territories than is indicated by REM. These factors would possibly have the effect of scaling REM down to levels closer to those indicated by official Israeli statistics for remittances. On the other hand, the figures presented in table 38 exclude remittances to the territories by Gaza Strip expatriates, who constitute a large proportion of the total permanent migrant labour force. Furthermore, remittances reported in these tables are only those transferred officially, and other unreported flows are not indicated or even estimated. The inclusion of unreported flows and Gaza Strip remittances would most likely push the figures back up to levels higher than the official Israeli series for total transfers.

233/ Though this is not always the case, as can be seen from the recent fall in aid through the Jordanian-Palestinian Joint Committee; see below.

234/ One of these, namely direct humanitarian and other aid by the Palestine Liberation Organization (PLO) to the territories, is not included in our discussion due to non-availability of data.

235/ This is understood as the "preservation of the underpinnings of the existence of the Palestinian people in the occupied homeland and their national identity, in its political, economic, cultural, psychological and ideological aspects", F. Bseiso, "A strategy for supporting national steadfastness in the occupied territories - the scientific and operational context", <u>Samed al Iqtisadi</u>, vol. 6, No. 49, 1984 (in Arabic).

236/ Algeria, Iraq, Kuwait, Libyan Arab Jamahiriya, Qatar, Saudi Arabia and United Arab Emirates.

237/ According to figures provided by the Joint Committee, Technical Bureau, Amman, 1986.

238/   The latter two issues became most apparent in 1986, when the Joint Committeee's activities were temporarily suspended. This followed a period when contributions to the Committee had been reduced to negligible levels. In fact, some of the contributions agreed upon were never made to the Joint Committee, while others were stopped or reduced after 1979 for a variety of reasons. For more information on the operation of the Joint Committee, reference is made to: (i) F. Bseiso, "A strategy..."; (ii) F. Bseiso, "The occupied homeland between the requirements of the support of steadfastness and the committments of the Arab boycott of Israel" in Shuoun Arabiya, June 1985, (in Arabic); and (iii) in Sayigh, Y., "Towards a more exemplary guidance of Arab economic assistance to the West Bank and Gaza Strip", unpublished study prepared for the Arab Fund for Economic and Social Development (AFESD), 1985 (in Arabic).

239/   From data provided by the Joint Committee, Technical Bureau, Amman, 1986.

240/   See A. Qassem, Funding sources for development in the occupied territories (Jerusalem, Arab Thought Forum, 1986) (in Arabic), Y. Sayigh, "The Palestinian Economy..." and George T. Abed (ed), Economic Development ..., for stimulating discussions of this issue. The subject again became the centre of debate following the proposal by Jordan in 1986 for a five-year "Development Programme" for the territories. See (i) Ministry of Planning, Hashemite Kingdom of Jordan, A Programme for Economic and Social Development in the Occupied Territories 1986 - 1990, Summary, (Amman, November 1986); and (ii) other views of the Programme in Filasteen al Thawra, 8 November 1986 (in Arabic) and Al-Fajr, 14 November 1986.

241/   "Programme implementation - special programmes of assistance - assistance to the Palestinian people, Report of the Administrator" (DP/1986/22), 13 March 1986, p. 2 and annex II.

242/   At the end of 1986, the Jordanian Government and PLO were engaged in attempting to raise Arab and international funding for their own separate aid/development programmes in the territories. In early 1987, reports indicated the possibility of a resumption of the activities of the Joint Committee, though not to the exclusion of each party's separate aid programmes. However, the present Arab economic climate is such that development finance at the level witnessed during the better years of Joint Commmittee operations will possibly not be available.

243/   Based on an analysis of projects submitted by three major United States-based PVOs to and approved or disapproved by the authorities - M. Benvenisti, U.S. Government Funded Projects in the West Bank and Gaza (1977 - 1983) (Jerusalem, West Bank Data Base Project, 1984).

244/   The report of the UNDP Administrator for 1986 states that "... approvals of proposed UNDP projects are being granted by the parties directly concerned at a faster rate than ever before" - "Programme implementation - special programmes of assistance - assistance to the Palestinian people, report of the Administrator" (DP/1986/22), 13 March 1986, p. 2.

245/   M. Benvenisti, U.S. Government Funded Projects ..., p. 8.

246/   Locally generated contributions amounted to $762,000 out of total project expenses of $1,754,000 in the West Bank and Gaza - Middle East Council of Churches, Annual Report 1984, Department on Service to Palestine Refugees (Geneva, MECC, 1985).

247/   When possible, these are managed by local Palestinian credit institutions, such as the Gaza Bank of Palestine, as discusssed in chapter II.

248/   Data provided by Save the Children, January 1987.

249/   It has been pointed out in connection with the apparent slow-down in demand for migrant labour in other areas that, "given this rather modest prospect for future growth in the demand for labour, it may be fruitful to ask whether there are alternatives to the movement of people for work. The benefits of migration, of course, go beyond that of earning foreign exchange; most importantly these include the generation of employment and earnings for large numbers of people. In a fundamental sense, therefore, it is important to ask whether there are alternative ways of generating this employment and income. Specifically, are direct foreign investment and trade feasible substitutes for labour movements? There is probably no single answer to this question, in the sense that there is no unique solution to a system where all the factors of production are freely mobile". G. Swamy, International Migrant..., p. 49.
